American Stranger

THE SUNY SERIES

HORIZONS OF CINEMA

MURRAY POMERANCE | EDITOR

Also in the series

William Rothman, editor, *Cavell on Film*

J. David Slocum, editor, *Rebel Without a Cause*

Joe McElhaney, *The Death of Classical Cinema*

Kirsten Moana Thompson, *Apocalyptic Dread*

Frances Gateward, editor, *Seoul Searching*

Michael Atkinson, editor, *Exile Cinema*

Paul S. Moore, *Now Playing*

Robin L. Murray and Joseph K. Heumann, *Ecology and Popular Film*

William Rothman, editor, *Three Documentary Filmmakers*

Sean Griffin, editor, *Hetero*

Jean-Michel Frodon, editor, *Cinema and the Shoah*

Carolyn Jess-Cooke and Constantine Verevis, editors, *Second Takes*

Matthew Solomon, editor, *Fantastic Voyages of the Cinematic Imagination*

R. Barton Palmer and David Boyd, editors, *Hitchcock at the Source*

William Rothman, *Hitchcock: The Murderous Gaze, Second Edition*

Joanna Hearne, *Native Recognition*

Marc Raymond, *Hollywood's New Yorker*

Steven Rybin and Will Scheibel, editors, *Lonely Places, Dangerous Ground*

Claire Perkins and Constantine Verevis, editors, *B Is for Bad Cinema*

Dominic Lennard, *Bad Seeds and Holy Terrors*

Rosie Thomas, *Bombay before Bollywood*

Scott M. MacDonald, *Binghamton Babylon*

Sudhir Mahadevan, *A Very Old Machine*

David Greven, *Ghost Faces*

James S. Williams, *Encounters with Godard*

William H. Epstein and R. Barton Palmer, editors, *Invented Lives, Imagined Communities*

Lee Carruthers, *Doing Time*

Rebecca Meyers, William Rothman, and Charles Warren, editors, *Looking with Robert Gardner*

Belinda Smaill, *Regarding Life*

R. Barton Palmer, Homer B. Pettey, and Steven M. Sanders, editors, *Hitchcock's Moral Gaze*

Douglas McFarland and Wesley King, editors, *John Huston as Adaptor*

American Stranger

Modernisms, Hollywood, and the Cinema of Nicholas Ray

Will Scheibel

SUNY PRESS

Cover image: From left to right: Natalie Wood, James Dean, and Nicholas Ray on the set of *Rebel Without a Cause* (Warner Bros., 1955). Author's collection.

Published by State University of New York Press, Albany

Printed in the United States of America

For information, contact State University of New York Press, Albany, NY
www.sunypress.edu

Production, Ryan Morris
Marketing, Anne M. Valentine

Library of Congress Cataloging-in-Publication Data

Names: Scheibel, Will, 1983– author.
Title: American stranger : modernisms, Hollywood, and the cinema of Nicholas Ray / Will Scheibel.
Description: Albany, NY : State University of New York Press, 2017. | Series: SUNY series, horizons of cinema | Includes filmography. | Includes bibliographical references and index.
Identifiers: LCCN 2016031490 (print) | LCCN 2016043817 (ebook) | ISBN 9781438464114 (hardcover : alk. paper) | ISBN 9781438464121 (pbk. : alk. paper) | ISBN 9781438464138 (e-book)
Subjects: LCSH: Ray, Nicholas, 1911–1979—Criticism and interpretation. | Auteur theory (Motion pictures)
Classification: LCC PN1998.3.R39 S34 2017 (print) | LCC PN1998.3.R39 (ebook) | DDC 791.4302/33092—dc23
LC record available at https://lccn.loc.gov/2016031490

10 9 8 7 6 5 4 3 2 1

Contents

Figures

Acknowledgments

The good people at SUNY Press have left me overwhelmed with appreciation for the way they shepherded the manuscript that became this book. Murray Pomerance, the Horizons of Cinema series editor, took an interest in my work with both editorial guidance and a generosity of spirit. James Peltz, co-director of SUNY Press, acted with industrious effort behind the scenes. My two referees pointed me to additional information and flagged areas to improve. Rafael Chaiken, Ryan Morris, and Anne Valentine aided in the pre-production, production, and marketing stages, respectively.

This book developed at Indiana University–Bloomington, and came to fruition at Syracuse University with the nurturing of friends and colleagues. The chair of the English Department, Erin Mackie, and my colleagues in Film & Screen Studies, Roger Hallas, Chris Hanson, and Matthew Fee (now at Le Moyne College), made Syracuse University the most hospitable place I could imagine to complete any sort of writing project. Steven Cohan, my departmental predecessor, is a wealth of kindness and knowledge of all things Classical Hollywood. A subvention from the College of Arts & Sciences gave me the funding to hire Staci Stutsman, Ph.D. Candidate in English, to prepare the index for the book, a job she undertook with painstaking diligence. At Indiana University, Barbara Klinger, Ed Comentale, Joan Hawkins, and Gregory Waller went above and beyond in commenting on first drafts. The late Alexander Doty offered recommendations that moved the project forward during a formative stage. James Naremore has been a model film critic and historian, and his ideas about film noir influenced many of the ways I approached studying a single figure. Joshua Vasquez and Laura Asbury not only lent advice for this book, but also vast personal support in the laboring to its completion. David Church shared suggestions and commiserations as he finished a book of his own. Jon Vickers, the director of the Indiana University Cinema, invited me to curate a Nicholas Ray program that allowed me to see some of Ray's films on the big screen—with an audience—for the first time. The staff at the Indiana University Herman B. Wells Library assisted me in tracking down primary sources, while my students both in Bloomington and Syracuse helped when I tested my analysis in the classroom (most of all in my courses on Hollywood directors of the 1950s).

Various academic organizations shaped material that went into this book, as well. The programming committees for the 2012 Modernist Studies Association conference, the 2013 Society for Cinema and Media Studies conference, and the 2015 International Association for Media and History conference enabled opportunities to present work in progress. A shorter, slightly different version of chapter 2 appeared in the *Journal of Gender Studies*, vol. 25, no. 2 under the title, "Rebel Masculinities of Star/Director/Text: James Dean, Nicholas Ray, and *Rebel without a Cause*," in April 2016. I thank my editor John Mercer and the readers he assigned to my manuscript for making it possible to publish an earlier portion of the book in the journal.

Fellow Nicholas Ray scholar Steven Rybin at Minnesota State University, Mankato is a valued collaborator and friend from whom I have learned a tremendous lot. This book benefited most recently from the inspiring notes he made on sections of the manuscript.

Writing a book seemed a little less daunting with the encouragement of my family, particularly of Andrea Scheibel, whose partnership alternately gave me counsel and respite throughout the entire process. I dedicate this book to her with love and gratitude.

Introduction

"I'm a Stranger Here Myself"

> There was theatre (Griffith), poetry (Murnau), painting (Rossellini), dance (Eisenstein), music (Renoir). Henceforth there is cinema. And the cinema is Nicholas Ray.
>
> —Jean-Luc Godard, "Beyond the Stars"

> Nicholas Ray has been the *cause célèbre* of the auteur theory for such a long time that his critics, pro and con, have lost all sense of proportion about his career.
>
> —Andrew Sarris, "Nicholas Ray [1911–]"

Why Nicholas Ray?

VENERATED AS THE QUINTESSENTIAL rebel auteur in Hollywood cinema, Nicholas Ray is famous for dreamy, stylish films such as *They Live by Night*, *In a Lonely Place*, *Johnny Guitar*, *Rebel without a Cause*, and *Bigger than Life*.[1] Although his films have been the subjects of a substantial corpus of auteurist criticism, as a director he remains cloaked in the shadows of his own legend, an ambiguous and elusive presence in cinema culture. With the limited academic scholarship on Ray since the reign of traditional auteurism, a question persists: what made him such an attractive figure to the cinema culture that gave robust life to his legend?

Fig. I.1. *The American Friend* (1977): The legends of Nicholas Ray tell of a Hollywood director who demonstrated artistic rebellion in postwar American culture, characterizing him as a homegrown version of the modern artist resistant to classical aesthetic norms, whose visions were perpetually compromised by institutional constraints and besieged by his inner demons. (Anchor Bay Entertainment, 2002; digital frame enlargement)

Apropos of the "sense of proportion about his career" to which Sarris refers above, this metacritical project examines the discursive work that built Ray's reputation as a director. Therefore, I approach the concept of authorship not in the terms of traditional auteurism, as the synchronic artistic expression of an individual creator, but as an art-historical category: the product of a complex interaction between and among various forms of enunciation and innovation. This book aims to enrich our understanding of Ray as a director, but, more broadly, it also explores interrelated questions of authorship, performance, identity, and taste in the production of a mediated public self. In this way, Ray's canonicity serves as a case study in how popular artists are culturally received and mobilized over time as modern icons.

Ray's tenure as a commercial director in the late studio system of Hollywood falls squarely in the postwar era from 1947 to 1962. For the French film critics of *Cahiers du cinéma* who pioneered *la politique des auteurs* in the 1950s, Ray embodied what Jim Hillier describes as "a particular conception of the filmmaker working within the system, always rebellious, often doomed, and a particular response to the modern world, as well as a particularly affecting style" ("Introduction" 76). The legends of Nicholas Ray tell of a Hollywood director who demonstrated artistic rebellion in postwar American culture, characterizing him as a homegrown version of the modern artist resistant to classical aesthetic norms, whose visions were perpetually compromised by institutional constraints and besieged by his inner demons. Meanwhile, in Hollywood of the late 1940s and 1950s, he was known as merely a technically competent director of genre pictures and star vehicles.

Prior to moving to Hollywood, during the 1930s Ray was a member of the Theatre of Action, a New York City agitprop group, and he also performed services for various New Deal agencies (the Works Progress Administration, the U.S. Department of Agriculture's Resettlement Administration, and the Office of War Information). Ray's directorial assignments began at RKO Radio Pictures between 1947 and 1952, where he worked under contract directing *They Live by Night*, *A Woman's Secret*, *Born to Be Bad*, *Flying Leathernecks*, *On Dangerous Ground*, and *The Lusty Men*, and was twice loaned-out to Humphrey Bogart's Santana Productions to direct the star in *Knock on Any Door* and *In a Lonely Place*. Howard Hughes, head of RKO from 1948 to 1955, gave the left-wing director shelter from the blacklist at the studio (Eisenschitz 124).

Throughout the 1950s, Ray went on to make films for Hollywood's other four major studios: *Run for Cover* at Paramount Pictures; *Rebel without a Cause* at Warner Bros.; *Bigger Than Life* and *The True Story of Jesse James* at Twentieth Century-Fox; and *Party Girl* at MGM. Ray's career also brought him through the major-minors, with Columbia Pictures' *Hot Blood*; the minors, with Republic Pictures' *Johnny Guitar*; and network television, with an episode of the CBS anthology series *General Electric Theater* titled "High Green Wall" (based on Evelyn Waugh's story "The Man Who Liked Dickens"). Directing *Bitter Victory* for the German-born Paul Graetz and *Wind Across the Everglades* for Budd and Stuart Schulberg, Ray had even worked under independent producers by the end of the decade.

The experience of shooting *Party Girl* for MGM in 1958 left Ray embittered by his treatment at the hands of the dying studio system. After completing the film, dependent on drugs and alcohol, he left for Europe to begin his next project. Shot in France, Italy, and the U.K., that film was *The Savage Innocents*, a semi-ethnographic tale of an Eskimo (Anthony Quinn) struggling to adapt to Western "civilization."[2] Ray then moved to Spain to direct a pair of big-budget, star-studded historical epics for American independent producer Samuel Bronston: *King of Kings*, a film about the life of Christ, and *55 Days at Peking*, a film about the Battle of Peking in 1900.

None of these European coproductions earned box-office or mainstream critical success, and the laborious conditions behind the scenes took a toll on Ray's mental and physical health. Bronston hired Andrew Marton and Guy Green to finish *55 Days* after Ray collapsed on the set in 1962—he remained in Europe and did not return to the United States until 1969. Toward the end of his period in Hollywood, Ray went from being a cult to "a living fictional character," in the words of critic David Thomson, "the American who wanted to make pictures and who had been forced out of his own country. His tattered life became the movie he could not quite make" ("Poet").

Despite the less celebratory attention he received in his homeland, Ray was eventually discovered and canonized by English-language critics and scholars in the 1970s, after he retired from commercial filmmaking. When Ray returned to the United States in 1969, he publically embraced his reputation as a cult hero to refashion his image as an active presence in the American counterculture. In addition to teaching at Harpur College (part of the State University of New York at Binghamton), New York University, and the Lee Strasberg Institute, he gave regular lectures and interviews, appeared in Wim Wenders's *The American Friend* (1977) and Miloš Forman's *Hair* (1979), and directed the seldom-seen shorts "The Janitor" (a chapter of the 1974 anthology film *Wet Dreams*) and *Marco* (shot with his acting students at the Strasberg Institute 1978).

After *55 Days at Peking*, Ray began various projects he was never able to see through to fruition, but his late career renaissance and practice of self-reflexive auteurism did yield two highly personal films: *We Can't Go Home Again*, an autobiographical collaboration with his Binghamton students in which he sought to achieve a new avant-garde language of cinema, and *Lightning over Water*, a pseudo-documentary he cowrote and codirected with Wenders that chronicled his last months as he battled cancer. *We Can't Go Home Again* premiered at the Cannes International Film Festival in 1973, but Ray continued editing the film until his death in 1979. A new version was restored under the supervision of Susan Ray, his widow, for release at the 2011 Venice International Film Festival, with the "making of" documentary *Don't Expect Too Much*, commemorating the centennial of his birth.

By the end of his life, Ray had come to personify an artistic mythology of rugged American individualism, and also a uniquely Western mytho-historical-ideological narrative: the white, masculine artist at odds with the forces of conformity, on a wandering, personal journey of enlightenment and creative expression. As David Thomson notes in *The New Biographical Dictionary of Film*, "he would not be a major figure if he did not have a fundamental conception of American legend and society" (732). But Ray was taken up as a rebel figure in more specific cases through which, as a discursive text, "the rebel" was activated differently: as an iconoclastic director at the vanguard of the Classical Hollywood style after World War II; as an innovative "actor's director" who experimented with "the Method" and worked with rebellious male stars; as a radical teacher of acting and filmmaking who spoke to new concepts in film form and politics; and as an antiestablishment model for hip art-house directors nostalgic for old Hollywood auteurism. The chapters that follow each consider different influences that shaped Ray's reputation between the 1950s and the 1980s. With particular moments of modernism conditioning ideas about Ray, we will see how his image as a rebel auteur has been drawn as a modernist symbol.

Film Authorship, Auteurism, and Reputation

This book is less a material history of industrial production or audience reception than it is an *intellectual history* that uncovers how a series of modernist contexts managed Ray's reputation: the development of auteurism in postwar France that extended certain American cultural front ideologies associated with Hollywood; the popularity of the Method in the United States during the 1950s as a modern acting style; the advancements of political modernism in cinema studies after 1968, when Ray came home to become a teacher; and the rise of international modernist art cinemas, where his influence is most apparent.

Biographical research and auteurist appreciations are the primary means by which film scholars have attended to Ray. Patrick McGilligan's *Nicholas Ray: The Glorious Failure of an American Director* and Bernard Eisenschitz's authoritative *Nicholas Ray: An American Journey* detail his life and working methods, and Geoff Andrew's *The Films of Nicholas Ray* is the standard critical study of his films (although now out-of-print). This book works differently by shifting the emphasis from Ray, the man, to the historical communities that set other parameters around how his films could be interpreted and evaluated. I do not claim to exhaust Ray's richness as a subject, of course, but I intend to bring new perspectives to a director whom conventional wisdom has called a "modern rebel." Yet, conventional wisdom does not tell us what exactly constitutes rebellion—or modernism—and my research proceeds from this theoretical problem.

As a study of a director, this book brings Ray in conversation with the poststructural developments in cultural studies, treating authorship as an organizing principle for the process by which films articulate meaning in their circulation through culture. This project therefore aims to show how film authorship is a discursive process: it is not only the instance of film production, but a series of diachronic events in which a director's films are read and "rewritten." Director reputation, or the public estimation of a director's authorship, accounts for one of the most important ways in which authorship is a contested locus of meaning that remains ideologically determined, historically and culturally specific, and always in flux. The longitudinal reputations of directors allow us to comprehend better the evolving significations of their films.

Auteurism was displaced almost as quickly as it entered the academy, as James Naremore reminds us, and the dominant methods followed under the rubrics of "apparatus theory" in the 1970s, and cultural studies in the 1980s. Yet, following Naremore, if the auteur theory is dead, so are the debates over the death of the author, and skepticism over "who is writing?" stunts the inquiry into the ideology of historical subjects who produce and reproduce culture. Not only is auteurism a small part of the discourse on authorship, as he claims, it is also a diverse and contradictory discourse at that. In the wake of disciplinary turns to ideologies of media and cultural production, and archival histories of industrial and reception practices, the auteur actually still has a great deal to teach us. Naremore contends that "writing about individual careers is necessary to any proper sociology of culture. Such writing helps us to understand the complicated, dynamic relation between institutions and artists, and makes us aware of performance, theatricality, and celebrity—issues we've just begun to analyze" ("Authorship" 21).[3] Directors are tied to aesthetic systems, responsive to politics, and embedded in histories than run deeper than those of individual productions. Thinking of the author as a cultural figure bears productive opportunities for readings of his or her life and work unbounded by individual creation as the final signified.

Rather than looking at issues of consistent style and personal vision alone (the provenances of meaning for traditional auteurists), this work is situated within the area of *reputation studies*, which has contributed to a small but fruitful body of scholarship on Classical Hollywood directors, including Charles Maland's *Chaplin and American Culture*, Robert E. Kapsis's *Hitchcock: The Making of a Reputation*, and Barbara Klinger's *Melodrama and Meaning: History, Culture, and the Films of Douglas Sirk*. As Klinger explains, the goal of a reputation study is to "grasp the dialogic relation between artistic reputations and history—the dynamic circumstances under which an author's status and the status of her or his works are established, sustained, transformed, unappreciated, or even vilified" (xiii). Charting the social and institutional currents that lead to Sirk's canonical status, Klinger navigates the public reception of his melodramas from the 1950s to the 1980s to "contribute to a broader understanding of the relations between the post-World War II melodrama and culture, from the genre's association with postwar attitudes about sexuality, masculinity, and mass culture to its more contemporary rewritings as subversive by film academics, classic by reviewers, and camp by mainstream audiences" (xv).

The other area to which this project is indebted is *star studies*. In his seminal book *Stars*, Richard Dyer outlines how star images are publically manufactured in the media by: (a) promotion, the material disseminated by the studio to market a star; (b) publicity, the (often staged and controlled) material that appears to capture the star spontaneously or candidly off-screen; (c) criticism and commentary, the material written or said about the star that gauges or influences popular opinion; and (d) films, which define these celebrities as "film stars" and give them roles based on character types, performances, and appearances (60–63). While the images of the stars whom Ray directed are important to his reputation, I also want to think about Ray himself according to Dyer's semiotic and sociological framework for film stardom. On the one hand, we can read stars as "a complex configuration of visual, verbal and aural signs" (34), which may signify in the films themselves according to performance codes and character types, or outside the films in reviews, studio announcements, press handouts, trailers, magazine advertisements, and information the press purports to discover. On the other hand, we can read stars as a kind of social reality, suggesting that "no matter where one chooses to put the emphasis in terms of the stars' place in the production/consumption dialectic of the cinema, that place can still only be fully understood ideologically" (34).

Directors are similarly ensconced in a complex network of social values and structures. Whether textually deduced by an oeuvre or publically manufactured by a larger media apparatus, a director's persona may function to uphold the status quo or expose and subvert surrounding ideological tensions. Engaging with primary sources in public discourse—biographical legends, interviews, reviews, articles in both national newspapers and international film magazines, and the promotional and publicity material of Ray's stars—I want to bring questions to bear on Ray's cinema that lie outside the borders of intentionality and privileged single films. What does it mean to sustain a reputation as a rebel auteur? What accounts for the change in meaning of an auteur's films throughout history? What enables the different significations of the name "Nicholas Ray" as a byword for rebellion in the wider discursive field of Hollywood cinema? What are the values of that name as user groups deploy it, and what do those values reveal about the ways in which cinema culture defines and measures rebellion?

Much of the analysis here also comes from close readings and thick descriptions of films themselves, which is where this book diverges from the reputation studies mentioned earlier. I am most interested in what

Ray's reputation says about aesthetics, as it was in certain philosophies and ideologies of aesthetics where his reputation took root. In the introduction to her anthology *Film and Authorship*, Virginia Wright Wexman states that among the poststructural approaches to director studies, scholars have dealt with "ways in which authorial discourses within and among filmic texts govern the ways in which they are read" (2). At its core, this book is such a study in *ways of reading*, unpacking the processes of interpretation and evaluation in reputation building. My own interpretations of films present some of the significations that different reading conditions make possible. Ray's films both illuminate and animate the discourses that formed his reputation, and over the course of this book I weave in and out of film texts—directed by Ray and others—to show what these various contexts afford them as sources of cinematic pleasure: aesthetic objects to be read, experienced, and appreciated.

Under the pressures of textual analysis, Ray's films provide an explicit, publically visible point of convergence for ideas about American modernism and artistic rebellion. Literary theorist Tony Bennett reminds us that interpretation of a text can facilitate "an intervention within the politics of reading, a particular activation of the text which aims to inscribe it within social and ideological relations of a particular kind" (13).[4] The task of the film critic who wants to reconstruct a director's reputation should not be to decode a film in order to access an interior meaning that remains inherent. Instead, it should be to contextualize the film in its diverse forms of material production, the social relations in which it is imbricated, and the conditions of possibility among its points of cultural contact. If texts are inseparable from their modes of production, circulation, and meaning, they are neither totally "closed" (bound to universal signification) nor totally "open" (available to any and all significations). What has been said about a text and how it is "used" are of greater relevance for us in what follows than the authority of the text and its author.

The notions of authorship that inform this book are guided by continental philosophers Roland Barthes and Michel Foucault, who continue helping critics work through questions about authors' relationships to textuality and communication. Barthes posits a semiological challenge to textual grammar and meaning as stable and rule-bound rhetorical systems that can be deciphered and explained through critique. If the linguistic relationship between sign and referent is arbitrary, language has multiple meanings and texts are polysemic in their form and content. Rejecting the authorial intent and authority (person, life, taste, passions, etc.) as the structuring absence of a text, Barthes decenters the author and finds the text liberated from a fixed essence, open to different reading strategies. Foucault puts forth the similar claim that authorship is an ideological construct or function of discourse that lays bare a range of discursive practices comprising society at large. The name of the author guarantees authenticity and serves as a description or classificatory term, but unmooring the text from the determinist control of the author opens it up to other uses, applications, readings, and "rewritings" that exceed the work itself.

Bennett, Barthes, and Foucault are familiar to the critical humanities, but I acknowledge their paradigm shifts in textual analysis here to reinforce the theoretical stakes of a reputation study within the discipline of cinema studies. An auteur study is a celebration of a director for his or her artistic genius wherein the director-as-author is the Master Key for an analysis of his or her coherent vision and style. This book, however, is an analysis of our investment in authorship as a category (reconstructing how an auteur becomes auteur, if you like). I do not see a false dichotomy with this distinction, advocating the abandonment of one approach for the other, but propose that one can pick up where the other ends as part of the same mission to study the significance of individual careers in cinema. In many ways, this book is a "prequel" to my largely auteurist anthology, coedited with Steven Rybin, *Lonely Places, Dangerous Ground: Nicholas Ray in American Cinema*, which attributes the stylistic, thematic, political, and technical aspects of Ray's films to Ray himself.

Both schools of thought speak to the two faces of authorship—an aesthetic signature and a public character—that often shape each other. "Even if we accept the poststructuralist conception of an omnipresent textuality and a fragmented subjectivity that is constantly in flux," writes Wexman, "we are still left with the presumption of some form of agency which is implicitly understood as having brought the work into existence" (*Film* 2). Directors have their own histories and realms of expectations like genres, and are often used for similar cultural work, governing the ways in which films are categorized, consumed, and understood. In contemporary cinema culture, a director may serve as a film's brand name for marketers and celebrity image for moviegoers.[5] The simplistic premise that the author is, of course, "dead" leads to an intellectual dead end. Selective, reductive interpretations of Barthes and Foucault have only prevented director studies from maturing by circumventing authorship and the difficult problems it raises altogether. This lasting power of film authorship is a force with which we still need to reckon.

Modernism, Modernity, and Mass Culture

As much as this book seeks to intervene in problems of film authorship, it is equally concerned with modernism as an artistic environment for cinema. Modernism in writing, art, and cultural production throughout the first half of the twentieth-century looked for new and alternative ways of representing reality. In his monograph *Modernism* from Routledge's "New Critical Idiom" series, Peter Childs defines the Anglo-modernist project as an effort "to modify if not overturn existing modes and subjects of representation, partly by pushing them towards the abstract or the introspective, and to express the new sensibilities of their time" (4). Breaking from traditional forms of articulation through experimental techniques came as a reaction to the crisis in language and knowledge that resulted from profound geographical, technological, industrial, economic, scientific, philosophical, and sociopolitical changes leading up to and following World War I.

Hope for salvation could only be found in medium-specific aesthetics of innovation, and autonomous authors and artists were therefore elevated above producers of mass culture ("make it new," declared Ezra Pound). Richard Pells explains the goals of modernism with a helpful preamble in his book *Modernist America*: "The point [. . .] was to force people to see, hear, and think about the world in entirely new ways, ways that made the bedlam of urban life, the unsettling effects of technological change, the transfer and 'cleansing' of populations, the terrors of totalitarianism, and the impersonal butchery of modern warfare seem more intelligible if no less disorienting" (x). Also consider the "heresy" that lured modernist creators, to which Peter Gay attests in his book *Modernism: The Lure of Heresy*, the drive that "impelled their actions as they confronted conventional sensibilities" (3). While disregarding bourgeois taste and morality, authors such as James Joyce, Virginia Woolf, T. S. Eliot, and Gertrude Stein exercised what Gay calls "a principled self-scrutiny, which entails an exploration of the self" (5). Literary modernism was authorship laid bare.

The elastic terms of art and modernity—modernism, high art, and the avant-garde—are related and vaguely defined, but they are not synonymous. I implement them loosely to respect an openness and flexibility in definition, but I do not mean to conflate them. Whereas I take *high art* as a bourgeois tradition of classical and romantic aesthetics, I refer to the *avant-garde* as experimental artistic or cultural formations within modernist contexts (Dadaists, Surrealists, Situationists, etc.), whose politically motivated activities often rely on industrial/mechanical reproduction to subvert social norms and undermine the authority of the autonomous author or of art itself. One of James Naremore and Patrick Brantlinger's clarifications in the introduction to their anthology *Modernism and Mass Culture* is that modernism "develops out of high culture, but is sharply critical, even deconstructive, of certain high-culture values" (9). According to their formulation, modernists were "[a]ggressively individualistic, contemptuous of bourgeois realism, and sometimes nostalgic for pre-industrial society," who "seemed at once reactionary and new" (10). Although the discourses of modernism in this book presume the broad and general understandings of modernism that I have just sketched, the storied reputation of Ray as a modernist film author does not fit a linear history of modernist aesthetics.

This book pushes back against the traditional definition of modernism as a homogeneous aesthetic practice reflecting a monolithic cultural era. Just as I do not adopt a hard-lined auteurist position, I also do not call for an art-for-art's sake return to high modernism. Rather, by investigating Ray as a director who was imagined as a late modernist via different conceptions of the rebel, I investigate the dynamic ways in which different historical and cultural sources after World War II conceptualized modernism. Ideas about modernism, much like ideas about rebellion, set the standards by which Ray's films were accepted as works of film art, but as these ideas changed, so did the standards of evaluation.

At *Cahiers du cinéma*, Ray was "modern," or a director of late modernity, representing the consistent style and personal vision of a modernist author or artist, but he was also a director of crime pictures, Westerns, and family melodramas for the Hollywood studios. Ray's films fused sex, violence, and sensationalism with social messages and topical subjects like juvenile delinquency and drug abuse, they blended generic formulas with expressionism and surrealism, and they combined commercial stars with experimental performances. They were about solitary men wrestling with their dark, unconscious Others in a wasteland of a postwar America, as well as the alienating, dehumanizing effects of consumerism, suburbanization, and paranoid Cold War fears. As he turned inward toward human subjectivity as a way to represent the existential despair and social upheavals of modern life, Ray reached an abstract directorial aesthetic. Responding to a modernist crisis in form and meaning, he ambiguously structured modes of articulation through embodiment, feeling, space, and movement. Consequently, it was in the star images and performances of his actors where that crisis was made most clearly legible.

The relationship between Ray and modernism does not end here. Ray's prescription to "the Method" puts him in a different context of modernism than what *Cahiers du cinéma* identified in film form. Different still was the political avant-garde of the 1970s through which Ray achieved a comeback in the American counterculture. There were even modernist movements Ray entered of which he was not a proper member, as art cinemas from the 1960s to the 1980s invoked his name and image. Modernism cast Ray as a rebel in particular historical moments of reception, publicity, self-promotion, and legacy that condition distinct ways of reading his films as modernist texts. The story this book tells about Ray is not hitched to a singular narrative of modernism, but revolves around a series of four *modernisms* that I track over the next four chapters, each illuminating a different side of Ray as a public face for multiple modernist causes.

The connections between cinema and modernity are in some ways fundamental to the discipline of cinema studies. Murray Pomerance persuasively argues in the introduction to his anthology *Cinema and Modernity* that "without cinema, modernity is unthinkable; and without modernity, cinema would not exist" (12). In addition to the birth of the department store, avenues, the railway, and the telegraph, and later the telephone, audio recording, and the photograph, and finally advertising and media, modernity witnessed the birth of cinema. "Modernity, the era of public illumination," Pomerance observes, "brought a new sense of exteriority: what had once been privately imagined was now dramatically depicted, broadcast, systematized for all to read and know" (11).

Yet, attempts to give modernist cinema a totalizing definition are in some ways futile considering cinema's murky relationship with modernism. Joe McElhaney astutely remarks in his book, *The Death of Classical Cinema*, that "from the moment that the cinema came into existence in the late nineteenth-century modernism was already substantially underway in other arts. The cinema had to, in a sense, learn to be classical and modernist at once, resulting in its various modernisms very quickly perceived to be as out-of-date as its classicisms" (10). Ray's films are not locatable in a historical period or national cinema of the high-modernist avant-garde, the way that Fritz Lang and F. W. Murnau belong to German Expressionism, Sergei Eisenstein and Dziga Vertov to Russian Formalism, and Luis Buñuel and Jean Cocteau to French Surrealism, and so forth. Moreover, the modernism of postwar filmmaking, what has been called "late modern" (Kovács 217) or "neomodern" (Orr 2), is generally associated with European art cinemas characterized by reflexivity, abstraction, and subjectivity (Kovács 217), as well as formal irony and a critical reaction to the epoch (Orr 2). Whereas Ray's films came out of Classical Hollywood, new movements in Europe signaled a break from neoclassical ideals of formal unity and seamless coherence: narrative causality and closure, goal-oriented action, invisible authorship and transparent realism, and conventional uses and understandings of time and space established through mise-en-scène, cinematography, and continuity editing.

Through Ray's reputation, we can see how cinematic modernism never exactly disappeared between its early and late iterations in the high-modernist avant-garde of the 1920s and European art cinemas after World War II, respectively. Repressed in the art produced by the American culture industry, modernism can be found in a more "impure" state between these two phases of film history where, for example, an avant-garde composer such as George Antheil and a popular film star such as Humphrey Bogart contribute to the same project in Ray's *Knock on Any Door* and *In a Lonely Place*. A filmmaker such as Ray, who worked in left-wing theater during the 1930s, while looking ahead to the political avant-garde and art cinemas of the 1960s and 1970s, reveals a hidden temporal continuum.

Ray evinced modernist tendencies in classical studio and genre systems, but for all of his flamboyance and stylistic flourishes, he never explicitly broke the rules of Classical Hollywood cinema. Therefore, the historical poetics of modernism, as the elite techniques circumscribed by a period style, cannot account for his films. Miriam Hansen's proposal of "vernacular modernism" lends a more applicable framework for theorizing modernism as a way to approach mid-twentieth-century modernity in its most popular and commercial forms. Hansen points out that modernism encompasses "a whole range of cultural and artistic practices that register, respond to, and reflect upon processes of modernization and the experience of modernity, including the paradigmatic transformation of the conditions under which art is produced, transmitted, and consumed" (60). Modernity and mass culture are thus closely linked. Mass-produced, mass-mediated, and mass-consumed texts, such as Hollywood films from the 1920s through the 1950s, brought about a new phenomenological horizon where modernity was worked through at the level of the senses in both quotidian and transnational dimensions.

Hollywood cinema here marks the shift from a literate bourgeois class to an affective visual and public sphere of mass culture, transforming the senses to make audiences hyperconscious of modernity. Classical cinema, Hansen argues, need not be thought of in opposition to modernism if it takes place in popular consciousness as a "scaffold, matrix, or web that allows for a wide range of aesthetic effects and experiences" (67). Ray then can be thought of as both a cinematic inheritor of the high-modernist avant-garde, a progenitor of Europe's postwar modernist art cinemas, and a product of America's cultural modernity at midcentury, felt by jazz, architecture, visual art and design, fashion, and photography. It was the machinery of the popular press that engineered his reputation as a modernist, publicly circulating reviews of his films, promotion and publicity of his stars, and interviews with the director. One of Ray's favorite sayings was, "I'm a stranger here myself," but it was this very identity as a stranger to Hollywood that bolstered his auteurist celebrity in the 1970s.[6]

Not only was Ray's modern world uniquely suited to spectacular cinematic representation and perception (i.e., new technologies of widescreen and color), it was also born from popular forms as opposed to classical literature. This notion of modernism was constructed by American mass culture and sold to French audiences, enamored with its images of postwar youth and rebellion that were banned during World War II, at a time when American mass culture was exported overseas and its art was recognized internationally on par with Europe. Arguably more so than any American director, Ray was heralded as a rebel auteur in this modernist context because of the innovative possibilities for which he stood in both Hollywood cinema (as a supposedly vanguard director) and in French national cinema (as a model auteur).

Ray was a modernist adrift in postwar mass culture. It is all the more significant that he worked in the culture industry, not outside of it, to be appreciated for his revolutionary potential. Critics championed this work of a popular artist not by abandoning a metanarrative of truth or welcoming the collapse of a "high"/"low" separation, but by subsuming Ray under a highbrow reading formation—intellectual and also nonacademic—based on the tenets of modernism. More importantly, his films could be marshaled as a challenge to bourgeois canons of quality and conservative middlebrow taste politics—the unpretentious antidotes to the literary adaptations of France's *cinéma de papa*—as vital for film culture as a Roberto Rossellini or a Robert Bresson.

Beginning with his critical reception, I map four contexts of modernism from which Ray's reputation gained purchase. Chapter 1 focuses on the discovery of Ray at *Cahiers du cinéma* after World War II, where his films were repurposed from products of American mass culture to antifascist works of art. Young French cinephiles appropriated Ray's films as vehicles for modern aesthetic ideologies that defied what had been officially sanctioned by the older, conservative generation and the recent Occupation. While *la politique des auteurs* in some ways granted a new lease on Hollywood's cultural front politics in the 1950s, its Anglophone translation as "the auteur theory" institutionalized Hollywood directors as the subjects of academic film criticism and cinema studies.

Chapter 2 hones in on particular films with closer analysis framed by the images of Ray's anti-authoritarian male stars. Ray's reputation as an "actor's director" is partly related to his interest in the Method, and James Dean in *Rebel without a Cause* embodied this modern performance style associated with hip, but sensitive young artists. Robert Mitchum in *The Lusty Men* and Humphrey Bogart in *In a Lonely Place* provide foils for Dean as older, tougher stars who worked with Ray, affecting personas as "bad boys," but they also employed Ray's improvisational and experimental techniques. In their characters' inabilities to signify as coherent, normatively masculine subjects onscreen, these three actors dramatize Ray's reputed struggles to articulate as an artist and also made those struggles commercially accessible.

Ray's own star persona is the subject of Chapter 3, which considers the ways in which he promoted himself as a rebel auteur in interviews, and literally played himself in his last two feature films, *We Can't Go Home Again* and *Lightning over Water*. As part of the political avant-garde and the American counterculture of the 1970s, Ray was able to speak to emerging theories and artistic practices that deterritorialized "authored" cinema (after all, both films were collaborative efforts). Paradoxically, he also enabled reevaluation and retroactive interpretation of his films through reading strategies tempered by his authority as the director, while anchoring *Home* and *Lightning* in his authorship through performances of self.

In chapter 4, we move from the avant-garde to art cinemas, where Ray's legacy is on display in films by directors he influenced: Jean-Luc Godard of the French New Wave, Wim Wenders of New German Cinema, and Jim Jarmusch of the New York Underground and American Independent Cinema. Godard first encountered Ray as a critic at *Cahiers du cinéma*, but Wenders and Jarmusch worked with him directly (Wenders in the films *Lightning over Water* and *The American Friend*, and Jarmusch as his student at NYU). This chapter covers the ways in which filmmakers from three generations of cinema gave Ray's films an afterlife through the intertextuality of homage.

The conclusion of this book takes up the preservation of Ray's reputation, which, following David Helpern and James C. Gutman's 1975 documentary *I'm a Stranger Here Myself*, has presented Ray less as a modernist than a socially conscious academic citizen. In addition to DVD and Blu-ray releases of his films and career overviews and retrospectives from online critics, the Nicholas Ray Centenary Project has sustained Ray's afterlife in the film culture of the millennium. Led by Susan Ray, the Nicholas Ray Foundation not only prepared *We Can't Go Home Again* for its 2011 premiere, but also produced the documentary *Don't Expect Too Much*. As a documentary and educational subject, Ray has become a humanist teacher of "responsible" rebellion in the new millennium. The next installment in the Centenary Project will no doubt crystallize this dimension to his reputation: *ACTION! Master Class with Nicholas Ray*, a full-length documentary funded by a Kickstarter campaign that will be edited from, among other sources, Ray's public talks and classes at NYU and the Strasberg Institute.

1

Cult of the Outlaw

Cinephilia, Film Criticism, and Mass Cultural Modernism

I think the reason you film buffs annoy me is that you ask so damn many questions, and I'm always afraid I won't have the answers. And I resent it if I don't have the answers. But hell, I don't have any answers.

—Nicholas Ray, *I Was Interrupted: Nicholas Ray on Making Movies*

Sites of Modernism in Ray's Biographical Legend

THE EVENTS OF AMERICAN modernity made an undeniable impact on Ray before he even began his career as a filmmaker. A student at the University of Chicago in 1931, he studied under Pulitzer Prize–winning author Thornton Wilder. An apprentice of Frank Lloyd Wright, he joined the renowned architect at his Taliesin Fellowship in Green Springs, Wisconsin from 1933 to 1934. A lover of jazz, during the early 1940s he was known to frequent America's first interracial nightclub, the Café Society in Greenwich Village (a hangout for Paul

Robeson, Langston Hughes, and Richard Wright), where he mingled with its jazz, blues, and folk musicians. An avid reader of literature, he held a special admiration for Thomas Wolfe, whose novel *You Can't Go Home Again* (1940) gave him the title for one of his final films.[1] Bernard Eisenschitz and Patrick McGilligan's biographies have detailed these and other events in Ray's life before he moved to Hollywood, as well as the various cultural influences on his career.

This chapter does not rehearse Ray's biographical details in the context of 1930s and early 1940s American modernity, but instead focuses on how his biographical legend and the critical reception of his films give his career a particular modernist import. Ray's modernism lies not on the purportedly high or low ends of the cultural spectrum, but can be found somewhere between them, as ideas about modernism were codified in terms of mass culture and sold to mainstream, middle-class consumers. We will see how his reputation in France as an auteur played a role in the modernization of French film culture after the Occupation, reviving a relationship between modernism and Hollywood cinema that began in the 1930s. Following different evaluative criteria, Anglo-American film culture then disciplined his auteurism through scholarly rereadings that paralleled the institutionalization of cinema studies in academic journals and university settings.

Ray's canonization is best understood as a result of what I call *mass cultural modernism*, a discursive practice by which cultural producers and consumers appropriate mass cultural forms and artifacts through a highbrow reading formation as a presumed weapon against hegemonic ideological and aesthetic systems. In order to nuance the historical generalizations about Ray as a "rebel," we need to undertake a precise investigation into the critical reception of his films, the conditions of their reception, and the ways in which different taste cultures broadly imagined him as a rebel according to their political and artistic investments.

To be clear, Ray was not a filmmaker who stood above or outside the culture industry, and critics did not canonize Ray in spite of his place within it. Rather, his appeal to the popular represented a late modernism constructed *by* mass culture at midcentury, wherein artists could express modernist ideas through popular idioms, thus rejuvenating (and also reinforcing) the traditions of high culture rather than contaminating them. In his book *Modernist America*, historian Richard Pells goes as far as to argue that "American culture is central to the modernist experience," the site of modern trends in art, music, and cinema, and that it always called the separation between high and low culture into question (xi). American culture imported international styles and techniques, while also exporting a modernity that made Americana legible in a global lexicon.

Despite the contempt that traditional European intellectuals held for its mass-produced commodities, Pells reminds us that "modernists abroad were always fascinated with American culture—with its novels, its movies, its jazz, its Broadway musicals, its cities and skyscrapers, and (after World War II) its Abstract Expressionist paintings" (xi).[2] The technical flaws or imperfections in Ray's films were not evidence of an incompetent artist, but the markers of modernism.[3] As Geoff Andrew muses in *The Films of Nicholas Ray*, "classical notions of balance, restraint, and tastefulness were neither Ray's forte nor, probably, his concern" (169). What French critics saw in Ray was not simply another commercial director of crime films, Westerns, and family melodramas, but an iconoclast with a distinctive style working to reinvent those forms through experimentation within the system, giving audiences a vehicle for cultural critique: popular entertainment as rebellion.

While Ray may not have been a Rossellini or Bresson (although French critics made those comparisons), he also did not operate in the most derided regions of the culture industry that produced the "vulgar modernism" famously identified by film critic J. Hoberman in 1982. Hoberman cites animation director Tex Avery, cartoonist-turned-director Frank Tashlin (best known for his comedies with Jerry Lewis), *Mad* magazine, and the early morning television programs of comedian Ernie Kovacs among the detritus of American mass culture from 1940 to 1960 that comprised "the vulgar equivalent of modernism itself" (72). These media artists and texts demonstrated what Hoberman describes as "a popular, ironic, somewhat dehumanized mode reflexively concerned with the specific properties of its medium or the conditions of its making" (72). Ray's modernism, while certainly a product of mass culture, was always mainstream in its projected audience of middle-class consumers and lacked this formal reflexivity.

Another way to put this is that Ray was the missing link between Tashlin and Rossellini. With films such as *The True Story of Jesse James* and *Hot Blood*, Ray rivaled Tashlin for colorful, widescreen spectacles and youthful, comic-strip subjects (e.g., Western outlaws and torrid gypsy lovers). Other films such as *Johnny Guitar* raised the moral, ethical, and spiritual questions of a brooding European art film, its social conscience concerned with a violent drifter who learns to love and renounce his past even in a world where violence is all he knows. If one reads Jean-Luc Godard, they are likely to see Ray for his delirious pop style, but reading François Truffaut illuminates his liberal humanism and poetic regard for dispossessed members of society. The line, however, is arbitrary, as Ray often proves both of these directorial tendencies at once. Classical Hollywood allowed for these sorts of slippages, and that was precisely what made directors such as Ray adaptable to the modernisms in which this book approaches him.

Before plumbing the reception history of Ray's films, where we will see how French critics such as Godard and Truffaut redeemed them by ascribing a subversive, anti-middlebrow aesthetic, we first need to understand exactly why a Hollywood filmmaker would matter for modernism. In his book *The Cultural Front*, historian Michael Denning explicates the American activities during the 1930s that allowed possibilities for American avant-garde work in a plebeian, leftist vein. Ray's pre-Hollywood activities in the 1930s contributed to this "cultural front," which was the result of a convergence of the Popular Front, a democratic social movement, and the culture industries of mass entertainment and federal education projects (xviii). A new technological apparatus of mass culture (motion pictures, recorded sound, and broadcasting) put industries of leisure and entertainment into motion, while a new bureaucratic apparatus of the state collected, subsidized, and distributed information, education, and the arts through networks of schools and agencies (38–39).

Denning argues that the left, or "the tradition of radical democratic movements for social transformation," did not make a significant impact on American culture until the era of the Popular Front (3). As he defines it, the Popular Front was "a radical historical bloc uniting industrial unionists, Communists, independent socialists, community activists, and émigré anti-fascists around laborist social democracy, anti-fascism, and anti-lynching" (4). The culture of the Popular Front was not a historical phenomenon demarcated by the periodicity of decades, but according to Denning, "a cultural charter for a generation," and thus lasted through the postwar years. For example, we can see continuity between Clifford Odets's play staged by the Group Theatre about a labor strike among cab drivers, *Waiting for Lefty* (1935), in which Elia Kazan had a minor acting role, and Kazan's Hollywood film about battles with union corruption among longshoremen, *On the Waterfront* (1954). Kazan was a member of the American Communist Party (CPUSA) when he appeared in *Lefty*, but even though he directed *Waterfront* after he broke from Communism, he was still working in the proletariat vernacular of the Popular Front (26).

This social movement did not speak for all of American culture, and it never became a dominant culture, but it cultivated a new working-class culture on the left whose stories were retold and preserved by American institutions. The remarkable influence of the Popular Front can be found in everything from Hollywood films and broadcast media to literature and system of higher education. Dance, popular music, vaudeville, musical comedy, radio, comic strips, and cinema were all mass arts that young American modernists used to combat the genteel European traditions of the classical arts, which had been the domain of the private sphere and the educated leisure class (Gilbert Seldes's 1924 book *The Seven Lively Arts* was practically a "declaration of principles" for this school of thought) (38–39).

What was once locally produced gained national exposure, what was once "classical" could be accessible and inexpensive, and what was once entertainment for the working class became available for "cultured" audiences. Denning brings up how the cultural front "was built on this 'popularization' of high culture and diffusion of 'proletarian' and 'folk' culture" (42). Yet, he also attributes the leftist political thrust of the cultural front to the emergence of the *émigrés* and the *plebeians*. The American modernists before them tied formal experimentation to what Denning calls "a new social and historical vision" (59–60). Émigré artists and intellectuals who fled fascism may have been Marxists, left-wing activists, or members of the cultural front in Europe, and they reconstructed that project of American modernism in areas such as New York and Southern California. Plebeians such as Odets and Kazan were second-generation immigrants from working-class families whose futures as artists and intellectuals were enabled by the cultural front (60–61). While technically neither an émigré nor a plebeian, Ray shares affinities with both groups.

A native of the Midwest, Ray was born Raymond Nicholas Kienzle, Jr. in 1911 to middle-class parents Raymond and Olene "Lena" Kienzle in Galesville, Wisconsin, and he grew up about twenty-five miles south in the town of La Crosse, where he and his family moved in 1919. On his father's side, his grandparents emigrated from Germany, and on his mother's side, from Norway (Lena's maiden name was Toppen). Raymond Kienzle began his career in theater, and in 1935 he moved to New York City, changed his name to Nicholas Ray, and joined the agitprop group the Theatre of Action. Adapted from the theatrical practices of postrevolutionary Russia, American agitprop theater ("agitation-propaganda") sought to educate the workforce of the 1930s in contemporary political issues, particularly regarding labor and class struggles, to create solidarity and critique bourgeois aesthetics of dramatic realism. The Theatre of Action was formed in 1929, and originally called the Workers' Laboratory Theater. Emphasizing the study of acting, community living, collaborative production, and proletarian mobility, it performed on the streets, at docks, factories, churches, and assembly halls, and before trade unions, strike committees, and political organizations. The socialist acting company took inspiration for its stage performance techniques from the film aesthetics of Soviet montage, and it was here where Ray also joined the CPUSA.

Through the company's association with the Group Theatre, Ray met Kazan and under his tutelage learned "the Method." Kazan and Theatre of Action cofounder Alfred Saxe directed a commissioned play titled *The Young Go First*, the company's first production on a legitimate stage, marking Ray's first appearance in mainstream theater. The play dealt with experiences in a Civilian Conservation Corps camp, a public work relief program that gave unskilled manual labor jobs to unemployed, unmarried young men, who worked on conservation and the development of natural resources in government-owned land during the Depression. With its unusual improvisation techniques, the play introduced themes about the exploitation of youth that Ray would return to in his films. In October of 1936, Ray accepted a job teaching theater for eight months at the socialist Brookwood Labor College in Katonah, New York, and while in New York he put on a production of "The Body of an American" from Dos Passos's *U.S.A.* trilogy at Madison Square Garden.

The various agitprop groups of the time such as the Theatre of Action were replaced by the Federal Theatre Project (FTP), the subsidized theater program of the Works Progress Administration (WPA) created in 1935 to employ actors and other theater workers, which appealed both to avant-garde sensibilities and popular tastes. Director Joseph Losey, who also hailed from La Crosse, hired Ray in 1936 as a stage manager on a controversial Living Newspapers play about the history of the American Labor movement, *Injunction Granted*, which opened in 1939 and became one of the most successful productions of the FTP.[4] Borrowing from mime, dance, cabaret, and cinema, the radically experimental play was, in Losey's words, "[a]n attempt to break with traditional theater practice, to establish a new relationship between the play and the public" (qtd. in Eisenschitz 36). Losey went on to earn a cult following for modest Hollywood films such as *The Boy with the Green Hair* (1948) and *The Prowler* (1951), but after he was blacklisted he spent the rest of his career in Europe.

In addition to his service for the FTP, Ray joined musicologist Charles Seeger (father of folk music icon Pete Seeger), singer Margaret Valiant, and artists Ben Shahn and Jackson and Charles Pollock in the Special Skills Division of the Department of Agriculture's Resettlement Administration (RA). Ray was the head of the division's Theatre Section and was responsible for organizing community theater groups and performances among the local residents of government-planned communities, where families across America were forced to relocate as a result of famine or eviction. During 1937, when the Farm Security Administration (FSA) absorbed the RA, he traveled along the Appalachians and through the South with his first wife, journalist Jean Evans, recording American stories and folk songs on the recommendation of his friend folklorist and ethnomusicologist Alan Lomax (son of the pioneering folklorist and ethnomusicologist John Lomax). After funds dried up at the FSA, the WPA Recreation Division employed Ray as a drama consultant in 1938, where his duties were similar to those with the RA. Again, he roamed the country, recording audio tracks for the Library of Congress collection.

When Ray returned to New York, frustrated by the WPA's bureaucracy and budget cuts, his knowledge of folk music and the rural America led to a brief career in radio. The WPA projects did not compete with the culture industry and would not serve as a model for government support of the arts, and as the WPA projects were eliminated during World War II, artists found new homes in information agencies (Denning 45–46). Ray reunited with Lomax in 1941 for CBS Radio's folk music program *Back Where I Come From*, which showcased performances by Woody Guthrie, Burl Ives, Lead Belly, and others, some of whom visited Ray and Evans in the house they shared with Lomax and his wife Elizabeth in Arlington, Virginia during Ray's tenure with the RA.

Taking Ray under his wing once more, Kazan brought Ray to Hollywood as his assistant on his directorial debut, the Twentieth Century-Fox film *A Tree Grows in Brooklyn* (1945), an adaptation of Betty Smith's novel about an Irish-American family and their tenement life in Brooklyn at the turn-of-the-century. The films that made Kazan's name were yet to come, chiefly *A Streetcar Named Desire* (1951) and *On the Waterfront* starring Marlon Brando, as well as *East of Eden* (1955) starring James Dean. Before Ray moved into the director's chair himself, he joined the Hollywood Writers' Mobilization Group in 1944, a war propaganda and information organization established by the Screen Writers Guild, which had already been investigated by the Motion Picture Alliance for the Preservation of American Ideals, a conservative pressure group that claimed to defend Hollywood from Communist infiltration. Ray's only screenplay work at this time was uncredited; he served as dialogue director on the B thriller *The Caribbean Mystery* (1945) at Fox and sold the original story of the musical comedy *Swing Parade of 1946* (1946) to Monogram Pictures.

Opportunities outside of Hollywood eventually secured Ray's career as a film director. Émigré producer John Houseman knew Ray from the FTP and was a fan of *Back Where I Come From*. When Houseman was named head of the Overseas Programming Bureau, he recruited Ray to assist him on Voice of America, the national radio program of the Office of War Information (OWI), from 1941 to 1944. Ray assisted Houseman on a variety of other media projects: an OWI short titled *Tuesday in November* (1945), a propaganda film about the American electoral college; a CBS television version of the radio thriller *Sorry, Wrong Number* (1946); and the 1946 Broadway musicals *Lute Song*, starring Yul Brynner and Mary Martin, and *Beggar's Holiday*, featuring the music of Duke Ellington.[5]

Ray's involvement with New Deal agencies and American folk culture made him an ideal choice to direct *They Live by Night*, a film Houseman was producing for RKO based on *Thieves Like Us*, Edward Anderson's 1937 crime novel of the Depression era South (Eisenschitz 90). In fact, close listeners may recognize Woody Guthrie's "Going Down the Road Feeling Bad" playing on the radio of the getaway car after the Zelton bank robbery. Transitioning from theater and radio to cinema was the logical next step for Ray, given that "[h]is interest seemed to be in new methods of communication, in neglected means of expression, rather than in artistic forms," as Eisenschitz reports in his biography. "Of course he dreamed, like those who preceded him, Kazan and Losey, of becoming a director" (73).

The liberalism of Ray's films is most acutely felt through what might be called the "aesthetics of social significance" that characterized the cultural front. Ray was not alone in these efforts and some of his fellow social filmmakers were eventually blacklisted. Between the private industries and foundations that manufactured and subsidized culture, respectively, and the rising unionism in news and entertainment outlets, a climate of both "multi-national" or "corporate" liberalism and a plebeian workforce facilitated left-wing cultural production (Denning 83). Among the liberal voices in postwar Hollywood included: Ray, Losey, and Odets; independent producers Mark Hellinger and Walter Wanger; radical writers Bertolt Brecht, John Howard Lawson, Howard Koch, and John Wexley; social conscience filmmakers John Huston, Jules Dassin, and Stanley Kramer; émigré directors William Dieterle, Fred Zinnemann, Michael Curtiz, Anatole Litvak, Ernst Lubitsch, F. W. Murnau, and Jean Renoir; and two resolute independents who would soon be recognized as auteurs in France, Charles Chaplin and Orson Welles. Former members of the CPUSA in the 1930s, Kazan and his *On the Waterfront* scribe Budd Schulberg testified as friendly witnesses before the House Un-American

Activities Committee (HUAC) in order to clear their names (Schulberg in 1951 and Kazan in 1952).

Hollywood studios were factories for films and genres stamped with the ideologies of the cultural front. Twentieth Century-Fox produced an earnest cycle of "problem" or "message" pictures under Darryl F. Zanuck, while Warner Bros. made populist crime films and antifascist action-adventures under Jerry Wald and Hal B. Wallis (vehicles for contract stars Humphrey Bogart, James Cagney, and Bette Davis). Émigrés such as Billy Wilder and Robert Siodmak, and plebeians such as Abraham Polonsky and Edward Dmytryk, directed films that would qualify as film noir. Blacklistees such as producer Adrian Scott and writers Albert Maltz, Robert Rossen, and Dalton Trumbo also worked on now classic examples of the genre. Over the first years of the Cold War, RKO intervened with urban thrillers and gritty melodramas under Dore Schary that have since been categorized as *film gris*, or "gray film." Los Angeles–based filmmaker, scholar, and educator Thom Andersen coined this term in 1985, referring to "a new genre of Hollywood films in the late 1940s, between the first HUAC hearings of October 1947 and the second of May 1951" that were created by the Hollywood Ten—the first group of blacklisted writers and directors—and "their artistic fellow travelers" (257). Of the thirteen films Andersen cites, Ray directed two: *They Live by Night* and *Knock on Any Door*.[6]

Andersen configures film gris as an outgrowth of film noir, embodied by the plebeian screen presence of blacklisted Method actor John Garfield, and distinguished by its "greater psychological and social realism." "The term seems appropriate because we have been taught to associate Communism with drabness and grayness," he remarks, "and these films are often drab and depressing and almost always photographed in black-and-white" (257). Humphrey Bogart chose Ray to direct *Knock on Any Door* for his independent company Santana Productions on the basis of the social realist tone he admired in *They Live by Night* (Eisenschitz 116). A courtroom drama about a Chicago defense attorney (Bogart) who tries to save an Italian-American juvenile delinquent (John Derek) from the electric chair, the film recalls Weegee's photographs of the Bowery in its shots of gray Skid Row streets (Eisenschitz 116).[7] The cinematographer Burnett Guffey specialized in what would be later termed *film noir*, and made Hollywood itself a shadowy, monochromatic landscape of deferred dreams in Ray's next teaming with Bogart, *In a Lonely Place*.

The "aesthetics of social significance" to which these names contributed reflects the prevailing "social realism" of documentary expression during the Depression (Denning 118–119). One need to look no further than the photographs for the FSA, a collectivizing agriculture program in charge of rehabilitating impoverished landowning farmers, sharecroppers, and tenants by resettling them on large plots of government-owned land to farm in groups. Journalist and poet James Agee (later an author, screenwriter, and film critic) and photographer Walker Evans published one of the most noteworthy examples of the form in 1941, *Let Us Now Praise Famous Men*, which documents the lives of three "Dust Bowl" families. Years after *They Live by Night* and *Knock on Any Door*, Ray's semi-ethnographic fascination with regional histories and indigenous peoples became more pronounced with *Wind across the Everglades*, a film about bird poachers in the early twentieth-century Florida Everglades, starring Burl Ives, and *The Savage Innocents*, a film about Eskimos based on archival research.[8]

We need not think of these aesthetic practices as approaches to realist representation and verisimilitude that are antithetical to the avant-garde innovation and experimentation in modernism. Denning insists that "the documentary aesthetic was actually a central modernist innovation" (118). What documentary projects such as the FSA photographs and Agee and Evans's book lay bare are the formal and political issues that this very mode of expression raises. Depression era cultural history and criticism reoriented its objects of study and terms of debate to pursue, as Denning describes, "the problematics of capturing the 'real,' the desire for the objectivity and immediacy of 'experience,' the dangers of manipulation and propaganda." Thus, the documentary of the Depression can be read as "a witness to Depression America's desire to see the 'real' and a cautionary tale of [its own] tragic superficiality" (119).

When viewed at the intersections of an American modernism in the 1930s and a French modernism of the 1950s, Ray is illuminated by a transatlantic dual-focus of modernism before and after World War II that makes the "use value" of American mass culture visible in a late modernist enterprise. The fusion between the Popular Front and the culture industries equipped American cultural producers to realize the socially democratic potential of mass arts, aligning them with a laborist avant-garde as opposed to elitist bourgeois traditions. However, for legions of young people in postwar France, the American pop of Hollywood cinema empowered them with the raw material for an antifascist revolution in the arts against the European *haute bourgeoisie*, whereby consumers could become producers of culture.

Postwar France was the primary context in which Ray's reputation first developed, and his American modernism was part and parcel of the modernization of their own national film culture by critics and cinephiles. During the war, the Axis powers had prohibited the exhibition of American films in Occupied countries, but after the collapse of the Vichy government, Hollywood was able to take advantage of reopened international markets as European countries attempted to rebuild their economic infrastructures. The American government supported the Motion Picture Export Association, which was created in 1945 to stimulate overseas business while exporting capitalism and democracy, and Hollywood's economic downturn from 1947 into the 1950s required the industry to look to foreign sales as compensation for domestic losses.[9] As a result of the influx of American consumer goods, and at a time when the country's economy prospered, European nations feared the spread of American imperialism and sought to preserve their own national identity in the face of competition with, among other things, Hollywood movies.

French culture was ambivalent in its response to this crisis of art and politics, and the import of American products engendered divisive stances within the nation. In his book *Seducing the French*, historian Richard F. Kuisel argues that the anti-American sentiments that characterized France transformed into "an assumption that the New World is a social model for the future" (ix). Kuisel shows how in the postwar years, "France became modern or 'Americanized' and yet remained French" through a process of "resistance, selective imitation, adaptation, and acceptance" (x). For example, as the country secured its standing within Europe's new geopolitical map and wage earners began to enjoy greater income, a rising consumer society in the 1950s fostered an alliance with American technology and mass culture that could potentially enhance its middle-class lifestyle.

The French intellectual establishment, however, debated concerns surrounding the Americanization of France: the homogenizing effects of consumerism; the social pressures to conform; the anti-intellectual privileging of leisure entertainments over art; and a sense of optimism employed for conservative ideological control. Kuisel finds that resisting the American way for the French intelligentsia meant preserving "a revolutionary posture or, at least, a critical social stance," as well as "a defense of national identity against a modern barbarism" (126). On the other hand, he adds, "America in the 1950s represented counterrevolution and mass culture" (127).

Pells has also probed French-American relations after World War II in his book *Not Like Us*. Unlike the older, more conservative generation, the youth of postwar France consumed mass culture in what they perceived as liberating acts of defiance against authority, which included their parents, especially if they had been pro-Nazi during the war.

Fashion statements were also rebellious personal statements, articulating an ethos of both freedom and fashionable alienation. In repurposing products of Fordist consumerism into works of modernist art, the young people incited a countertradition in France. As Pells explains, "For the young, American culture was attractive precisely because its pleasures were unauthorized—because of its vulgarity, its primitivism, its indifference to the pretensions of art and philosophy. From the 1940s on, youthful Europeans identified with those elements in American society that appeared marginal, alienated, and definitely not middle-class" (241). No wonder that a generation inspired by Beat poetry, jazz, and rock and roll would identify with a juvenile delinquent played by James Dean in *Rebel without a Cause*—as Godard taught us, these were the children of Marx and Coca-Cola. John Derek's catchphrase from *Knock on Any Door*, "Live fast, die young, and have a good looking corpse," could have been the mantra for French moviegoers of a certain age.

Hollywood movies were a particular source of inspiration for an emerging group of young French cinephiles. Under the leadership of Henri Langlois, the Cinémathèque Française was cofounded with Paul-Auguste Harle, Georges Franju, and Jean Mitry in 1936, and introduced French audiences to America's genre films and the populist directors of the 1940s and 1950s who would shape *la politique des auteurs*. By the outbreak of World War II, Langlois had acquired one of the largest collections of films and related materials in the world, and when the Nazis threatened to destroy his collection, he and his colleagues hid caches in unoccupied areas of France, where they remained protected until the end of the war. The Cinémathèque would therefore be remembered as a testament to the antifascist, revolutionary spirit of cinephilia, and it became an international nonprofit center for film exhibition, preservation, and education.

During World War II, French intellectuals had also been enthusiasts of modernist American literature and praised its tough male authors such as Ernest Hemingway, William Faulkner, John Dos Passos, and Dashiell Hammett. A generation of American modernists had also crossed over into Hollywood (both Faulkner and Dos Passos, as well as F. Scott Fitzgerald, Nathanael West, and Raymond Chandler), although they had limited success in the film industry. Pells notes that while some French intellectuals "read American novels surreptitiously as a 'symbol of resistance' to the Nazi occupation," others related to "the depiction of desperate human beings caught in extreme situations" (*Not* 248).

This fascination with proletariat writing—a rejection of stale French literary traditions, European gentility, and elitist bourgeois culture—was also reflected in their discovery of American films as a hip antidote to "official" French cinema. Critics Nino Frank and Jean-Pierre Chartier (writing in *L'Ecran Francais* and *Revue du Cinéma*, respectively) were so impressed by the existential and surrealist worldview of the dark, urban melodramas, mysteries, and crime thrillers coming out of Hollywood, that in 1946 they grouped these films under the term *film noir* in homage to the Poetic Realist cinema and the *Roman Noir* from their own national heritage.[10]

In her book on horror cinema and the avant-garde, *Cutting Edge*, Joan Hawkins refers to a homoerotic romance with American machismo at Pierre Rissient's Cinema MacMahon in Paris, where Ray's films found a home. Swooning over the violent action films of Joseph Losey, Budd Boetticher, and Raoul Walsh, members of the theater and its journal *Présence du cinema* waxed rhapsodic over Hollywood's masculinist orientation and, as Hawkins observes, an aesthetic that "drew equally from high and low culture" (18). Among other things, the misogynistic phenomenon of MacMahonism launched a Charlton Heston cult led by *Présence* coeditor Michel Mourlet, who published a tribute to the star in *Cahiers du cinéma*, France's most influential film magazine. It would become the most important international site for the propagation of Ray's directorial reputation in the 1950s.

Founded in 1951 by André Bazin, Jacques Doniol-Valcroze, Joseph-Marie Lo Duca, and Léonide Keigel, *Cahiers du cinéma* developed from a forerunner titled *Revue du cinéma* and drew members from the Parisian cine-clubs Objectif 49 and Ciné-Club du Quartier Latin, and the monthly *La Gazette du cinéma*. The first generation of contributors included Jean-Luc Godard, François Truffaut, Claude Chabrol, Jacques Rivette, and Éric Rohmer, some of whom were MacMahonists and all of whom became filmmakers of the *nouvelle vague*. If there was any orthodoxy to this heterogeneous, polemical, aphoristic, and passionately evaluative writing on film during the 1950s, it was *la politique des auteurs*, a "paradigm shift" that Peter Wollen describes as "the last of a series of twentieth-century critical revolutions in the name of 'modernism' and against the *ancien régime* of artistic values" (*Paris* 218).

The critical project at *Cahiers du cinéma*, both aesthetic and impressionistic in nature, was to celebrate cinema on separate but equal terms with the other arts as a unique form of creative expression. Truffaut published "A Certain Tendency of the French Cinema" in 1954, a manifesto that decried the pretentious psychological realism and "Tradition of Quality" dominating plot- and character-driven French cinema after

World War II. According to Truffaut, the stuffy, middlebrow literary adaptations of the era upheld bourgeois values and aesthetic philosophies, whereas Hollywood cinema (in addition to Italian Neo-Realism) offered a model for the future of filmmaking in the auteur, or a director with a personal vision and signature style. An auteur demonstrated consistency and progression over his body of work at the level of mise-en-scène. The *Cahiers du cinéma* axiom therefore advocated, above all else, the director as artist or author: the single, controlling force who organizes the entire film in its stylistic, thematic, and ideological structure. What the young cinephiles at the magazine did not take on were the social and political issues of the day, such as Indo-China and the Algerian War, as either contexts for or subjects of contemporary cinema. Despite accusations of conservativism, particularly when compared to the rival left-bank magazine *Positif* (Bickerton 27–28), this French critical writing of the 1950s in some ways inadvertently picked up where the American "cultural front" left off in its commitment to the avant-garde potential of American mass culture.

Authorial significance registers differently in these contexts of production and reception, but is still connected to progressive cultural work. For example, Dos Passos's experimental "Newsreel" and "Camera Eye" sections in *The 42nd Parallel* (1930), *1919* (1932), and *The Big Money* (1936), which comprise his *U.S.A.* trilogy, are evidence of what might be called a "cinematic writing." Read in light of the cultural front, he was a radical author whose social realism revealed the modernist crisis of the documentary impulse in the 1930s. The Dos Passos of postwar France, on the other hand, was a Sartrean existentialist who resonated with readers traumatized by years of Nazi Occupation, and who understood their reliance on individual action and consciousness to navigate a modern world of absurdity and meaninglessness.

Hollywood auteurs were in many ways extensions of the American modernists for French critics, and comparing literary authors with film directors was an effort to rescue cinema (or at least certain types of cinema) as serious art. At *Cahiers du cinéma*, Hollywood auteurs were also celebrated for their unabashed populism: their command of movie stars (e.g., Humphrey Bogart), their interpretation of genres (e.g., the Western), and, most of all, their deployment of cinematic technologies that emphasized the spectacle and sensory effects of the medium during Hollywood's competition with television for audiences in the 1950s (e.g., color and widescreen).[11]

The auteur was not necessarily the historical person who exercised complete autonomy in the making of a film (this attribution would be difficult to establish without empirical evidence of the film's production, to which the *Cahiers du cinéma* critics did not have access). More of an imaginary figure, the auteur was the director's "second self" fabricated in the creation of an oeuvre. As Cecilia Sayad remarks in her book *Performing Authorship*, this performative quality of authorship underscores the director's always already "conscious or involuntary impulse to masquerade" (4). Ray's "image" here was the organizing principle for his films, as well as a face for the rebellion acted out in and through them, long before he embodied the persona of the auteur in his public celebrity and film performances as himself. Partly constructed by the director, this image is also constructed by critics. Outlaws of "official" French cinema, the *Cahiers du cinéma* critics formed auteur cults that made-over Hollywood directors as authors/authenticators of cinematic outlawry, and thus "Nicholas Ray" guaranteed rebellion as a symbol of both modernism and mass culture.

Ray's Reception at *Cahiers du cinéma,* 1953–60

Saving cinema as an art form was not enough; *Cahiers du cinéma* was also committed to saving film criticism from pedantic, sanctimonious scholarship. The Hollywood directors most important to its critics at this time included the American-born Orson Welles, Anthony Mann, Robert Aldrich, Samuel Fuller, and Vincente Minnelli, along with émigrés such as Joseph von Sternberg, Fritz Lang, Otto Preminger, Douglas Sirk, Max Ophuls, and Edgar G. Ulmer. Alfred Hitchcock and Howard Hawks served as their Alpha and Omega, but Ray was their test case for *la politique des auteurs*. "Early contributions on Nicholas Ray bring out the distinctiveness of each critic," writes Emilie Bickerton in her book *A Short History of Cahiers du cinéma*, pointing out the eclecticism of the magazine (24). Whereas "Godard and Rivette celebrated the unprecedented in Ray," she continues, "Rohmer drew out timeless issues of morality and tragedy" (25), while "Truffaut was aggressive, prescriptive and darkly comical" (24). The following reception history will look closely at the particular ways in which each of these critics found validation of their aesthetic principles in Ray's films.

The auteur was conceived at *Cahiers du cinéma* as a point of conjunction between modernism and mass culture, but also among modernism, romanticism, and the avant-garde. James Naremore sees an "old-fashioned enthusiasm" about movies in Godard and his cohort that went out of vogue in 1960s cultural criticism (think of Andy Warhol's cool detachment and Leslie Fielder or Susan Sontag's condescension toward the medium) ("Authorship" 18). The cinephilia of the magazine's critics opposed both heavy-handed traditions of quality and the binary between modernism and mass culture. If *la politique des auteurs* resounds with a nostalgia for a preindustrial conception of authorship and high art, it also looks to the media technologies of modern machine culture as potentially liberating, and therefore straddled the line between romantic aestheticism and surrealism ("Authorship" 16).[12]

Godard defended even Ray's most disparaged films—especially those films, in fact—such as *Hot Blood*, which stars Jane Russell and Cornel Wilde as feuding newlyweds from two gypsy tribes in Los Angeles (former Group Theatre member Luther Adler plays the gypsy king) (see fig. 1.1). Ray's medium-specificity was the chief attribute Godard cited in his review, a modernist idea that was typically conceived in terms of painting or literature, but Ray's mastery of Technicolor and the CinemaScope frame put him in the category of cinema's greatest artists. "If the cinema no longer existed," Godard proclaimed, "Nicholas Ray alone gives the impression of being capable of reinventing it, and what is more, of wanting to" ("Nothing" 116). What brought his films to life for Godard was Ray's "innate sense of cinema," much like the automatic manner of the early surrealists ("Nothing" 117). This comparison runs contrary to the ways in which auteurs would be conceived in later contexts as controlled technicians.

Comparing him to Kees van Dongen, an early twentieth-century modern painter known for his portraits that accentuated garish colors over realist representation, Godard praised Ray's "deliberate and systematic use of the gaudiest colors to be seen in the cinema: barley-sugar orange shirts, acid-green dresses, violet cars, blue and pink carpets." *Hot*

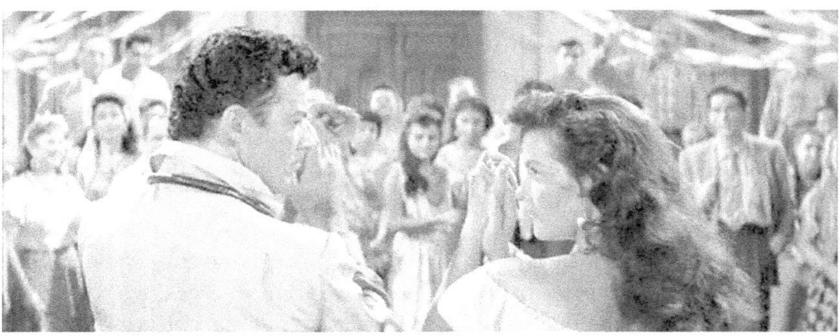

Figure 1.1. *Hot Blood* (1956): Jean-Luc Godard defended even Ray's most disparaged films—especially those films, in fact—such as *Hot Blood*, which stars Jane Russell and Cornel Wilde as feuding newlyweds from two gypsy tribes in Los Angeles. (Warner Home Video, 2010; digital frame enlargement)

Blood was Ray's third Technicolor film, following *Flying Leathernecks* and *Run for Cover*. Godard also acknowledged his use of contrast to create depth of focus, given the short focal length of the CinemaScope lens ("Nothing" 117). The medium-specificity Godard valued was central to the *Cahiers du cinéma* critics' investment in Ray and also to his long-term appeal with cinephiles.

Ray's films represented cinema itself, the exciting power and potential unique to the medium as a modern art form. "After seeing *Johnny Guitar* and *Rebel without a Cause*," Godard professed, "one cannot but feel that here is something which exists only in the cinema, which would be nothing in a novel, the stage or anywhere else, but which becomes fantastically beautiful on the screen" ("Nothing" 116). Auteurs such as Ray achieved what was known as "pure cinema," in which films made aesthetic meaning through the essentials of the medium: editing, sound, camerawork, movement, and elements of mise-en-scène. In other words, his films were "nothing but cinema," as the title of Godard's review announced.

Indeed, *Hot Blood* is just the sort of hyperkinetic, candy-colored piece of American popular culture that would have delighted Godard with its audacity and excesses, and could have only been possible in the medium of cinema. Behind the color and contrast that he attributed to Ray's "innate sense of cinema," the film also evinces Ray's preoccupation with folk culture from his days with the cultural front. The original idea for the film was based on ethnographic research Jean Evans conducted over weeks in New York City interviewing store-front gypsies on First, Second, and Third Avenues on the Lower East Side in 1951 (Eisenschitz 258). Ray had wanted to take advantage of this material and make an on-location film about urban gypsy life in contemporary America, collaborating with screenwriter Walter Newman on a first draft of the script while under contract at RKO.

Although it never moved into production at his old studio, it attracted attention from Russell (Eisenschitz 186). Independent producer Howard Welsch and Columbia Pictures gave the film a green light in the mid-1950s, when Ray abandoned the original script and began improvised research for a new script by Jesse Lasky, Jr. (Evans had lost interest by this point). Ex-boxer Roger Donoghue, Ray's assistant and consultant on *Rebel without a Cause*, helped with the research and writing (Eisenschitz 257–58).[13] No longer shot on location, but in Columbia's soundstages, *Hot Blood* plays less like an ethnographic film than a sexy melodrama with colorful musical overtones. Russell and Wilde perform an S&M style "whip dance," and Russell delivers an inner monologue in the form of a song written specifically for the film, "I Could Learn to Love You," which she sings in voice-over while miming the sequence with Wilde (Wagner 163). Ray had always aspired to direct a musical (Andrew 20). Although he never achieved his goal, one can find traces in the set pieces here, and later in the dance sequences of *Party Girl* with Cyd Charisse and *King of Kings* with Brigid Bazlen.

The color Western *The True Story of Jesse James*, produced by Twentieth Century-Fox, directly contributed to Ray's outlaw persona by turning to a legendary American outlaw and folk hero as the subject (the role of Jesse went to the young contract player Robert Wagner, who was about to marry Natalie Wood, one of Ray's recent discoveries).[14] Godard's review deemphasized the importance of traditional storytelling, social message, and fidelity to source material in evaluating the film's direction. Calling Ray "the most peculiarly modern of filmmakers," he went on to commend his framing of actors and his rendering of abstract ideas through widescreen compositions, attention to décor, and the editing of dialogue scenes in his films. Rather than faithfully adapting James D. Horan's 1949 novel of the James Gang, *The Desperate Men*, which itself was based on archival sources, Ray made, in Godard's words, "a more detailed *Rebel without a Cause*" (*Godard* 60).

Twentieth Century-Fox had successfully brought Horan's *The Desperate Men* to the screen in 1939 with *Jesse James*, directed by Henry King, and *True Story* was conceived as a straight remake for the studio that could reuse footage from the earlier color film in CinemaScope.[15] *True Story* also returned Ray to his cultural front roots with Benjamin A. Botkin's 1944 volume, *A Treasury of American Folklore*, produced from Botkin's work with the Federal Writers Project, from which Ray drew as a source (Eisenschitz 290). From 1942 to 1945, Botkin was assistant director of the Archive of American Folk Song at the Library of Congress (eventually succeeding John and Alan Lomax as director), where he and Ray first met.

After scrapping the first draft of the script by Russell S. Hughes, Ray brought in *Hot Blood*'s original screenwriter, Walter Newman, to write a new version with a flashback structure (Eisenschitz 284–85), which reached a kind of modernist fragmentation in the narrative. British writer Gavin Lambert, Ray's assistant and lover at the time, worked with Ray on revisions, as well as on the development and improvisation of new scenes, but studio-imposed changes continued during filming (Eisenschitz 285). At Fox's behest during postproduction, old scenes were cut, others were reshot, and new scenes altogether were added, in addition to colored, misty inserts to transition between past and present. That Ray ultimately "lost control" over the production, forced to relinquish it to studio head Buddy Adler and producer Herbert B. Swope, Jr., makes it especially apt for close readings by cinephiles such as Godard, in search of a textual unconscious, those fleeting or incomplete moments that bear the hallmarks of an auteur. Godard's review demonstrates the way Ray's "second self," or the *idea* of Ray as auteur, often surpassed Ray as a historical person in the *Cahiers du cinéma* discourse on authorship.

Thus, Ray earned his status as an auteur not simply through his modern techniques, but in his image as an antiestablishment employee of the studio system, rebelling against studio traditions in order to champion a personal artistic vision. Godard wrote:

> Where the crafty businessman saw in *The True Story* a means to attract spectators tired of a story which had already been dished up in every conceivable manner, the filmmaker on the other hand saw the legend already taking shape behind the true facts, and behind the existence, the essence. Which explains the constant battles between producer and director. Like Orson Welles before him, Nicholas Ray left Hollywood before shooting ended, defeated, slamming the door behind him (*Godard* 58).

Ray left Hollywood to shoot *Bitter Victory* for Paul Graetz's French-based company Transcontinental Films. This World War II film follows two men in the British Army—a cowardly German captain, David Brand (Curd Jürgens), and a South African major, James Leith (Richard Burton)—sent on a mission to Libya to seize secret documents from the German headquarters.[16]

Godard named *Bitter Victory* the best film of 1957, and in his review heralded "[t]he world of modern cinema," a cinema that transcends the power of individual stills, objects in a frame, and even the medium itself ("Stars" 118). "For *Bitter Victory* is not a reflection of life," wrote Godard, "it is life itself turned into film, seen from behind the mirror where the cinema intercepts it. It is at once the most direct and the most secret of films, the most subtle and the crudest" ("Stars" 119). Former French Resistance member René Hardy wrote the script with Ray and Lambert, adapting his own 1956 novel, *Amère victoire*, and Graetz later asked American author and sports writer Paul Gallico to join the team as a script doctor. The film was censored to downplay its antiwar themes, eliminating the cynical ending for its release in most countries (in which the lying and murderous Brand is awarded the Distinguished Service Order by his commanding officer after Leith sacrifices his life for him). Running 102 minutes, it was edited down to 90 minutes for Britain, 87 minutes for the French-dubbed version, and 82 minutes for American audiences (Eisenschitz 308). Although it was completed in 1957, and played internationally (competing for the Golden Lion at the Venice Film Festival), it did not receive an American release until Columbia Pictures distributed it in 1958.

The "blinding" truth Godard witnessed in the film, though, comes not from the screenplay or its critique of military bureaucracy ("Stars" 119), but from the editing, from Jurgens and Burton's performances ("Stars" 118), and from Ray's discovery of a cosmic aesthetic beyond fiction and reality: "The stars, maybe, and men who look at them and dream" ("Stars" 119). Only the heavens, for Godard, seem to do justice to the film, with its stark black-and-white location shooting and lateral framings of the desert moonscape within the CinemaScope aspect ratio (see fig. 1.2).[17] It is as if to say the film's otherworldly images belong exclusively to the dreamlike experience of cinema, but also require a new kind of language with which to talk about cinema. By declaring that "the cinema is Nicholas Ray," Godard reiterated the medium-specific thesis of his review of *Hot Blood*: a great film must be personally authored according to cinematic form, and that meaning is produced from the union of form and content.

François Truffaut's writing on Ray was less hyperbolic and more humanistic than Godard's. Attracted to Ray as a young, outsider artist, Truffaut took to him as a director of misunderstood films about characters on the

Figure 1.2. *Bitter Victory* (1957): Only the heavens, for Godard, seem to do justice to the film, with its stark black-and-white location shooting and lateral framings of the desert moonscape within the CinemaScope aspect ratio. (Sony Pictures Home Entertainment, 2005; digital frame enlargement)

fringes of society, who was himself marginalized by audiences, critics, and the industry. In Truffaut's review of the bizarrely eccentric Western *Johnny Guitar*, he remarked that *In a Lonely Place*, *On Dangerous Ground*, and *The Lusty Men* "went virtually unnoticed by all but the most discerning," and that "Ray's films bore the public, irritated as they are by the films' slowness, their seriousness, and indeed their realism, which shocks them by its extravagance" ("Wonderful" 107). The *Cahiers du cinéma* critics had been exposed to *They Live by Night* in 1949, when it was prominently featured at the *Festival du Film Maudit*, a series for unjustly neglected films ("Wonderful" n108). For Truffaut, Ray was a modernist in that he shared a closer kinship with a European art director than one of his American contemporaries; he was the "Rossellini of Hollywood" and "the poet of nightfall," but "in Hollywood everything is permissible, except poetry" ("Wonderful" 108).

The lurid Trucolor palette of *Johnny Guitar* was a primer for an "extravagance" of realism that his color films portrayed throughout the second-half of the decade (see fig. 1.3).[18] Color enhanced its theatrical

Figure 1.3. *Johnny Guitar* (1954): The lurid Trucolor palette of *Johnny Guitar*, Ray's second color film following the Technicolor outing *Flying Leathernecks*, was a primer for an "extravagance" of realism that his color films portrayed throughout the second half of the 1950s. (OliveFilms, 2012; digital frame enlargement)

mise-en-scène as a stage for explosive emotional conflicts and sublimated psychosexual tensions, allowing Ray to play further with the depth, contrast, figural positions and movements, and rich textures that he began in his black-and-white films. Truffaut called *Johnny Guitar* "the *Beauty and the Beast* of Westerns, a Western dream" (*Films* 142), grouping Ray with the French high-modernist Jean Cocteau, another auteur with a penchant for grotesque beauty.

Despite comments about Ray's "beautiful positioning of figures within the frame," Truffaut saw Ray's greatest success in the emotion with which he imbued each shot, his sincerity and sensitivity, his "triumph of the heart," not necessarily his formal harmony (Truffaut accused Ray's films of being technically "disjointed") ("Wonderful" 108). *Johnny Guitar*, he determined, tells the same story as Ray's other films: "the story of a violent man who wants to stop being violent, and his relationship with a woman who has more moral strength than himself. For Ray's hero is invariably a man lashing out, weak, a child man when he is not simply a child" ("Wonderful" 107). Although it was Ray's imaginary "second self" who received much of the acclaim at *Cahiers du cinéma*, his historical subjectivity was not unacknowledged. Truffaut's review alludes to the ways in which Ray's troubled life paralleled his characters onscreen, just as Truffaut would be known for autobiographical trademarks in his own films ("Wonderful" n108).

Despite its reputation as one of Ray's signature masterpieces, the authorship of *Johnny Guitar* remains one of the film's many ambiguities. Star Joan Crawford purchased the rights to the novel from its author, her friend Roy Chanslor, before he published it in 1953. Chanslor wrote the first draft of the script, but Philip Yordan, who claims to have joined the production *after* filming began, took the sole writing credit. Yordan often hired "surrogate" writers to work under his name, including his longtime secretary and some blacklisted writers. The person responsible for Crawford's prominent role in the film was none other than Crawford herself, who demanded that Yordan beef up her character, even though her estranged lover Johnny Logan was ostensibly the protagonist (McGilligan 244–55). Although Ray may have enjoyed more freedom on this film at Republic Pictures than he was used to at RKO, studio head Herbert Yates held the real authority, and his primary concern was the happiness of his $200,000 star (Eisenschitz 203). So contentious was Crawford and Ray's relationship that it actually inspired Lambert's "The Closed Set," one of the Hollywood Babylon stories collected in his 1954 book *The Slide Area*.

More than any of Ray's films, *Johnny Guitar* is symptomatic of Ray's cultural front politics. Yordan has explained that the film was intended as an anti-McCarthyist allegory (McGilligan 415). As a saloon owner planning to build a train depot on her property, who is driven off her land by local cattlemen opposed to the coming of the railroad, Vienna (Crawford) represents victims of the blacklist. The puritanical rancher Emma Small (Mercedes McCambridge), who leads the cattlemen in a lynch mob (read: "witch hunt"), represents HUAC. Ward Bond, a member of the Motion Picture Alliance for the Preservation of American Ideals, plays the "red-baiting" lawman who accuses Vienna of acting as an accomplice in a stagecoach robbery and murder. By contrast, the gunslinger-turned-guitar player whom Vienna hires for protection is played by Sterling Hayden, a former member of the CPUSA who "named names" for HUAC in 1951.[19]

Ray had been saved from the blacklist by Howard Hughes, Dore Schary's replacement as head of RKO, who extended Ray's contract and assigned him to direct the World War II aviation film *Flying Leathernecks*, a piece of right-wing propaganda for the U.S. Marine Corps starring John Wayne. Although Hughes's patronage spared Ray a summons to appear in court and testify, Ray was forced to testify in private. Nothing is known about his statement except that he accused his ex-wife Evans as having invited him to the Communist Youth League, an allegation she later denied (Eisenschitz 124). Whether Yordan was retroactively guiding critics' readings of *Johnny Guitar* in a way that was never intended, and whether Ray had much involvement in the film's writing at all, is a matter of conjecture. The film was not interpreted as a response to McCarthyism at the time of its release. However, this allegorical reading has certainly informed contemporary critical discourse, and even abstracted from the repressive Cold War context, the film remains a biting critique of xenophobia, mob rule, and authoritarian regimes at odds with liberal American democracy.

What intrigued the *Cahiers du cinéma* critics about *Johnny Guitar* is not the control Ray may have exerted over the production, but the ways in which his own "poetic" style comes through despite his industrial limitations as a director. The film does not reflect the stated or conscious intentions of a singular filmmaker (uncovering directorial intentionality was never what *la politique des auteurs* was about, contrary to assumptions and generalizations). Rather, it reflects what an auteur did with those limitations, transcending the sort of studio-commissioned project in which a lesser filmmaker would have floundered, and subsuming a third-party screenplay into a personal worldview.

Like *Johnny Guitar*, *Bigger Than Life* was maligned by mainstream American reviewers in the 1950s,[20] but for Truffaut, it brought the revelatory experience of Ray's films to a feverish climax. A family melodrama about an intellectual schoolteacher (James Mason) addicted to cortisone, and the horror that he reins down on his wife and son, the film was adapted from Berton Roueché's nonfiction story "Ten Feet Tall" published in the *New Yorker* in 1955. Godard included it on his list of the ten greatest American sound films, published in the December 1963–January 1964 issue of *Cahiers du cinéma* (*Godard* 204), and Truffaut named it one of the best films of 1957, its year of release in France.

Describing the close-ups as among the most beautiful he had ever seen in CinemaScope, Truffaut compared Ray to the great surrealist Luis Buñuel, but he was once again most enamored with Ray's presentation of solitude and violence:

> In his first films Ray treated violence and the moral solitude of the violent with a certain approval. Gradually he has set out to demonstrate the vanity of violence and the importance of clearheadedness. Now, he gives us again the portrait of a man whose intransigence leads him to moral solitude, but, although he shows him as wrong, he nevertheless, while demonstrating the emptiness of violence, also offers proof that lucidity is not an end in itself; his hero is an escapee from the hell of logic. (*Films* 146)

Truffaut first saw *Bigger Than Life* at the Venice Film Festival, where it competed for the Golden Lion and where his fellow critics dismissed it for unconvincingly finding the tragedy in an ordinary cortisone overdose. However, the dialectics between truth and countertruth, between logic and irrationality, were more important to him than claims to the believable psychology of contemporary tragedy. Truffaut read the film instead as a fable, a commentary on the limits of science, and a critique of so-called medical miracles and miracle drugs.

The film was to be another entry in Twentieth Century-Fox's postwar social problem cycle. Once the studio agreed to let Ray adapt the *New Yorker* article, Mason, also the film's producer, hired Cyril Hume and Richard Maibaum to write the screenplay. Ray was interested in the film as an indictment against the underpaid salary of public schoolteachers and the "keeping up with the Joneses" mentality of middle-class America, and thought that Hume and Maibaum's approach felt more like a medical case history faithful to the *New Yorker* story. After Ray recruited Lambert to doctor the script, he brought it to his old colleague in leftist theater, Clifford Odets, who reworked it further. Odets gave the film some of its pessimistic themes about the gradual abandonment of idealism as one settles into middle age (Eisenschitz 273), while the dynamic camera movements, baroque angles and lighting, lush colors, and expressionistic CinemaScope compositions were the stuff of Ray's medium-specific style.

The antihero Ed Avery, who has resigned to what he perceives as a life of "petty domesticity," is diagnosed with a rare, degenerative inflammation of the arteries that may leave him with only a few more months to live. Spending after school hours as a switchboard operator for a taxicab company in order to compensate for his low wages, Ed also suffers from embittered feelings of inadequacy as an emasculated patriarch, failing to perform his socially prescribed role as the breadwinner and head of the household (at one point he even refers to himself as a "male school marm"). Ray and Lambert rejected Odets's villainization of Ed's wife as a spend-crazy social climber (Eisenschitz 273), but Ed's latent resentment toward his family is still apparent in the first act of the film.

Another *Cahiers du cinéma* critic who supported *Bigger Than Life* was Éric Rohmer. Both Truffaut and Rohmer suggested that the cortisone Ed takes for his illness does not create his problem, but exacerbates the problem that was always already there. This experimental "medical drug" allows Ed to see more clearly than ever before. Cursed by a mad lucidity of mind, he sets out to become "bigger than life" and "ten feet tall," striving to rise above dull, petit bourgeois mediocrity by insisting Lou shop at an upscale designer clothing store and holding impossible standards for his son Richie to achieve. Innocuous activities such as playing football with Richie in the backyard and checking his homework turn into pathological systems of abuse. Paradoxically, Ed's despotic mission to become an extraordinary individual is both alienating (he is an outlaw of cultural convention) *and* conformist with the normative American standards of the postwar suburban family ideal (he tyrannically upholds the values of consumerism, education, athletics, etc.).

Echoing Truffaut's liberal humanism, Rohmer dubbed Ray "the poet of violence" and "perhaps the only poet of love," and like Godard, he revered Ray's tendencies toward comic strip aestheticism, referring to him as "more of a colorist, even in his black-and-white films, than a plastic artist" ("Ajax" 112). In his review of *Bigger Than Life*, he proposed that Ray was both another Dreyer, one of the preeminent directors of the high modernist period, and another Rossellini, one of the preeminent directors of the postwar modernist art movement (*Taste* 145) (see fig. 1.4). More of a traditional European intellectual than Godard and Truffaut, Rohmer had confessed to the mistrust of Hollywood that he once shared with his countrymen ("America" 88), acknowledging the

Figure 1.4. *Bigger Than Life* (1956): In his review of *Bigger Than Life*, Éric Rohmer proposed that Ray was both another Carl Theodor Dreyer, one of the preeminent directors of the high modernist period, and another Roberto Rossellini, one of the preeminent directors of the postwar modernist art movement. (The Criterion Collection, 2010; digital frame enlargement)

economic power of the industry's producers and distributors, its mass appeal, global publicity, and "bad taste" ("America" 89). Yet, he had also expressed his fondness for Hollywood Westerns, thrillers, and comedies, his admiration for Hammett, Faulkner, Hemingway, and Dos Passos, and his respect for confident, restrained directors such as Ray, whose films demonstrated the efficacy and elegance by which he characterized auteurist American cinema after World War II.

Rohmer insisted that postwar American cinema was even more modern than American literature of the machine age ("America" 92). American cinema reached "a greater psychological subtlety," he argued, whereas "the charm of these [literary] works lies more in the delirious romanticism of their heroes and the modernism of their technique." As he explained, "Hollywood, shy of them for so long, suddenly noticed their existence, and a breath of the avant-garde made the studios tremble" ("America" 91). According to Rohmer, Ray was the greatest of the new generation of American filmmakers ("Ajax" 111), who introduced a tone and style "foreign to the ordinary rhetoric of the screen" and ultimately independent of literary content. Ray was more of an artist than an author in Rohmer's estimation, both an architect in his use of the set and the frame, and a painter in his use of expressive colors and gestures (*Taste* 143).

The conception of Ray gleaned from Rohmer's critical writing, in particular, also shows how *Cahiers du cinéma* conceptualized modernism in the 1950s. Rather than abandoning classicisms, the modernism of its critics posed *a new relationship with aesthetic traditions*, an inquiry into the outmoded conventions that needed to be overturned, the old forms that needed to be preserved, and the new practices that needed to emerge. Following in the footsteps of T. S. Eliot and Charles Baudelaire, these critics were less interested in breaking from the past than in rethinking and reanimating the history of art. After all, a medium as young as cinema had yet to develop a classical age of its own, and part of the magazine's goal was to discover what that could be.

For example, Rohmer imagined Ray as a tragedian, whose films were as modern as they were mythic. Invoking the ancient Greek warrior Ajax and the eleventh-century Castilian knight El Cid, Rohmer deemed *Rebel without a Cause* Ray's masterpiece.[21] Rohmer stressed in his review how "the constraints exercised by the production companies on filmmakers are such, the manpower, the managers, and the good foremen so numerous, that the presence of a leitmotif is *a priori* an auspicious sign." The title of the film, he noted, "aptly illuminates the author's purpose: *Rebel without a Cause*, the cause for which one fights" ("Ajax" 111). *Rebel* explicitly derives from the tradition of Greek tragedy, chronicling a single day in the lives of three Los Angeles high school students. One of the characters is an implicitly gay, mentally unstable teenager named after the Greek philosopher Plato, who, in the film's climax, is killed on the steps of the Griffith Observatory (a proscenium for his death). Inspired in design by Greek architecture, the Observatory is connected to the Greek Theater at the base of the Griffith Park hill (Schleier 370). This theatrical mise-en-scène imbues the film with the moral imperative and timeless drama that puts its "modern" 1950s setting in dialogue with the historical past.

A counterpoint for Rohmer at *Cahiers du cinéma* might be Jacques Rivette, one of the most esoteric members of the *nouvelle vague*, although their ideas were hardly mutually exclusive. Rivette contributed much of the received wisdom we now have about Ray as Hollywood's rebel archetype. Whereas Godard idolized Ray as something of a proto-pop artist, Truffaut as a dark poet of the disenfranchised, and Rohmer as an epic hero, Rivette viewed him as a revolutionary figure in a new *mal de siècle*—a generation that also included Mann, Aldrich, and Richard Brooks. Challenging traditional definitions of cinema in terms of genres, actors, and producers, Rivette welcomed "the age of *auteurs*," in which young directors are all "motivated by the same desire to produce work that is modern" ("Notes" 96), but each spans multiple genres, privileging their own themes over rules and conventions. This revolution was in the name of those tenets of modernism, autonomy and medium-specificity. Rivette wrote:

> [F]or all of them it's a question of more or less unequivocally refusing the dictatorship of the producers and trying to create a work that is personal. [. . .] The repudiation of the traditional rhetoric of script and *mise en scène*, that flabby and anonymous formula imposed by company executives since the first talkies as a symbol of submission, has first and foremost the value of a manifesto. ("Notes" 95)

What set Rivette apart from his colleagues was where he located the modernism of these directors, who cracked "the classical cement" of cinema with "[m]odern bitterness and disenchantment" ("Notes" 96) articulated through violent action.

As Rivette determined, violence in their films was an affect brought on either by their "immediacy of expression" or a textually deducible sign of rupturing aesthetic norms ("Notes" 95). Ray, Brooks, Mann, and Aldrich deployed violence to various ends: to unleash emotions through narrative cadences and techniques of mise-en-scène instead of script and plotting; to demolish shopworn systems of editing through an abrupt, discontinuous style; to annihilate the self as author through practices of critical reflection; and, quoting Rivette, "to make physical contact with an audience insensitive to anything new, imposing oneself as an individual, insubordinate if not rebellious" (95). Rivette claimed that Ray was the "greatest and most secret" of these directors, and the most "spontaneously poetic," who shared their "rediscovery of naiveté." The age of auteurs both violently rejected certain traditions and delicately returned to others, such as the "lyricism, powerful feelings, [and] melodrama" that Rivette associated with D. W. Griffith. Rivette identified continuity with that "naive" history in Ray, highlighting the "childlike clarity of his look" and "the provocative humility of his narratives" ("Notes" 96).

This thesis underlies Rivette's review of *The Lusty Men*, a film distributed by RKO that Ray directed for independent producers Jerry Wald and Norman Krasna about the vanishing American rodeo circuit. The "clumsiness" Rivette described in the film—Ray's "accidents of imagination"—could be thought of as violent disruptions from the profilmic real. Rivette asked that we do more than excuse the mistakes and lack of polish or evenness in Ray's films, but also show "a little love" for the "youthful exaggeration" and "simple pleasure of filming" Ray unabashedly enjoys. Instead of engaging with conventional modes of spectator address, Ray's films purportedly turn to abstract, subjective, and embodied forms of articulation, to jazzlike improvisations. Ray's profound ideas, Rivette contended, are channeled through the spontaneity of mise-en-scène, sacrificing all "to expression, to efficacy, to the sharpness of a reflex or a look" ("Imagination" 104). The film's intentional or unintentional idiosyncrasies that Rivette fetishized are evident in the gestures, disquiet, and paroxysms of individual shots or marginal details.

Lee Garmes's melancholy black-and-white cinematography has been compared to Walker Evans and the FSA photographers (Eisenschitz 184–85), and the film excited Rivette by foregrounding the representation of physical or indexical reality as a fundamental cinematic property. Before shooting began, the film was conceived as a more "authentic" Hollywood production, and, apropos of its documentary aesthetic, it also paradoxically recognizes cinema's inability to capture the real. Adapted from Claude Stanush's 1946 *Life* magazine article about rodeo cowboy Robert "Wild Horse Bob" Crosby, the film underwent a string of different drafts and screenwriters as Ray and star Robert Mitchum worked on improvisational acting techniques. To prepare for the role, Mitchum actually learned how to ride and rope cattle from real-life rodeo cowboys ("Rodeo" D3). *The Lusty Men* contains location footage shot at rodeos, including the Pendleton Round-Up in Oregon, and evokes Ray's background with American folk communities in the WPA, where he rekindled his childhood love for the rodeo, or, as McGilligan puts it, "a sort of Western people's theater" (218).

Ray's reputation in the 1950s was built more by film criticism than by his own role in the press, but it is worth flagging his 1958 interview with Charles Bitsch in *Cahiers du cinéma* to see the continuity between criticism and self-promotion. The interview revealed quite a lot about Ray's methods, philosophies, and intentions that inform his biographical legend and auteurist reception, disseminating a dominant reading to which critics consented. We see authorial confirmation of one of his main encoded messages in his films: "no human being [. . .] is all good or all bad" and everyone has the potential for violence. Ray explained how audiences should be able to recognize their own weaknesses in characters onscreen and therefore identify with their heroic acts (120).

Moreover, Ray was outspoken about his improvisational techniques with actors, a topic to which he would return regularly throughout his career. Other topics he discussed included the importance of nonconformity (and how conformists were more likely to commit antisocial acts), the solitary quest for a fulfilled life, and his favorite saying, "I'm a stranger here myself," drawing out themes that had already been established by critics. Reflecting on his training in architecture, he mentioned Wright's influence on his affinity for CinemaScope and the horizontal line.[22] As for his career in Hollywood, Ray addressed how he was "forced to choose from an often discouraging list of projects" and direct "films to order" while under contract with the studios (122).

By the time *Cahiers du cinéma* published Fereydoun Hoveyda's review of *Party Girl*, Ray had already left the Hollywood studios for good and the first wave of the magazine's critics had begun making films. Hoveyda called the pulpy melodrama "Ray's most interesting film to date" (130), occasionally citing Bitsch's interview as support, but by practically all accounts it was a critical and commercial failure for Ray at home. Ray himself dismissed it as "[a] bread-and-butter job" for MGM and "a shit film" (qtd. in Eisenschitz 346). The auteurist position Hoveyda took to reclaim it was no different from his colleagues, but his review deliberately overstates his opinion. Even if *Party Girl* is "a commissioned piece with an imposed screenplay" (122) and "has an idiotic story" (123), he asserted, "Long live this rubbish which so dazzles my eyes, fascinates my heart, and gives me a glimpse of the kingdom of heaven" (127). Although he conducted a closer reading of the film than was typical at *Cahiers du cinéma*, he essentially used *Party Girl* as a vehicle for a larger valorization of "a particularly modern cinema" characterized by "Ray's need of instant and direct expression, his *discontinuous* technique and rejection of conventions" (123), and by "torrents of inventiveness" (125). This definition of modernism according to rejection of or discontinuity with convention takes us back to Godard and medium-specificity. Hoveyda attributed of Ray's "inventiveness" to his "instant and direct expression" in mise-en-scène alone, eschewing the narrative and genre formula of the studio's assigned script.

An elegy for the Classical Hollywood gangster picture, the film was part of a nostalgic cycle in the late 1950s and early 1960s about organized crime in the era of Prohibition. Cast against type, Robert Taylor plays a defense attorney for a Chicago mob (a change of pace from his "nice guy" roles), and Cyd Charisse plays a showgirl and prostitute (deviating from her star persona as a refined ballerina). The aging actors were both accumulating salaries at MGM and losing favor with audiences, and *Party Girl* was to be their last film under contract at the studio (Eisenschitz 340). It was also the final film Ray directed in the late studio system, ending where he started not only in the crime genre, but in the Midwest territory of the 1930s.

The screenplay evolved through a series of drafts, first a 271-page story by Leo Katcher that MGM bought in 1956, then treatments by

William Ludwig later the same year, and finally synopsis and subsequent versions by George Wells in 1957 (Eisenschitz 339–40). "When I couldn't contribute as much as I wanted to the script," Ray said, "I tried to do the next best thing in color and performance, to give the kind of bizarre reality there was, which permitted people who lived that life to believe that theirs was the only reality" (qtd. in Eisenschitz 346). Ray directed the film for producer Joe Pasternak's company Euterpre, which operated through MGM, and although Ray kept an amicable relationship with Pasternak, he was still beholden to the studio (Eisenschitz 340–41). Manipulating MGM's splashy house style, "*ars gratia artis*," or "art for art's sake," Ray made *Party Girl* all about retro fashions, super-saturated colors, and high-key lighting, shot in Eastmancolor and CinemaScope. Robert Sidney choreographed two vibrant dance numbers for Charisse, and her husband Tony Martin sung the title song written by Nicholas Brodszky and Sammy Cahn. In the end, *Party Girl* stood for the sublime power of mise-en-scène, that which elevates an "imposed screenplay" into a director's film, and allowed Hoveyda to single out Ray as the standard bearer for the prevailing philosophy of aesthetics at *Cahiers du cinéma* after World War II. This film may have been the apotheosis of *la politique des auteurs*, but Hoveyda's euphoric review became the center of controversy over debates about film authorship in the first years of the 1960s.

Ray's Reception in the Academy, 1960–79

The second phase of Ray's critical reception, as we will see in the following history, coincided with two decisive formations: his reputation in English-language cinema culture and cinema studies as an academic discipline. Before "the auteur theory" fully traveled across the Atlantic at the end of the decade, culminating in Andrew Sarris's publication of his landmark book, *The American Cinema* in 1968, director-based film criticism blossomed in Great Britain. As it was conceived in the pages of *Cahiers du cinéma*, *la politique des auteurs* was not an academic enterprise, nor was it even a theory, but a gnomic, potentially scandalous avant-garde practice that could be at once absurdly ironic as satire and earnestly poetic as critique. The cavalier attitudes and outrageous claims of critics such as Hoveyda were profound rhetorical strategies, perhaps saying more about what the critic remembered from the film than what may have actually been there. However, as film criticism developed into more institutional contexts among Anglophone writers affiliated with the discipline of cinema studies, it also bifurcated into two staunch camps.

One followed a Romantic aesthetics model in the periodical *Movie*, while the other adopted a more literate, politically correct outlook in

Sight & Sound, a magazine published by the British Film Institute (BFI).[23] Both of these approaches, however, differed from Sarris's schematic classification system and the subsequent structural-linguistics turn led by film theorists Peter Wollen and Alan Lovell. Ray did not shy away from espousing his own auteurist myth, granting interviews with Penelope Houston and John Gillett for *Sight & Sound* in 1961, where he appeared alongside his Wisconsin compatriot Joseph Losey, and with the *Movie* staff in 1963. He had already published a *Sight & Sound* piece in 1956 about the filming of *Rebel without a Cause*, in which he anticipated the sentiments at *Cahiers du cinéma*: " 'It was all in the script,' a disillusioned writer will tell you. But it was never all in the script. If it were, why make the movie?" ("Story" 70).

V. F. Perkins was one of the first English-language writers to give Ray serious critical attention, and his first published work on Ray was an essay in a 1960 issue of *Oxford Opinion*, a precursor to *Movie*, the undergraduate journal of the Oxford University film society. Here, Perkins introduced ideas he took further in his better-known treatise, "The Cinema of Nicholas Ray," published in *Movie* in 1963. Meticulously cataloguing Ray's "use of the entire vocabulary of film" (253), he concentrated on issues from expressive performances, to décor that establishes particular times and places, to a directness and clarity in his cinematic communication. Perkins was equally attuned to the rhetoric of Ray's dynamic and subjective shot composition, editing, and camera movement. The central theme that cuts across Ray's career stems from these aesthetic tendencies, what Perkins referred to as "The Blind Run," the title of Ray's seventeen-page treatment for *Rebel without a Cause*: a rebellion against the "view of life as a too rapid journey under no guidance with no apparent direction or purpose" (257–58). In his reviews of *King of Kings* and *55 Days at Peking* in *Movie*, both critical and box-office disappointments, Perkins situated Ray's last two commercial films within this intellectual framework.

Sight &Sound favored socially aware directors who tackled important subjects (e.g., juvenile delinquency) over directors they considered apolitical stylists. A film such as *Rebel without a Cause* was therefore prized, whereas films such as *King of Kings* and *55 Days at Peking* were not. Houston, the new editor at the magazine, saluted Hollywood's new social protest cinema, made up of films such as *The Wild One* (1953), *On the Waterfront*, *Blackboard Jungle* (1955), *The Man with the Golden Arm* (1955), and *Rebel*, which she affirmed made a timely statement about "the responsibility of parents for the sins of their children" ("Rebels" 180). Likewise, in his review of the film, Derek Prouse honed-in on its themes of "social maladjustment" and "the decadent nature of various patterns in American family life" (161).[24] To whatever extent Ray was seen as a rebel, his choice of subject matter dictated the standards of evaluation, not his contributions as the director.[25]

Authorship was not a point of debate in *Sight & Sound* until Houston and Richard Roud each wrote polemics in 1960 that accepted cinema as a director's medium. In Houston's article "The Critical Question," complete with stills from *The Savage Innocents* and Satyajit Ray's *The World of Apu* (1959), she asked provocatively, "Nicholas Ray or Satyajit Ray?" Prior to her editorship at *Sight & Sound*, Houston was one of the founding editors of the Oxford journal *Sequence*, which, she reminded readers, first noticed Ray and helped him land a London screening of *They Live by Night* in 1948 (164). Like *Cahiers du cinéma* and *Movie*, *Sight & Sound* was now playing the directors game, but Houston's question asks what type of cinema the critic should preoccupy him- or herself with extolling. Should a critical method privilege Nicholas Ray's aesthetically pleasing achievements in a film such as *Party Girl*, or Satyajit Ray's naturalistic representations of modern Bengali society and cultural history in *The Apu Trilogy*? (see fig. 1.5). Houston wrote, "reviewing a film in terms of half a dozen striking shots, and of what their emotional impact and technical brilliance meant to you, is like walking around in a fog without a torch" (163).

The article was less a critique of Ray than a call to arms, a reaction against the "aesthetic approach" that came to define his significance as a director. "We might not be able to pull down a film aesthetic out of the clouds," she concluded, "but we should be able to get closer to defining

Figure 1.5. *Party Girl* (1958): Should a critical method privilege Nicholas Ray's aesthetically pleasing achievements in a film such as *Party Girl* or Satyajit Ray's naturalistic representations of modern Bengali society and cultural history in *The Apu Trilogy*? (Warner Home Video, 2009; digital frame enlargement)

the cinema's place in the world we live in" (165). Roud's article, "The French Line," was equally explicit about this critical objective. One of the hypocrisies of the aesthetes at *Cahiers du cinéma*, he argued, is that they delight in nonintellectual films and are skeptical about serious subjects, while at the same time they draw comparisons with philosophers, artists, and literary authors. Directly responding to Hoveyda's review of *Party Girl*, Roud wrote, "To Hoveyda, as to many French critics, *x* number of beautiful shots equals a great film" (170). He continued, "But the problem remains, unlike a painting, a film exists in time, and there must be something to link all those shots together" (171). The *Cahiers du cinéma* critics were guilty of eschewing "the human situation" in cinema, Roud lamented, and instead fixated on matters of "spacial relationships" (163).

Movie was much closer in spirit to *Cahiers du cinéma* than the more self-righteous *Sight & Sound*, but while *Cahiers du cinéma* and *Movie* both shared an investment in director-based aesthetic criticism during the 1950s and 1960s, respectively, *Movie* grounded analysis of a director's style in the material evidence of mise-en-scène. That is to say, reading the film text at *Movie* was motivated by a rigorous empirical methodology that isolated cinematic details, stylistic patterns and relations, and individual techniques to ascertain formal functions and textual meaning.[26] This type of criticism is premised on the classical ideals of the organic unity of art and presumes that film texts make meaning through uniquely cinematic language. On the other hand, *Cahiers du cinéma* never laid claim to a methodology or formula, and took a more irreverent position on cinema, exercising playful interpretation over analysis, while documenting the affective impressions of style over the ways in which films work as textual systems. The project at *Cahiers du cinéma* was not about an academic cineliteracy, but about recording the pleasures of film experience, through which one not only finds a love of cinema, but a love for the language of thick description (however inadequate it may be) that illustrates a personal encounter with the medium.

As we have seen, these idiosyncratic readings were also implicit critiques of fascism and politically responsive essays on art and taste, seeking to undermine the hegemony of the middlebrow, bourgeois film culture in France that prioritized classical literature over cinema. The accusations of apoliticism from *Sight & Sound* are therefore disingenuous. It is more accurate to say that if *Cahiers du cinéma* believed in the revolutionary possibilities of the auteur through cinematic artistry, *Sight & Sound* believed in the director as an author of cinematic content. The latter magazine determined a director's radical potential by what social issues and subjects he addressed with the medium rather than how he deployed the medium itself. When Godard famously stated, "Tracking shots are a question of morality" (Domarchi et al. 62), in a roundtable discussion with the *Cahiers du cinéma* editorial board on Alain Resnais's *Hiroshima mon amour* (1959) and modern French cinema, he was dissolving the line between form and content. The question then was not about aesthetics and politics, but about the politics of aesthetics.[27]

Ray moved from *Cahiers du cinéma* to *Movie* and *Sight & Sound* as an instrument for these new ideas about cinema. Critics transplanted him from his modernist roots in postwar France to more institutional practices of film criticism within the establishment of cinema studies. Both *Movie* and *Sight & Sound* made indispensible contributions to the development of the discipline, but it was not until the political modernism of film theory in the 1970s, during which time Ray put himself in American cinema culture as a transgressive teacher of experimental filmmaking, when he lived up to his reputation in France.

Beginning in the 1950s, Ray's reputation in America followed a more circuitous path than it did in Europe. *Rebel without a Cause* was Warner Bros.'s highest-grossing film of 1956, one of the most commercially successful films of the year, and Ray's most popular film with American audiences (McGilligan 317). Nominated for three Academy Awards, including Best Supporting Actor (Sal Mineo), Best Supporting Actress (Natalie Wood), and Best Story (Ray), it was also well-received by the industry. American reviewers, on the other hand, were more mixed in their reactions.[28] If the film fared better than Ray's other titles, it is because it appeased certain politics of taste that held sway at the time.

Bosley Crowther of the *New York Times*, chair of the New York Film Critics, was the most influential and respected tastemaker of the 1950s. Primarily concerned with the social consciousness of a film, he typically praised downbeat message movies that argued for social reform or diagnosed social ills. Conversely, he often condemned films that ignored socially responsible themes and subjects for generic conventions and escapist Hollywood artifice. As we have seen, Ray's films often blurred the lines between realist social commentary and commercial formula, which Crowther indicates in his review of *Rebel*: "There is [. . .] a pictorial slickness about the whole thing in color and CinemaScope that battles at times with the realism in the direction of Nicholas Ray" ("Delinquency" 28). Crowther's reviews of Ray's films could be far more scathing.[29] Films that he charged with excusing or romanticized crime received the brunt of his criticism, and he was particularly hard on Ray's sympathy for outlaw characters. Reviewing *They Live by Night*, he noted that it "has the failing of waxing sentimental over crime" ("*Night*" 33). On the juvenile delinquency melodrama *Knock on Any Door*, he reflected, "Not only are the justifications for the boy's delinquencies inept and superficial, as they are tossed off in the script, but the nature and aspect of the hoodlum are outrageously heroized" ("Humphrey" 31). At the same time French cinephiles flocked to Ray's films during a process of decolonization, compelled by the existentialism of his outlaw heroes, Crowther recast the American outlaw as a harmful effect of popular culture and he ignored the legacy of the cultural front that Ray's films possessed.

Among American reviewers of the time, Ray never achieved the prestige of a "major" Hollywood director such as John Ford, John Huston, George Stevens, and William Wyler, and among the general public, he never enjoyed the celebrity of Alfred Hitchcock or Frank Capra. Ray was recognized as more of a practical young man than a stylist, who entered the industry with a postwar generation of workmanlike directors who comprised an "economy wave" for increasingly standardized Hollywood productions (Scheuer, "Crop" D1). For example, *They Live by Night* opens with a helicopter shot of a speeding getaway car by Paul Ivano, which was the first time a helicopter was used in an action shot. The decision to shoot from a helicopter saved Ray $10,000 in production costs ("Film" 7). In this context, Ray was a professional craftsman, whereas an old-line director such as Ernst Lubitsch (who also wrote and produced) was an individual artist, and it would take a shift in the taste politics and reading strategies of American film criticism for the two directors to share the same status as auteurs.

An alternative strand of American film criticism emerged in the postwar era through the "cultism" of Manny Farber in magazines such as the *New Republic* and the *Nation*, as well as Parker Tyler's exercises in "camp" in the journal *Film Culture*, both of which were truer to the modernist cinephilia of *Cahiers du cinéma* than anything else at the time. Although neither Farber nor Tyler were devotees of Ray (he would have been too middle-class for their tastes), these modernist discourses influenced the larger reclamation of noncanonical American films and directors during the 1960s and 1970s. Farber's hip school of cult criticism supported marginal art and pulp styles that defied the prevailing and pretentious standards of good taste, backing "underground films" from the Depression onward that were neglected by theater patrons and reviewers. Violent B-movies and low-budget genre pictures from "termite artists" such as Mann and Fuller challenged Hollywood's glossy, "white elephant" spectacles. Equally countercultural (and subcultural) were Tyler's avant-garde deployments of camp criticism, but his appropriation of mass cultural texts entailed the manipulation of the cultural meanings of texts through a personal control over one's symbolic identity and a defiance of the culture industry. A "trashy" melodrama such as *Mildred Pierce* (1945) in this way could be appreciated for its concealed Freudian narrative that enriches the psychological and emotional depth of character, dimensions perhaps unintended by the screenwriters and unapparent to the casual viewer.[30]

American film noir emerged as a critical category in the 1970s, giving violent pulp films from marginal directors of the 1940s and 1950s a belated cachet. The nostalgia for noir can be traced to various factors: the institutionalization of auteurism in mainstream film criticism, the rise of college film societies and film cults, the pre–home video culture of the New York Underground, the recycling of old movies on television, and the dawn of the Film School Generation, in which directors such as Francis Ford Coppola, George Lucas, and Martin Scorsese learned their trade by watching Classical Hollywood films at UCLA, USC, and NYU, respectively. Critics such as Raymond Durgnat adapted surrealist taste to the trendy pop art atmosphere of the youth scene, while a new generation of cinephiles identified with dark, postwar genre films in the wake of the Vietnam War, the assassinations of the Kennedys and Martin Luther King, Jr., the Kent State massacre, and the riots in Watts and at the 1968 Democratic convention (Naremore, *More* 29, 34).

Adding to this list of cultural and artistic influences, we might also include the Museum of Modern Art retrospective *The American Action Movie, 1946–1964*, which ran from April 24 to June 6, 1969, and Lawrence Alloway's 1971 monograph companion *Violent America*. Alloway claimed that Hollywood action genres drew from current convention and conservative folklore, compounding topical events and traditional plots and formulas, therefore revealing America's covert culture of violence when "decoded" by the critic. Ray's noir film, *In a Lonely Place*, was one of the films in the program.

It was during this historical moment when Ray emerged from relative anonymity as a studio director for hire to become immortalized as a folk hero for American film culture in the 1960s and 1970s. Ray's films could share the same cultural capital as Dennis Hopper's *Easy Rider* (1969), Robert Altman's *McCabe & Mrs. Miller* (1971), and Martin Scorsese's *Mean Streets* (1973) (Hopper and Scorsese both greatly respected Ray, and Altman remade *They Live by Night* under the title *Thieves Like Us*). One of the ironies in this critical discovery is that suddenly it was a "highbrow" posture to rescue "lowbrow" directors from obscurity, and those left in the middle were carefully reassessed (the influence of Bosley Crowther had long since faded). Whereas *Cahiers du cinéma* fought to defend Ray as a modernist in disguise, rebelling against the studio system, he was now sanctioned by the academic institution of American cinema studies as a serious artist worthy of teaching and scholarship in the system of higher education.

Sight & Sound continued giving Ray critical attention, no longer adhering to Houston and Roud's dogmatic rubric, reconstructing Ray in the image and likeness of New American auteurism. Following the exhibition of the unfinished version of *We Can't Go Home Again* at the 1973 Cannes Film Festival, American critic Jonathan Rosenbaum published the notable article "Circle of Pain." Rosenbaum touched on practically all of Ray's films, exploring his ahead-of-his time politics and traits that range from "romanticism to anarchistic violence, pop imagery to 'cosmic' abstraction, symmetry to choreography" (218). The following year, another American critic, Robert Kolker, published a three-way analysis of *They Live by Night*, Anderson's 1937 novel, and Altman's 1974 film, a more faithful adaptation of the novel and quite different from Ray's original version. Focusing on the noir elements of both films, Kolker found that "[t]he formal realization of the novel in the Ray and Altman films represents a transformation of cinematic genres that points the way to some major changes in American cinema from the late 1940s to the early Seventies" (236). Less concerned with reclaiming the film as a lost masterpiece, Kolker instead concluded that Ray's film (and film noir as a genre of the 1940s) enabled a "new *film lumière*" for the 1970s, in which auteurs such as Altman allowed their characters "a certain triumph to their lives" (239), even in dark and hopeless narratives.[31]

When Ray died in 1979, *Sight & Sound* ran a careerwide retrospective written by David Thomson that described him as "the first man to film what we now regard as the convulsions of the 1960s" (217). Published thirty years after *Cahiers du cinéma* started its auteurist lobbying, the article conveys the nostalgia that English-language critics already experienced for old Hollywood auteurism practically at the same moment when the term and concept had taken hold in English-language criticism. Thomson yearned for the kind of American cinema Ray represented—"difficult, original, intelligent, humane movies"—that he regrets had evaporated by the end of the 1970s, replaced by the corporate logic of high-concept blockbusters and sequels (220).

As cinema studies gained visibility as an academic discipline in the 1970s, criticism published at universities had also become entrenched with the auteur theory.[32] Just when auteurism reached critical mass, however, it seemed as though it was becoming a "traditional" mode of scholarship before it even had a chance to mature, whereas applied theories of political modernism—and their allegedly decentralized role of the author—came into fashion, redefining modernist aesthetics for the field (Ray's place within this discourse is the subject of chapter 3). Ray's films sparked interest among young film scholars influenced not so much by *Cahiers du cinéma*, but by the synthesis of *Movie*'s aesthetic analysis and *Sight & Sound*'s ideological critique that Rosenbaum, Kolker, and Thomson demonstrate.

Scholars tended to conceptualize Ray's rebellion in terms of his growing celebrity as a self-fashioned outlaw. For example, in the *Brighton Film Review*, the University of Sussex film journal and a precursor to *Monogram*, Thomas Elsaesser published a two-part article on Ray in 1970 that worked through various problems of form and meaning. Inspired by Ray's 1969 lecture at the National Film Theatre (now the BFI Southbank) accompanying a retrospective of his films, Elsaesser identified Ray's recurring themes of solitude and violence, friendship and maturity, and the rebel and society, surveying how they appeared, developed, and varied from film to film in Ray's career. Further, he discussed Ray's narrative structure derived from triangular patterns of character relationships and the spatial relations of his architecturally influenced mise-en-scène.

On one of his many other visits to college campuses, Ray screened *Johnny Guitar* and taught a practicum for film students at the University of Wisconsin–Madison in 1973 (McGilligan 480). *The Velvet Light Trap*, then an auteurist film journal edited by the university graduate students and Madison cinephiles, featured Ray in a two-part article by Mike Wilmington published the following year (the first of which included an interview with the director). Wilmington examined Ray's career at RKO from 1947 to 1952 through close readings of his films at the studio. According to Wilmington, Ray was "our last great Romantic" and the most passionate American directors in the 1950s in his portrayal of "the individual's rebellion against injustice" ("RKO" 46). The RKO years epitomized Ray's "real 'underground' period" for Wilmington, when after *They Live by Night*, "he was forced to be devious and circumspect, to work with scripts that appalled him and to express himself against the grain of the material—to work, in other words, in the classic manner of the Sarris-Farber subterranean auteur" ("RKO" 47). In a follow-up piece for the *Velvet Light Trap* on *Johnny Guitar*, Wilmington speculated that Ray's greater freedom at Republic allowed him, with Yordan, to deliver a critique of McCarthyism rather than a run-of-the-mill Western. Quoting Wilmington, "that freedom apparently enabled him to spring a number of subterranean currents; to plumb deeper, less conscious emotional levels [. . .]."[33] Influenced by the groundbreaking research on the business and economics of Hollywood at the University of Wisconsin, and the ideological sensitivity of film criticism of the 1970s, Wilmington's essays gave auteurist preoccupations a footing in both studio practices and sociopolitical context.

As a filmmaker who literally spoke to academic communities such as the National Film Theatre and the University of Wisconsin, Ray helped guide career overviews such as Elsaesser and Wilmington's with his autobiographical legend. Other critics attempted to reclaim individual films that had been overlooked by American audiences. A young academic named Robin Wood wrote a "Film Favorites" column on *Bigger Than Life* for a 1972 issue of *Film Comment* shortly before it became the official magazine of the Film Society of Lincoln Center in New York City. Wood interpreted the film not as a cautionary tale of prescription drug addiction, but likeTruffaut and Rohmer, he read it as a treatment of "the illness of man-in-society rather than of a particular individual" (59). What Wood, Wilmington, and Elsaesser make clear is the way director-based criticism in the 1970s followed a larger academic investment in "textual politics." The questions for these scholars were not about film form, function, and effect or the social consciousness of a filmed subject, but about the ways in which the aesthetics of a film text subvert the superstructures of Classical Hollywood. Ray was thought to be a progressive auteur whose films proved to be exceptions to the ideological rule.

More traditional auteurist writing from academic film scholars still persisted in the 1970s, but once secondary formal contexts of Ray's films such as genre and performance now received more systematic and sustained analysis. Douglas Gomery published a *Velvet Light Trap* article in 1972 devoted to *They Live by Night*, in which he called Ray "the least examined of the major 'discoveries' of the auteur theory by critics writing in the English language" (25). While commenting on the production history of the film and Ray's combination of technique with theme, Gomery also showed how *They Live by Night* is a film noir—a relatively new term in American cinema discourse. Another example is George Morris's "Old Hollywood" column on *On Dangerous Ground* in a 1975 issue of *Film Comment* (Morris would go on to help found the Austin Film Society). Morris called it a "masterwork" that rivals any of Ray's mid- to late-1950s films, and admired the "motif of touching, reaching out," not only between stars Robert Ryan and Ida Lupino, but with Sumner Williams, who plays the disturbed young killer in the film (23).

Over these micromoments of reception—bringing Ray in dialogue with 1960s and 1970s, progressive reading strategies, and wider formal contexts—Ray's authorship helped justify cinema as an academic pursuit in the critical humanities. Yet, this scholarly project was quite different from the *Cahiers du cinéma* campaign that launched his reputation. For postwar French cinephiles, Ray represented an existential cinema in populist packaging, an avowal against fascism, middlebrow taste politics, and bourgeois traditions. The reception practices of the 1950s that generated *la politique des auteurs* also renewed the relationship between Hollywood cinema and American modernism born in the cultural front. By contrast, the loose "translation" of auteurism into English, as it was taken up by journals and university programs, legitimized the discipline of cinema studies even as it contained or "tamed" the modernism of the Hollywood auteur. Under auspices of "the auteur theory," a more institutional version of *la politique des auteurs*, Hollywood directors were the subjects of film canons and their films were the objects of study in the academy from sociopolitical or art-historical perspectives.

The transatlantic circuit of critical reception was not the only conduit by which Ray's reputation traveled. When we look more closely at Ray's Hollywood films, we will see how Ray's male stars enact aesthetics of rebellion, embodying images in the public that are then layered over Ray behind the scenes. Ray's stars retroactively inscribe him into his films, making him legible through a "portrait of the artist" as actor. In the next chapter, I focus on how the performances Ray directed from James Dean, Robert Mitchum, and Humphrey Bogart personify rebellious masculinities, how their star personas as rebels brought modernist discourses into mass culture, and how their performances work through modernist problems of articulation.

2

Performance of Authorship

Film Directing, Male Movie Stars, and Modern Acting Styles

[. . .] cinema stands on the borderline between the novel and the theater. Once again, the only method I can claim to have is to work on the actor. I attach great importance to the actor.

—Nicholas Ray, Charles Bitsch, "Interview with Nicholas Ray"

An Actor's Director

We have seen how Ray's reputation as a rebel auteur originated in France during the 1950s through the criticism and commentary of the influential cinephile magazine *Cahiers du cinéma*, and subsequently through Anglophone versions of director-based film criticism. However, Ray later confessed that he did not believe in "the auteur theory," as it came to be called by the end of the 1960s, and never even considered himself a "film buff" (Ray, *Interrupted* 151). Proceeding from Ray's admission, this chapter turns to another face of his public image. Ray's background was in theater, not cinema, having worked in the 1930s with the Theatre of Action in New York City, the Federal Theatre Project and Recreation Division of the Works Progress Administration, and (as head of the Theatre Section) the Special Skills Division of the Department of Agriculture's Resettlement Administration. As we will see, the star performance texts of his male actors complicate his presumed directorial autonomy and yet also contribute to his auteurist reputation.

Ideas about "the Method" as an innovative and experimental approach to realist film performance gave the cinematic figure of "the rebel" a certain prominence in the postwar era. Rebels sold the modernist project of the Method to the public, and the most celebrated performance Ray elicited as a director can be found in *Rebel without a Cause*, starring Method actor James Dean. Critic Martyn Auty concludes, "The real director of *Rebel without a Cause* [. . .] may be James Dean," quoting David Thomson's description of Dean " 'redirecting the picture by virtue of sheer presence' " (78). Auty posits that "Ray was taking advantage of this opportunity to play Dean as his *alter ego* and extend the art of performance so that Dean can be seen as acting out Ray's romantic fantasy" (78). In this chapter, I focus on the ways in which Dean's rebel persona, constructed by the film and the popular press, forms a larger metanarrative for Ray's reputation ex post facto. With points of comparison and contrast to Dean's hipster intellectual, I also look at Robert Mitchum in *The Lusty Men* and Humphrey Bogart in *In a Lonely Place*, stars from an "old school" generation of Hollywood actors, whose rebel personas carry different implications as disaffected loners and "bad boys" of the backlot.

By creating an interpretive framework of star/director/text, Ray's actors planted the discursive seeds for his future reputation, enabling us to map their images retroactively onto his own (see fig. 2.1). Michael Goodwin and Naomi Wise once told Ray in a 1977 interview, "we think that in many, if not all, of your most interesting films the leading actor portrays Nick Ray—Dean as a rebel, [Richard] Burton as a cynical, self-destructive intellectual, [James] Mason as a potential psychotic, [Robert] Taylor as a charming prostitute." Agreeing with their assessment, Ray added Humphrey Bogart and Farley Granger to the list of on-screen surrogates (20). Beyond anecdotal and apocryphal accounts, we can never know whether Ray truly envisioned his male actors or characters as versions of himself, and this issue is not one I wish to argue. Moreover, I am not interested in the empirical processes by which Ray collaborated with his actors or how they crafted their roles, as those private working negotiations would not have impacted Ray's reputation in a public way. Rather, this chapter concerns the ways in which Dean, Mitchum, and Bogart mediate or "perform" his authorship by embodying and enact-

Figure 2.1. *Rebel without a Cause* (1955): By creating an interpretive framework of star/director/text, Ray's actors planted the discursive seeds for his future reputation, enabling us to map their images retroactively onto his own. (Warner Home Video, 2005; digital frame enlargement)

ing a particular ethos of masculinity that their respective films ask us to view as rebellious. We need not shift the attribution of authorship from Ray to his actors to understand this relationship between star and director, but instead consider the way certain actors can be read as symbolic stand-ins for Ray through their publicity, promotion, and performance aesthetics as iconic male stars.

The expressive performances in Ray's films also reveal the ways in which he turns to gestural modes of articulation as a modernist response to failures in linguistic communication and knowledge of epistemological truth. An authorial and narrational stance predicated on a reflection of the self was a distinguishing feature of modernist art cinemas (Orr 2), and in this way Ray warrants further comparison with auteurs of postwar Europe. Speaking to Goodwin and Wise, he said that "it is the role of the poet or the artist—and every artist hopes to be a poet—to expose himself" (20), and the interviewers pointed out that "by their refusal to compromise," Ray's characters "put themselves up against absolutely impossible odds" (21). Biographer Patrick McGilligan attests, "The struggle for self-expression was at the core of [Ray's] personality, and his art. And wasn't it the most poignant handicap an expressive artist can have—the inability or powerlessness to express himself, to realize his art fully?" (220). How fitting that the title of his memoir is *I Was Interrupted*, taken from his dying words in *We Can't Go Home Again*.

During the 1950s, Ray's films were advertised not as "films by Nicholas Ray," but as vehicles for the numerous male stars he directed, including John Derek, Robert Wagner, Jeffrey Hunter, Robert Ryan,

Sterling Hayden, John Wayne, James Cagney, Charlton Heston, David Niven, Anthony Quinn, Cornel Wilde, Christopher Plummer, and Burl Ives. Ray was regarded in the studios as an "actor's director," drawing from his Method training at the Theatre of Action even when directing actors who rejected the Method, such as Bogart and Mitchum.[1] For instance, in order to prepare for his role in *Party Girl* as a disabled lawyer for the mob who walks with a limp, Robert Taylor went with Ray to the top bone specialists in Southern California to study hip dislocations. "It was a strictly method [*sic*] approach," Ray told interviewers (Goodwin and Wise 18), although Taylor was not a Method actor per se. This mystique continued to fascinate those who knew Ray and his more contemporary admirers.[2]

Biographies by McGilligan, Bernard Eisenschitz, and others have characterized Ray as a private director who made intensely personal and confessional films. In addition to projecting Ray's biographical legend, the self-reflexive performances in his films inhabit fractured spaces of midcentury American modernity that externalize the postwar anxieties of his male antiheroes and problematize certain archetypes of masculinity: discovering that social power is legitimated by age alone, juvenile delinquent Jim Stark (Dean) stands on the edge of a chasm between generations in *Rebel*; bourgeois husband and father Ed Avery (James Mason) succumbs to a cortisone addiction in *Bigger Than Life* when he is unable to fulfill his role as head of the house; rodeo cowboy Jeff McCloud (Mitchum) faces the vanishing of the frontier and the idea of an authentic home in *The Lusty Men*; New York City police detective Jim Wilson (Robert Ryan) grows weary of the "bad cop" routine in *On Dangerous Ground*, as the act seems to have lost all effect; and in *In a Lonely Place* screenwriter Dixon Steele (Bogart) attempts to make a comeback amid the fall of the Hollywood studio system and the paranoia of the HUAC era.

What Ray's stars bring to light is the integral role publicity played in his reputation, not simply the advertising and marketing of his films, but their actual state and quality of being public. Ray's critical reception constructed an abstract body for him through printed discourse, but his stars were explicitly visible in the public sphere, endowing Ray's otherwise disembodied authorial presence with an affective iconicity that could be consumed by what social theorist Michael Warner calls a mass-public subject (something impossible in a literate private sphere, where discourse could be anonymous). By way of philosopher Jürgen Habermas, Warner explains that "public persons derived their power in part from being on display" (388), and that in a variety of body images on display in nearly every media context, these figures "increasingly take on the function [. . .] of actualizing the otherwise indeterminate image of the people" (388). If "the cinema is Nicholas Ray," it is because his reputation is a byproduct of cinema itself, and difficult to imagine without the circulation of images that largely displayed white, male stars who concretize a collective bourgeois public, inscribing Ray into his films.

Before examining Dean, Mitchum, and Bogart, specifically, a brief background of the Method is necessary for the purposes of contextualization. Marianne Conroy offers this useful definition:

> In American acting parlance, "the Method" refers to three related contexts: the studiously naturalistic style of performance popularized in mid-century American theater and film, in which actors produce the effects of emotional intensity through "ordinary" voice and everyday gesture; the theory of preparation for performance that supports that style through its emphasis on the actor's emotional identification with characters; and the institution that formally introduced both the style and the preparation technique to America: the Actors Studio. (242)

We might supplement her definition with a series of specific techniques that Virginia Wright Wexman underscores in her book on film performance *Creating the Couple*—"improvisation, relaxation, the cultivation of psychologically meaningful pauses, and the use of emotionally charged objects"—all of which "are designed to reveal psychic conflict" (162). Constantin Stanislavski pioneered these techniques for the Moscow Art Theater, which he founded in 1897, working to establish a mode of Russian drama independent from the classical European plays and styles. What came to be called "Stanislavski's system," laid out in his seminal book trilogy *An Actor Prepares* (1936), *Building a Character* (1949), and *Creating a Role* (1961), was both a theory of performance and a training program for actors based in "affective memory."

The Method, the version of Stanislavski's system Lee Strasberg modified for American theater in the 1930s, moved the emphasis from ensemble performances to individual actors, who were taught to substitute their own feelings for those that their characters experienced. To be clear, the Method refers not to an orthodoxy of performance, but, as James Naremore shows in his book *Acting in the Cinema*, to "a series of quasi-theatrical exercises, often resembling psychological therapy, designed to 'unblock' the actor and put him or her in touch with sensations and emotions" (197). Strasberg was the director and acting teacher for the Group Theatre, the left-wing New York City collective he cofounded in 1931, which, like the Moscow Art Theater, sought to break away from the dominant European tradition and foster a national theater.

The Group's members included Stella and Luther Adler, John Garfield, Lee J. Cobb, Karl Malden, and Elia Kazan, and its favorite playwrights were Tennessee Williams, Arthur Miller, and especially Clifford Odets. Along with members Robert Lewis and Cheryl Crawford, Kazan left the Group to found the Actors Studio in 1947, a professional school that institutionalized the Method and prepared actors for careers in theater and cinema. In 1949, Stella Adler established her own training school, the Stella Adler Studio of Acting, in New York City. Strasberg became the Group's artistic director in 1951, a position he held until his death in 1982. The teachings of Stanislavski made a formative impact on Ray at the Theatre of Action (where Strasberg served on the advisory committee) and through its affiliations with the Group, Ray studied the Method under Kazan. Ray started teaching at the Lee Strasberg Institute in 1977, and by the end of his life, he determined that he had "been working according to the principles of [*An Actor Prepares*] for 40 years" (qtd. in Eisenschitz 29).

Thinking of the Method as a coherent methodology of performance with intrinsic cultural value would be misleading. The Method may have been inspired by highbrow dramatic purpose to abolish stodgy and antiquated performance styles. However, the publicity apparatus and fashionable celebrity associations with Dean, Marlon Brando, and Montgomery Clift in the 1950s called claims to authenticity into question, belying the modernist presumption that the Method "unblocked" the actor from an authentic authorial self. In their book *Reframing Screen Performance*, Cynthia Baron and Sharon Marie Carnicke remark that "rather than presenting actresses as hapless butterflies or multigaited horses, journalists had discovered they could sell behind-the-scenes articles about screen stars learning to produce natural performances" (24). Whereas prior to this point, the American press reflected the studio promotion that stars effortlessly relied on their natural charm, beauty, and talent, glimpses inside the Actors Studio (not to mention Strasberg's own celebrity) provided a new way to advertise the film star to the public. Baron and Carnicke address how "the American public's interest in the Actors Studio was a response to publicity that the Method represented a radical departure from the slapdash methods and inauthentic approach used by older generations of actors" (28). This image of the actor derived from the film star at work, a commercial portrait of the autonomous film artist, not unlike that of the modernist painter presented to the general public at this time.[3]

Discourses on the Method are deeply rooted in modernist notions of highbrow aesthetic distinction (Conroy 246), subjectivity and psychoanalysis (Wexman, *Creating* 246), innovative forms of articulation (Braudy 212), and autonomous, medium-specific authorship (Pells, *Modernist* 344). Much in the way Ray's critical reception codified modernist ideas in terms of mass culture, the Method similarly challenged the purported divide between high and low culture in modernism. Conroy attends to "the familiar fifties' publicity discourses in which Method actors appeared as rebel heroes and hipster intellectuals," with Brando, for example, strategically balancing discussions of motorcycles and Freudian analysis in his interviews (243). "For fifties' audiences," she elaborates, "the appeal of such images lay in the way they appropriated and endorsed the critiques of the conformist American 'mass man' popularized in the mass market fiction and non-fiction of the period" (243). On the other hand, as her reception history details, intellectuals of the era saw Method acting as part of the new middlebrow stratum of taste for the ways in which the actor identified with a "high" performance style and yet conformed to the consumerist demands of a "low" mass culture, promoting a popular and institutional understanding of theatrical realism.

Through Dean, *Rebel* is one of the films that introduced the Method to American audiences in the 1950s. With Dean's celebrity came both a new representation of vulnerable masculinity onscreen that, in turn, helped dictate the style of *Rebel*. Leo Braudy makes the compelling case that the Method demonstrates not just a new type of screen acting, but "how a postwar ambiguity about the actor's authority, rooted in the fragility of male self-definition, affected still other sources of artistic authority—in film direction, plotting, and characterization" (194). Hollywood's poster boys for the Method were social symbols and therefore could be imitated, not merely idolized. As emblems of the postwar era, they were "models for being" at a time when the personal and social identity of the male was under revision (195). Method actors reflected the hyperconsciousness of emotion and the performing body in both the arts and everyday life. The 1950s had seen years of physically and psychologically damaged World War II veterans re-acclimatized to the home front, only to give us the "organization man," the individual expected to conform and commit to the collectivist work ethic of America's new managerial culture. *Rebel* posed a challenge to the "man in the gray flannel suit" with the red-jacketed teenager Jim Stark (Dean), but the very question about *how to act* on both Dean and Jim's part is a salient metaphor for the bourgeois pressures to perform socially acceptable masculinity, from loyalty to one's corporation to fatherhood in one's home.[4]

Dean took classes at the Actors Studio, but Ray preferred to coach actors less by a "method" than through private conversations and exercises. In the following analysis of *Rebel*, we will see how Dean's persona of the "rebel male hero" was constituted by the promotion of his self-fashioned authenticity, his nonnormative sexuality, the publicity surrounding his death, and the identification with an alternative family structure his role invites.[5] This star image was the cultural manifestation of a masculine style, complimented by Dean's body language and inarticulacy, which occupies a central place in the performance legacy of Ray's cinema.

James Dean: Last Night When We Were Young

In addition to being symbiotic rebel artists, Dean and Ray were also good friends (the two men even shared the same psychiatrist). On an episode of the half-hour CBS program *Camera Three* in 1977, Cliff Jahr interviewed Ray at the time his cult was growing in the United States. Although they covered a variety of topics related to Ray's career, they spent most of the episode discussing Dean and *Rebel*. Jahr opened the interview with this introduction to the aging director: "On the outside, Ray had the tough-guy charm of his drinking buddy, Humphrey Bogart—inside, the anguished sensitivity of his friend James Dean—a contradiction that helped Ray shape both actors into bravura performances." Despite its enduring place in American popular culture, Dean's performance as Jim remains one of the most elusive points of meaning in the film.[6]

Jim's problems articulating himself are both literal—just as his parents are unable to understand him, he is unable to communicate with his Los Angeles high school peers—and existential. For the rebel star type, as Richard Dyer tells us in his book *Stars*, "inarticulacy (a symptom of anomie) is the defining characteristic [. . .], and it inhibits him/her from any analysis of the situation" (53). As Jim and his classmates learn from a lecture on a field trip to the Griffith Observatory, they are on course for an apocalyptic Big Bang:

> And while the flash of our beginning has not yet traveled the light years into distance, has not yet been seen by planets deep within the other galaxies, we will disappear within the blackness of the space from which we came, destroyed as we began, in a burst of gas and fire. The heavens are still and cold once more. In all the immensity of our universe and the galaxies beyond, the Earth will not be missed. Through the infinite reaches of space, the problems of man seem trivial and naive, indeed, and man existing alone seems himself an episode of little consequence.[7]

Envisioning a different film than Ray's nocturne for the nuclear era, Warner Bros. had acquired the rights to a 1944 book by prison psychologist Robert M. Lindner titled *Rebel without a Cause: The Hypnoanalysis of a Criminal Psychopath*. The studio saw commercial potential in the book and sought to capitalize on growing public concerns about middle-class juvenile delinquency. Ray, on the other hand, was uninterested in Lindner's case history and decided instead to tell his own story. The studio later assigned Leon Uris to collaborate with Ray on the script, but Ray eventually replaced him with Irving Shulman. The shooting script, however, was written by Stewart Stern.

Rather than attempting to explain Jim's actions through banal psychological realism, Ray followed Lindner's title itself. Jim is a rebel without a cause; or, to put it another way, the cause of Jim's angst is beyond language and cannot be identified. Murray Pomerance notes that Jim is "a kind of icon of modernism, having been forced to grow up in a perpetual state of motion as he is lifted out of one high school after another, transplanted from community to community, in order that his troublesome eruptions of temper and adolescent anguish do not tarnish his career options (or his father's)" ("Stark" 35). And as an icon, he is a relatively flat character with no stable identity, an empty signifier reduced to Dean's wails, moans, giggles, utterances, shrugs, squints, smirks, pouts, nervous ticks and twitches, and facial contortions that the film can barely contain.

Always in motion onscreen, Jim is a gesturing body that never fully takes shape, hungry to "live it up" before he burns out as the threat of annihilation hovers in the background with Atomic Age allusions. "I don't know what to do anymore," he laments at one point, "except maybe die." Development of character happens subtly through Dean's fragmented performance, rather than through novelistic means of dialogue or narration. Shuffling and slouching, speaking in mumbles and stammers, puffing on a cigarette, and depicted in promotional material leaning against a brick wall with his shoulders hunched, he is a fluid and formless physical presence. A queer figure of almost feminine male beauty, he also refuses to identify with a clear-cut sexual or gendered category. Jim is a rebel because his body does not conform to the world around him, and Dean's hesitant performance thus constantly calls attention to itself, oscillating between tough, cool composure and awkward, painfully insecure affectation. The overall weirdness of a twenty-four-year-old playing a teenager is a sight unto itself—Dean's costars Natalie Wood and Sal Mineo were sixteen. In his review of Kazan's *East of Eden* (1955), Bosley Crowther of the *New York Times* derisively called Dean a "mass of histrionic gingerbread" (33), but he makes a point with this description. Quite simply, Dean does not fit in.

Borrowing from James Joyce, Ray gave special attention to Dean in a chapter of his memoirs titled, "James Dean: The Actor as a Young Man," reprinted from a 1956 story he wrote for the *Daily Variety*. Ray put it this way: "Riding a motorcycle, he traveled by himself. Sleeping in a studio dressing room, he had complete solitude. [. . .] He shied away from all manners and social convention because they suggested disguise. He wanted his self to be naked" (Ray, *Interrupted* 107). Of course, this tribute reinforced Dean's allure as a genuine artist and an authentic American rebel, but Ray also superimposed Dean's star image over his directorial reputation. Even though Ray would contradict himself with this comparison during his lifetime after *Rebel*, its truth matters less to his reputation than the myth he helped propagate. Ray mused over how "[t] o work with Jimmy meant exploring his nature; without this his powers of expression were frozen. He wanted to make films in which he could personally believe, but it was never easy for him" (109). The underlying theme in Ray's meditation was that he was capable of "exploring Dean's nature," as esoteric as it was, and that *Rebel* gave them both a potential opportunity to satisfy their impossible ambitions of achieving artistic action in which they fully believed. When Ray talked about Dean's vulnerability and defiance, as David Thomson has observed, he implicitly identified those qualities in himself and "must have marveled at the lucid enactment of his own anguish" ("James" 81). Others have suggested that Dean modeled himself after Ray, even copying his sartorial choices and speech patterns (Kashner and MacNair 108).

Entering the film in the opening credits, Jim sways down a deserted street late at night and falls to the ground alongside the littered remains of a gift (wrapping paper, a bow, and a wind-up toy monkey). This shot is as much an introduction to the character as it is to the droopy-eyed Dean, whose messy pompadour and disheveled suit immediately show that he is no clean-cut boy next door. We see Dean's grinning face in close-up as he winds the monkey and watches it clap a pair of symbols. He then blankets the monkey in the wrapping paper, places the bow under its head, and curls up to sleep next to it. In this short, improvised moment, Jim is both an innocent child (playing with a toy, sleeping in the fetal position) and a protective parent (tucking in a child before bed), and he will perform both of these roles, sometimes simultaneously, in the film.

Shooting began on *Rebel* in black-and-white, but Warner Bros. was forced to switch to color in order to shoot the film in CinemaScope. Twentieth Century-Fox had developed CinemaScope technology in 1953, and licensed the process to the other studios under the condition that films shot in CinemaScope must also be shot in color. As an added incentive, color could better show off Dean and it also elevated Rebel to the status of a "prestige picture" (Rathgeb 111). Of course, Dean was one of several Hollywood "pretty boys" who came of age after World War II and worked with Ray, but after skyrocketing with *East of Eden* just months before the release of *Rebel*, his star outshone them all.

A "newcomer" to the industry following a stint on Broadway, Dean was often compared to the slightly older Brando and the new "school" of naturalism in American cinema he was said to have inaugurated. "No matinee idol of the Valentino-Barrymore-Gable tradition, James Dean belongs to the Marlon Brando-Montgomery Clift 'school' of acting," wrote columnist Louella Parsons, "the professionally unwashed, unmannered, unconventional actor's group that—East or West—flourishes under the brilliant direction of Elia Kazan" (44). Both his "unconventional" performance style and "unwashed, unmannered" appearance in his films and at public events aligned his rebel image with a greater authenticity and outsider independence in Hollywood than its glamorous leading men possessed. Columnist Hedda Hopper named Dean one of the "stars of tomorrow" in a piece titled "Young Men of Hollywood," in which she praised his "sensitive performance" in *East of Eden*, marked by "a mesmerizing tenseness, amazing flexibility of facial expression, and an ability to project an ever fleeting mood" (57).

The press also framed Dean's authenticity and outsider independence in terms of his rural, Midwest roots as an Indiana "farmboy" (he was born in Marion and grew up in Fairmount) and his New York City home as a serious stage actor, where he could pursue his interest in the arts. Dennis Stock's renowned photo essay in *Life* reported that his Quaker aunt and uncle "brought him up, encouraging his talents and accepting his eccentricities." Dean was illustrated in one photo surrounded by his uncle's cows with a caption that reads: "Not overly fond of farming, he has always liked animals because, he says, they accept him on his terms" (127). Yet another photo depicted Dean walking in the rain down Time Square with this caption: "His top floor garret on Manhattan's west side is no more home to him, he says, than the farm in Indiana. But he feels that his continuing attempt to find out just where he belongs is the source of his strength as an actor" (128). The article described him as "[i]ntense and introspective," prone to "incessant self-analysis" (127), and also referred to his "militantly independent offstage behavior and his scorn for movie convention" (125).

Dean would play this part in interviews, as well. For example, when Hopper mentioned how Dean was known to "tear around" Hollywood on his motorcycle, he corrected her by suggesting the motorcycle was a vehicle for intellectual and artistic self-exploration: "Yes, I have a motorcycle. I do not tear around on it. I intelligently motivate myself through the entanglements of your streets" (L40). Dean was not shy in interviews about his philosophies on acting, which solidified his rebel image as an artist who took his work seriously, not simply a studio cash cow. "To me, acting is the most logical way for people's neuroses to manifest themselves," he told the *New York Times*, "in this great need we all have to express ourselves" (Thompson X5).

The James Dean moviegoers read about in newspapers and magazines, an authentic actor and outsider-independent in Hollywood, gave them a conception of the rebel star that his film performances would corroborate and expand, and in a way it was his articulacy in the press that legitimated his inarticulacy on-screen. Consider the scene in the precinct station that immediately follows the opening credits in *Rebel*. Two police officers carry in Jim's limp body and we quickly realize that he is intoxicated. Propped up against a wall, he spies an attractive teenage girl, Judy (Wood), waiting to be called for questioning. When a benevolent detective, with the over determined name of *Ray* Fremick, brings her into his office, she sobbingly recounts how she ran away from home after her father called her "a dirty tramp" for wearing too much makeup (later in the film, it becomes clear that Judy still desperately seeks attention from her father, while he has grown threatened by her blossoming sexuality).

Meanwhile, sitting slumped in a chair outside the office, Jim mimics the sound of a police siren, as a third, more disturbed teenager is revealed to us. John "Plato" Crawford (Mineo) sits shivering with his African American nanny, having been picked up for shooting a litter of puppies, and in an oblique reference to the opening scene, Jim offers him his jacket. The glass partition in Fremick's office separates Judy from Jim and Plato, but the CinemaScope aspect ratio draws together all three of these alienated characters by capturing them in the same frame, foreshadowing how their lives will dramatically intersect through the film, united by mutual anger, confusion, and fear. Creating "frames within a frame," as Geoff Andrew describes in *The Films of Nicholas Ray* (91), Ray shows an early example of his fascination with multiple image techniques that he would later take to experimental extremes in *We Can't Go Home Again*.

Jim's parents arrive at the station with his grandmother, straight from a country club party, and he drunkenly proceeds to mock them. Humming Wagner's "Ride of the Valkyries" to himself, he listens to his family bicker and finally interrupts them to howl out the film's most famous line: "You're tearing me apart!" Dean compounds the grotesque image of Jim literally being torn apart, suggesting the very instability of his body, with his overwrought line delivery. After holding his head in his hands and then looking up with a rubber-faced grimace, he points at his parents and waves his arms in the air continuing to yell ("You say one thing, he says another, and everyone changes back again!"). Jim tucks his head down and hugs himself in exasperation as Fremick escorts him into his office, where Jim then delivers a punch to the detective. After deflecting the attack and throwing Jim to the ground, Fremick encourages him to hit his desk and release his frustration. Breaking down and crying, he flies into a spasmodic, out-of-control fit, reigning blows on the hard wood until he reels back and winces from the pain. So legendary was Dean's physical performance that, according to Ray, he was driven to the hospital after the shot and set-up changes only to learn he had broken a knuckle (*Interrupted* 41).

This masochistic episode enables Jim to open himself emotionally to Fremick, and through swallowed words convey the dysfunctional relationship among his controlling, judgmental grandmother, his materialistic, status-conscious mother, and his passive, ineffectual father, as well as his own concerns about being perceived as a "chicken."[8] Both Jim and Judy are outlaws in part because their middle-class parents are hardly the sexual role models or authority figures they seek. However, because of his absent parents, Plato occupies the most liminal position of the three characters. Raised by his black nanny, he is associated with discourses of femininity, as well as opposing discourses of blackness and high class.

The making of *Rebel* was fraught with sexual tension, rivaling the sexual tension in the film, and Dean's promiscuity was well known on the set.[9] As he walks to his first day of school, Jim recognizes Judy from the police station, and when he says he remembers where he saw her, she cuts him off with a sharp glance as if to repress the incident earlier in the film. Judy dismisses Jim and rides to school with a local gang led by Buzz Gunderson (when Jim asks where she lives, she replies jadedly, "Who lives?"). At school, Jim catches Plato's eye gazing at him longingly from his locker adorned with a photo of movie star Alan Ladd. The film codes Plato as gay, and his admiration for Jim as a fatherly role model is tinged with an unspoken romantic desire for this mysterious stranger.[10] Mineo bears a resemblance to Farley Granger and John Derek, and also to a young Ray, and one wonders whether the director saw himself in these dark, boyishly handsome stars he directed—gentle and delicate, as well as brooding and potentially dangerous.

A more explicit way in which both Mineo/Plato and Dean/Jim are discursively linked to Ray is through their reputed bisexualities.[11] Ray was rumored to have slept with both Mineo and Dean (Kashner and MacNair 101–02). By the late 1960s, Mineo's bisexuality was eventually made public, as reported by his biographer Michael Gregg Michaud, while Dean remains a more ambiguous case. Although Dean, like Ray, was always evasive about his sexual orientation, numerous biographies and memoirs have referred to him in nonnormative terms.[12] Sexually ambivalent and vaguely androgynous, an outsider star who desired rebellion and assimilation in his films, and a bachelor rumored to have slept with both men and women, Dean is now considered a gay and lesbian icon.[13]

When Ray realized that Mineo was developing a real-life crush on Dean, he encouraged the actors to take advantage of these emotions to develop Plato and Jim's relationship further (Frascella and Weisel 85), knowing that Dean "swung both ways" (qtd. in Frascella and Weisel 181). "Warners didn't know what the hell I was doing," Ray said (qtd. in Frascella and Weisel 172), but Mineo and Dean were certainly aware of the implications.[14] Mineo later credited Plato as "the first gay teenager in films" (qtd. in Frascella and Weisel 87).[15]

Despite studio publicity and Dean's efforts to get better acquainted with Wood before their love scene, Dean and Wood did not become an item during filming, although like Mineo, she was very much in awe of the new star (Frascella and Weisel 166). Behind the scenes, Wood's sexual attention was divided between Dennis Hopper, who plays a member of Buzz's gang, and Ray, igniting jealous antagonism between Ray and Hopper throughout the production. Ray "drew on his own life to understand and probe the bisexuality of Dean and Mineo," recalls Gavin Lambert in his biography of Wood, "and as Natalie's lover, he knew the intensity of her need for love" (334). The triangulations of desire in *Rebel* (Jim-Plato-Judy, Jim-Buzz-Judy) are compounded by these sexual dynamics that penetrate the text from the outside (Dean-Ray-Mineo, Wood-Ray-Hopper), adding deeper structures to the meaning of the film, the stardom of its performers, and the reputation of its director.

When Jim's class attends the lecture at the observatory, the homosocial relationships in *Rebel* are clearly established. Students look up at a projection of star constellations and watch in terror as the Milky Way galaxy explodes in a "burst of gas and fire," accompanied by the lecturer's comments on the loneliness of man in the universe, a chilling echo of Judy's sarcastic quips to Jim earlier that morning ("Stop the world," "life is crushing-in on me"). Hiding behind the seats, Plato cowers in fear until Jim reassures him, "You can wake up now. The universe has ended." Jim's attempt to attract Judy's attention again raises the ire of Buzz and his gang, who challenge him to a switchblade duel on the outdoor balcony of the observatory. According to Hopper, in another story about Dean's physical commitment to the part, Dean reprimanded Ray for cutting when he was actually nicked by Allen's blade (Eisenschitz 247). Ray stages the fight like a homoerotic dance, a widescreen display of Dean and Allen's bodies parrying and thrusting to Leonard Rosenman's jazzy score.

The centerpiece of the film is not the knife fight, however, but the "chickie run" sequence, in which Buzz makes an even more dangerous challenge to Jim: meet in the evening at a nearby bluff and speed to the edge in their respective stolen cars. Whoever jumps from his car first is a "chicken." The threat of being a "chicken," or not living up to the socially prescribed roles of normative masculinity, hits particularly close to home for Jim when on returning from the planetarium he finds his father dressed in his mother's apron, serving her dinner in bed while she rests from a headache. Infuriated by his father's inability to stand up to his mother or provide him with direct advice as to how to prove one's honor in a life-threatening situation, Jim bolts from his house wearing a white T-shirt, blue jeans, and red jacket.

Dean's onscreen appearance in color should not be taken for granted. Color is not a function of narrative in the film, but a "spasm of motive," to quote Murray Pomerance's book on film experience, *The Horse Who Drank the Sky*, a "part of the way Jim Stark lived" that gave Ray and Dean "agency in the performance" (41). While his stooped posture in jeans and a T-shirt deliberately evokes a working-class aesthetic, the vibrancy of his red jacket in his gray, flannel world matches Judy's red coat and lipstick, in addition to Plato's mismatched sock, as a symbol of youthful transgression. Jim also demonstrates a potentially positive transgression compared to Buzz, who sports a "bad" black leather jacket. Moreover, it refers back to the red cloud of gas and fire from the show at the planetarium, signaling the increasing volatility of Dean's body, while it too anticipates further bloodshed. On a larger, political scale, the color red resonated with the conservative climate of the 1950s, connoting left-wing subversion with its implications of the Communist "red scare," which undermines the patriotic colors—red, white, and blue—of Dean's costume.

In the theatrical "chickie run" sequence, bodies transform from volatile to explosive. A crowd of adolescent spectators (not unlike those who flocked to see this film) waits for Jim, including Judy and Plato. Buzz greets him with surprising sympathy, and the two young men formally introduce themselves, shake hands, and engage in a curious series of nonverbal rituals in preparation for the fateful drive. "Why do we do this?" Jim asks, to which Buzz replies, "You've gotta do something. Don't you?" The shots of Dean behind the wheel eerily predicts his real-life death in his Porsche Spyder at the junction of California Highways 41 and 46 near Paso Robles, colliding into another vehicle en route to a sports-car race in Salinas, and today these close-ups read like death's head masks. It is not Jim who perishes in the "chickie run," however, but Buzz. Catching his sleeve on his door handle, he plummets over the cliff in his car and dies in an explosive "burst of gas and fire," while Jim leaps to safety and acrobatically somersaults on the ground (see fig. 2.2).

Rebel was released in the United States on October 27, 1955, almost a month after Dean's death, and by "living fast" and "dying young," his rebel star image could live on immortally in popular culture. At least six records were available in 1956, with tribute songs and film scores, turning Dean into a folk hero reminiscent of another one of Ray's mythic Americans, Jesse James (Goodman 80). The closed-casket funeral, in which hardly anyone saw Dean's body, led to many fans' refusal to accept that Dean was actually dead, believing someone else was buried in his grave (Goodman 75). A rumor circulated that only his face was badly mutilated in the crash and that he was undergoing facial repairs in hiding until the release of his final film, George Stevens's *Giant* (Mitgang 112). As the marketing apparatus for *Rebel* was already in place at the time of his death, Dean was actually billed as if he was still alive, and an almost necrophilic cult followed the film's release.

Massive coverage ran in fan magazines, complete with photographs of the deceased star and interviews with just about anyone who knew him

Figure 2.2. *Rebel without a Cause* (1955): Catching his sleeve on his door handle, Buzz plummets over the cliff in his car and dies in an explosive "burst of gas and fire," while Jim (James Dean) leaps to safety and acrobatically somersaults on the ground. (Warner Home Video, 2005; digital frame enlargement)

(the fan magazine *Rave* even featured a thirty-page life story of Dean in November of 1956—narrated in the first person!). Fan activity emerged from more than fifty fan clubs ("Stars" 122), and included pilgrimages to his gravesite. At his funeral in Fairmount—a community of 2,700 people—600 attendants crowded the Quaker Friends Church, while 3,000 stood outside (Mitgang 112). By 1956, flowers had been anonymously placed on his grave on the thirtieth of each month, and forty baskets and bouquets were found there on his posthumous twenty-fifth birthday (Mitgang 112). The Griffith Observatory served as another shrine, where visitors retraced Dean's steps (Scullion 126). Although Ray began a book about the making of *Rebel*, which he never completed, he did not "want to be associated with this bandwagon" ("Stars" 122). Hoping to reign-in the near religious adoration for Dean, with morbidly bizarre discourses of "resurrection" and "reincarnation," Warner Bros. worked with civic leaders in Fairmount to establish the James Dean Memorial Foundation. With only three starring roles to his name (*Giant* was released in 1956), Dean would be remembered as an eternally young actor whose greatness was cut short. Thus, *Rebel* was seen as his defining moment on screen and Ray his most attuned director.

Warner Bros. had received an outpouring of letters by the end of 1955 from teenagers who identified with the film's characters, parents who appreciated its social message, and sociologists and psychiatrists who admired its treatment of child-parent misunderstanding ("*Rebel*'s" 2, 71). Roughly five thousand letters were sent to Wood and over one thousand letters to Ray ("*Rebel*'s" 71). In death, Dean received more fan mail and requests for photographs than James Stewart, John Wayne, and Spencer Tracy (Mitgang 112), exceeding any mail he received while he was living (Weales 41). Among the eight thousand letters sent per month to Dean by 1956 were fan requests for everything from pieces of Dean's hair and clothing to parts of his car (Goodman 75). Fans wrote to Warner Bros. begging for his jacket in *Rebel*, and they were directed to Mattson's in Hollywood, where it was originally purchased. The store quickly had a run on red jackets for $22.95 (Goodman 80).

The experience of watching *Rebel* is nearly impossible to disassociate from Dean's death, just as Dean's performance is nearly impossible to dissociate from his public persona. One of his Hollywood acquaintances implied that Dean had a sort of death-drive: "He was always racing somewhere because he didn't believe he would live very long. He had a premonition of death" (Korman F18). The death cult of James Dean also manifested itself in a variety of macabre fetish objects, including a gold medallion for watch chains and necklaces (Weales 41), a long, wicked knife called "The James Dean Special," amateurish oil paintings of Dean that ran from $40 to $200 apiece (Mitgang 112), and three-inch-high stone sculptures of his head, as well as life-size casts made from flesh-like plastic (in addition, a more expensive bronze edition was issued) (Goodman 80). Dean's wrecked Porsche Spyder, which he nicknamed "Little Bastard," was sold to a West Coast couple, who displayed it for a fifty cent admission (Mitgang 112).

Attempts to present the "real" Dean after his death in biographical accounts or explanations of his appeal only perpetuated the romantic image of the Baudelairean aesthete that he cultivated through the press and his films while he was alive. As *Variety* reported, Dean stood as "a symbol of disoriented youth in the U.S." ("In Death" 2). The press responded to his death by again invoking his eclectic tastes and eccentric behavior to show the "man" behind the late star—his interests in motorcycles and racing cars, classical music and jazz, and bullfighting and bongos were documented in a *Colliers* article, as was his fondness for the music of Bartok and Schönberg and the writing of Genet, Malaparte, and Heard (Roth 65)—only to make this rebel in his private world seem somehow more than a man. Dean, the Indiana farmboy, was given equal attention in articles that made claims to "truth" and "facts." We meet the anemic child who never got over the death of his mother when he was nine, who developed a sensitive, artistic disposition as an adolescent, and who the *Chicago Daily Tribune* observed "adopted a certain coolness toward strangers as a defense against those who, professing friendship, would distort his words in order to hurt him" (Nielson L22).

The scene in *Rebel* in which Jim returns home from the "chickie run," perfectly tailored to Dean's moody silences and his hysterical convulsions, crystallizes this image of a loner with family trouble that the press made available as a reading strategy for the film. In a state of shock, he walks into his living room, gulping milk from the bottle (another image of Jim retreating into an infantile past) and cooling his face with the glass. Jim sees his father asleep in front of the television, and he sprawls out upside-down on the couch across from him. When his mother frantically descends the staircase in a 180-degree vertical turn showing Jim's point-of-view, they both rise as Jim explains the night's events. Ray attested to improvising this moment with Dean in his own living room, and had the set designed as a replica (Bitsch 122).

Although Jim feels obligated to go to the police, his parents urge him to remain quiet about his involvement with Buzz's death. Moving to the staircase, he flails his arms between his parents, his domineering mother standing a few steps above him and his father sitting below them both submissively. Again infuriated by his father's unwillingness to "stand up" as the patriarch, Jim pulls him by the collar, spins him around, and pushes him into the floor. As Jim begins to strangle his father, his mother jerks him away, and Jim staggers out of the house, kicking a hole through a portrait of his grandmother on his way out the door.

Teenagers related strongly to Dean's character, even if the exact source of his connection with audiences is a bit mysterious, but after his death they must have also related to Judy and Plato, whose fascination with Jim borders on idolatry in the second half of the film.[16] Jim and Judy take comfort in each other, both traumatized by Buzz's death and disappointed by their parents' lack of understanding and compassion. Buzz's gang trolls the streets for Jim, fearing he will talk to the police, while Plato, armed with a handgun for protection, tracks down Jim and Judy at an abandoned, decaying mansion in the Hollywood hills. The trio forms a surrogate family, with Jim and Judy as parents to the short, baby-faced Plato, but Jim also plays Peter Pan to Judy's Wendy and Plato's "lost boy" in a Neverland of eternal, carefree adolescence. By "playing house," they also play act the adult roles against which they were rebelling, gently poking fun at the postwar domestic ideal and still desiring the perceived stability of the suburban nuclear family. Plato pretends to be a realtor selling the property to wealthy newlyweds Jim and Judy, and then he falls asleep like a child under Jim's watchful eye as Judy hums him a lullaby. Submitting to their romantic feelings that have intensified over the past few hours, Jim and Judy decide to explore the mansion together.

Buzz's gang finally infiltrates the mansion and awakens Plato, who thinks his friends have abandoned him. The police arrive just as Plato shoots one of the gang members and flees to the nearby observatory with Jim and Judy in pursuit. Jim manages to remove the magazine from Plato's gun and, after pledging his sincere and loyal friendship, he convinces him to exit the observatory (where, unbeknownst to Plato, the police are waiting with Jim's parents). In another reference to the opening scene, Jim gives Plato his jacket, a gesture that marks Plato as the film's most transgressive character and thus marks him for a regrettable death: the rebel who cannot properly fit or function in normative society.

Our most discerning interpreter of Ray's dramaturgical methods, Pomerance conducts a lengthy reading of *Rebel* in *The Horse Who Drank the Sky*. While he acknowledges that "Dean in life and in death overshadowed the film" (37), he urges us to watch the *action* of actors such as Dean to experience the "lines of tension between characters' motives" (37) that Ray achieves and the lines of thought they stimulate in us.

Ray makes his frame equal to the action of performance in order to capture all of its nuance, and makes plot and story the space where this mode of expression is possible (37–38).[17] The viewer's eye, Pomerance suggests, "needs to follow the game the actors initiate in following out this tension" (38). Pomerance shows how in different moments of *Rebel*, "action is carried through, rounded out, concluded with pregnant meaning for the story and the sensibility of the film" (*Horse* 56), whereby Jim finally learns to become a man (*Horse* 61). This climactic sequence is the culmination of Dean's/Jim's line—the continuity between Dean's "in the moment" action and Jim's "felt need and impulse" (*Horse* 39)—as the character struggles to liberate Judy from her repressive family and protect Plato from Buzz's violent foot soldiers. Where we find this character at the end of his line, having weathered the storm of juvenile delinquency and society's attitudes toward youth, is a position closer to normative masculinity (i.e., domestic fatherhood), but the gestures of rebellion we have just witnessed are now compromised.

When the police see Plato holding his gun, they shoot him on the steps of the observatory only to discover that Jim holds possession of the bullets. The camera tilts sideways, as if to briefly assume Plato's point of view, and then levels itself as he drops to the ground. As Jim weeps over Plato, Jim's father crouches down and promises to be strong and dependable, offering to "stand up" with him. Jim's father lifts up his body and, in turn, Jim zips his bright red jacket over Plato, a friend whom he tried to protect. Proving his honor in the face of authority, Jim also sacrifices his rebel status to assimilate into his new family unit with Judy. One recalls Jim's warning to Plato that the end of the world will not come at night, but at dawn. The single figure walking up to the planetarium as the sun rises was said to have been Ray himself, an authorial punctuation mark on this "episode of little consequence" (Rosenbaum, "Looking" 72).

Whereas Kazan found Dean difficult to work with and actually advised Ray against casting him in *Rebel* (Lambert, *Natalie* 97), Dean and Ray were kindred spirits, giving the film an intuitive, free-form charge to which we attribute their riffing as actor and director, as muse and "spiritual father." Holding auditions and rehearsals at his Chateau Marmont bungalow, Ray avoided theoretical approaches with his actors and instead preferred interpersonal collaboration. The way Wood tells it, "He always felt it was important to know a lot personally about the actor, so that at a given moment, if he needed something in a scene, he might say something not totally relevant to it, but relevant to the person" (qtd. in Lambert, *Natalie* 95). Dean's performance also grew out of the freedom Ray allowed him on the set, to the point that his costars actually recounted the film's making with Dean as the author.[18]

Robert Mitchum: Wild Man Blues

By 1952, when *The Lusty Men* was released, Mitchum was an acting relic, a holdover from the Classical Hollywood of the 1940s. One of the last members of an "old school" generation of leading men, the middle-aged star had given way to sensitive young artists such as Dean, Clift, and Brando in the 1950s. Mitchum's performance in the film conveys the nostalgic ache to return to an idealized home from one's past with the sad realization that this old, familiar place may never have actually existed outside of memory. As such, the rootless, displaced Jeff McCloud becomes a vessel for Ray's often-quoted maxims—"I'm a stranger here myself" and "we can't go home again"—on a metaphysical journey through the inauthentic landscape of a postwar Wild West Show. By regressing to the outdated morals and mores of the frontier, Jeff's directionless rebellion is premised on the rejection of the idea of family, and a middle-class life of consumerism and conformity in the suburban developments of America. Refusing to "settle down" is therefore his defiant response to the failure of the American Dream.

The Lusty Men is one of Ray's most elegiac meditations on homelessness, a recurring theme in his work, in part because the film seems so liberated from obligations to plot. In *The Films of Nicholas Ray*, Geoff Andrew praises the film's "relatively loose, ballad-like structure" that allowed Ray to focus on character and mood (64), which also gave him more freedom to experiment with performance. Originally titled *Cowpoke*, the film was one of the backlogged properties of RKO producers Jerry Wald and Norman Krasna, and was based on a 1946 article in *Life* magazine by Claude Stanush titled "King of the Cowboys."[19] Stanush was hired to write a treatment and a full script, and he then collaborated on a new draft of the screenplay with director Robert Parrish and David Dortort, the latter of whom went on to create and produce the television hit *Bonanza* (1959–73). When Ray was brought in to direct after Parrish left the project, Wald recruited Niven Busch and eventually former reporter and pulp writer Horace McCoy to revise the script.[20]

Shooting began after a series of delays and, according to Ray, they only had "about twenty-five or thirty pages of script," which required him to adopt an improvisational method of directing his actors (qtd. in Eisenschitz 180). Ray claimed the following: "We wrote every night. So there wasn't much beside instinct and reactions of my actors to what we had done the day before" (qtd. in Eisenschitz 180). In his biography, Eisenschitz points out, "Working like this, Ray happened—by chance if not by design (at least for the moment)—on a method practiced by European art cinema (by Renoir, for example), constructing each scene as a separate entity. He knew how to find what he later called 'a common language with actors' " (180). Working closely with Mitchum on his scenes in particular, Ray earned the nickname "the Mystic" (McGilligan 225).[21]

Between its ongoing problems of articulation in its own production context and the psychologically ambiguous performance by its laconic, publically self-effacing star, *The Lusty Men* is also one of Ray's most challenging films to penetrate. The parade of script contributors, Ray's limitations as director, and his purported collaborations with his actors make any sense of singular authorship equally difficult to attribute. Paradoxically, Ray's reputation as a modern artist toiling to see his personal vision realized under these conditions no doubt makes the film appealing for auteurist critics and cinephiles. Jacques Rivette delighted in Ray's "accidents of imagination" ("Imagination" 104), finding his directorial signature in the ideas imprinted on mise-en-scène, especially through "a certain dilation of expressive detail" and "a certain breadth of modern gesture" ("Imagination" 105).[22] Even Crowther, one of Ray's toughest critics, gave the film a positive review, acknowledging that "Robert Mitchum, Susan Hayward, and Arthur Kennedy do credible jobs in the leading roles." Crowther added, "Mr. Mitchum is most authentic as a hard-bitten rodeo 'tramp' " ("Lusty" 12).

Jeff's washed-up career reads as an ironic point of juxtaposition against Mitchum's, which could have been ruined in one of Hollywood's most famous celebrity pot busts. One of RKO's screen "tough guys" in Westerns, noir films, and war pictures, Mitchum was a already a popular, respected star and idol of the Bobby Soxers by the end of the 1940s, having been nominated for an Academy Award for his supporting performance in *The Story of G.I. Joe* (1945) and attracting notice for films such as *Crossfire* (1947), and especially *Out of the Past* (1947). However, his real artistic passions—writing poetry, songs, and plays—were left unfulfilled by his $3,000-a-week contract work for the studio, as George Eells explains in his biography, and he was known to turn to alcohol, marijuana, and the company of friends to medicate his loneliness and depression (101). "His use of grass earned him membership in a group that considered themselves hip and scorned nonusers as square johns and janes," writes Eells, and Mitchum quickly became friendly with Hollywood party girls. Eells observes, "Never before had they seen a prominent star make himself such a high-visibility risk, strutting around as he did in a straw Stetson and cowboy boots, with a reefer tucked behind each ear or carrying a package of cigarettes in which the regular ones were alternated with hand-rolled joints" (102).

On September 1, 1948, Mitchum attended a pot party with his friend Robin "Danny" Ford at the Laurel Canyon home of actress Lila Leeds and her roommate Vicki Evans, where they were arrested. Two narcotics officers of the Los Angeles Police Department made the arrest, a result of the campaign against "the killer weed" led by the new Commissioner of the United States Treasury's Bureau of Narcotics Harry J. Anslinger (Eells 2). "Well, this is the bitter end of everything," he told reporters, "my career, my home, and my marriage" (qtd. in Eells 104). In the face of conservative, moralistic diatribes against Mitchum and Hollywood, RKO released his latest film, a Western titled *Rachel and the Stranger* (1948), to national box-office success.

Mitchum, Ford, Leeds, and Evans were indicted on the counts of marijuana possession and conspiracy to violate the State Narcotics Act. The trial was postponed until January 10, 1949, and hoping to persuade the judge either to grant Mitchum parole or postpone his jail term, RKO rushed into the production of *The Big Steal* (1949), a film noir that would reteam Mitchum with his *Out of the Past* costar Jane Greer. RKO did not get its wish, and Mitchum, Ford, and Leeds were found guilty of conspiracy to possess. On February 9, Mitchum and Leeds were sentenced to a year in the county jail. The judge suspended those sentences and placed them on probation for two years, the first two months of which were to be served in the Los Angeles County Jail. Evans had fled to New York City on bond and was eventually acquitted in March, while Ford was held on another marijuana charge, but given the same sentencing as Mitchum and Leeds ("Vicki Evans Back" 2; "Vicki Evans Freed" 2; "Mitchum's Pal" 2).

If anything, Mitchum's widely publicized court appearances and jail term gave his career a boost and added to his anti-authoritarian yet apathetic image (a photograph even circulated of the star mopping the floor in his prison uniform). Fan magazines played an integral role in recuperating his image, divulging information about the pot bust, but not condemning Mitchum. In fact, many of them were sympathetic to the star, producing the rehabilitating rhetoric that he may have smoked marijuana to improve his confidence, and that marijuana, after all, was not as harmful or addictive a drug as heroin (Desjardins 216). Mary Desjardins reports that *Photoplay*, for example, "praise[d] the actor for pleading guilty and sparing Hollywood and the nation—especially the young teenagers who idolized him—the scandal of a long trial and the subsequent sensational press coverage" (216). RKO arranged for his transfer from county jail to the Sherriff's Wayside Honor Farm in Castaic, California. Mitchum received a ten-day reduction in his sentence and was released from custody on March 30, 1949, immediately resuming work at RKO to finish *The Big Steal* (Eells 117–25).

The studio knew that his legal problems would not harm his future in the industry when *The Red Pony* (1949), an adaptation of John Steinbeck's novella for which Mitchum was loaned to Republic Pictures, scored a hit with audiences. Mitchum gained sympathy when on review of the case in 1951, his arrest was exposed as part of a set-up to catch Hollywood dope smokers. Probation was terminated and the Los Angeles courts and District Attorney's office expunged the records of the case. On the other hand, Leeds never recovered her career and was instead offered a part in the antimarijuana exploitation film *She Shoulda Said "No"!* (1949), an attempt to capitalize on her role in the Mitchum scandal (Schaeffer 242–45).

Mitchum's rebelliousness was partly understood through the notorious pot bust and other run-ins with the law—in 1951, he was involved in a Colorado Springs saloon brawl ("Just a Saloon Hassle" 2)—but also through his opposition to the Hollywood glamour that his contemporaries possessed as romantic leading men of the screen. Described by the *Los Angeles Times* as a "rugged individualist," Mitchum was devoted to outdoor life and coveted his privacy, so much so that he built a removable cabin that sat on the rear of his Ford truck in order to travel into "rugged country which a car and trailer couldn't penetrate" (Scott E1). The article recounted Mitchum's fishing trip with his two boys to the High Sierra, the wilds of Idaho, Arkansas, and Mississippi, and the Colorado Rockies, a vacation that he arranged with RKO to start promptly after his theater tours to promote his Korean War adventure *One Minute to Zero* (1952). "I hate crowds" (Scott E1), Mitchum told the newspaper, adding, "So at every opportunity I head for tall timber" (Scott 3). Within the industry, Mitchum's contempt for the Hollywood establishment was no secret—this was the same actor who supposedly slapped Otto Preminger (Hirsch 188) and spread Limburger cheese on the engine block of Joseph von Sternberg's car (Kashner and MacNair 159).

Released at the height of his stardom, *The Lusty Men* gave the Hollywood troublemaker another rebel role, but it also allowed him to play to his artistic side that the movies had not yet tapped, perhaps not that far from Dean's in *Rebel*. In Method-like preparation for the part, Mitchum and his costar Arthur Kennedy were even tutored in the ways of "bulldogging," "calf roping," "bronc riding," and "Brahma bull riding" from real-life rodeo cowboys Les Sanborn, Gerald Roberts, Bob Burrows, and Jerry Ambler ("Rodeo" D3). *The Lusty Men* authenticates Mitchum's rebellion by guaranteeing his image as an outsider, much in the way *Rebel* ensured a similar image for Dean through his Method-based celebrity and premature death.

As a melodrama of domestic malaise, *The Lusty Men* bears further comparison to *Rebel*. Instead of the physical disruptions of the male body we see in Dean's performance, in Mitchum we see a kind of blankness, a flat affect that absorbs and internalizes problems of articulation. Jim is a soft young body struggling to come into form, but Jeff is an aging body whose form has been broken, hollowed, and, perhaps most importantly, disarticulated. Limping across a deserted rodeo arena as he emerges from a cloud of dust in the opening sequence, the wind picking up debris that blows past him, Jeff looks not unlike a specter of the Old West. In *Lightning over Water*, Ray tells an audience at Vassar College, "this film is not a Western. This film is really a film about people who want to own a home of their own. That was the great American search at the time this film was made."[23]

A lost drifter, Jeff is unable to embody the domestic breadwinner's role as the unified, coherent national character of the American male. As Steven Cohan reminds us in *Masked Men*, his book on masculinity and Hollywood stardom of the 1950s, spaces of domesticity were nodal points in the construction of national ideology and gender identity (male/breadwinner, female/homemaker) for postwar America. "Because the society in which Americans actually lived was no longer synchronous with the one they imagined as 'America,'" he explains, "home acquired renewed value after the war as the metonymy of the nation. The uniformity of home life in popular representations of domesticity conveyed a unity and coherence that U.S. society itself lacked" (52). Jeff, the homeless rodeo cowboy, in this way is much like Jim, who cannot enter the Symbolic Order without the proper male role model (i.e., father as head of the house) to whom he can emulate.

Unlike Jim's cries and gesticulations at the police station, Jeff enters the world of the film without losing control of his body or even producing much of an audible sound. After hitching a ride from the rodeo arena to the rural town where he grew up, he hobbles to his childhood home, now in disrepair, and finds the front door locked. Crawling underneath the house, he discovers remnants from his youth hidden under the cobweb-infested joints: a broken pistol, a tobacco can containing two nickels, and a rodeo handbill (see fig. 2.3). The close-up of Mitchum's face looks ahead to Dean playing with the toy monkey in the opening shot of *Rebel*, his eyes hooded and his mouth smiling as his cowboy facade dissolves in front of the camera to reveal an innocent boy. When the current owner confronts Jeff, pointing a rifle at his back, Jeff stands up and remarks, "I didn't think nobody lived here . . . I was lookin' for something I thought I'd lost."

The old, wiry man introduces himself as Jeremiah Watrus and invites Jeff inside for coffee, when he explains that he lived in the house twenty years ago. Jeff admits to Jeremiah that he always aspired to make enough money to come home and buy the house, and they both reflect on their life of solitude, disappointment, and failure. Mitchum's baritone voice, slow movements, and stiff, thick appearance lend a necessarily wooden quality to Jeff. Crippled by an accident that aborted his career, and left without a family or home, he lacks the traditional markers of an

Figure 2.3. *The Lusty Men* (1952): Crawling underneath the house, Jeff (Robert Mitchum) discovers remnants from his youth hidden under the cobweb-infested joints: a broken pistol, a tobacco can containing two nickels, and a rodeo handbill. (Warner Home Video, 2014; digital frame enlargement)

identity, but loss and emptiness actually come to define it. "Man comin' back to his home place, findin' it like this," says Jeremiah, "kinda like visitin' a graveyard."

Leaving his homestead behind him, along with his past and his plans for his future, Jeff is picked up by an ambitious young couple hoping to buy his old property, amateur rider Wes Merritt (Kennedy) and his wife Louise (Susan Hayward). Wes recognizes Jeff from his rodeo stardom and recruits him to work as a fellow cowhand on a ranch nearby. While Wes is captivated by Jeff's stories and seduced by the prospects of fast money, Louise disapproves of the reckless lifestyle that comes with the rodeo. Much to her chagrin, Jeff agrees to take Wes under his wing, but his motivations are ambivalent other than to share the profits. On the one hand, Jeff is obviously attracted to Louise, but on the other, he maintains a homosocial desire for Wes. He can live vicariously through Wes and Louise to satisfy his impossible dream of having a family and owning a home (specifically his actual former home), but mentoring a younger protégé also allows him to relive his glory days and avoid a life of bourgeois institutionalization.

Jeff's quest to own a home is also a microcosm for the modernist project of the postwar American suburbs in bridging the country and the city. In his book *Rebels*, cultural historian Leerom Medovoi argues, "Suburbia, then, as a bourgeois ideal for sublimating these lifestyles, has always promised continued access to the city's modern opportunities while recreating the peacefulness and pastoral values of the country" (95). The most interesting scenes for Mitchum's performance are not the rodeo sequences, which consist of stock footage and process shots, but are those of his body enclosed by the domestic milieu of the film. After Wes earns his first check from riding a bull, he and Jeff decide to quit their jobs at the ranch and travel the rodeo circuit. Louise storms into her barn to find Jeff pitching hay, striking an iconic Western pose in his cowboy hat and denim attire.

As she tries to talk him out of the idea, she tells him that she came from a family of fruit pickers and grew up in tents and camps: "We never had a house. Got so I was always jealous of people who lived in houses, and stayed in one place and had somebody to love." Jamming his hands in his back pockets, Jeff also strikes a typical Mitchum pose, standing over Hayward with his broad shoulders, barrel chest, and stone-faced expression. Of course, Louise's sentiment is one that Jeff knows all too well, and this scene lays bare the contradictory impulses that drive his character. Jeff wants the same stability as Louise, but, like Wes, the only way he feels he can achieve it is by surrendering any commitments to home and family, and living a transient existence.

With a cowboy ethos conceived from nineteenth-century notions of the American frontier, Jeff remains incompatible with the modernity of the postwar era, rendering home and family in his rustic terms increasingly obsolete. Mitchum's performance, therefore, can be understood as a double-layered masquerade: Jeff deliberately performs the anachronistic role of the American cowboy as a gesture of resistance, both masking the same "feminine" domestic yearnings as Louise with the image of a red-blooded man who will not be "tied down," and translating those same ideals of hearth and home into a "masculine" folk idiom of the pioneer spirit. Jeff's hard, lumbering body is a blank slate where these ideologies of the home converge, and through Mitchum it becomes a site of embodied meaning that invites us to interpret him less as a character than as a collection of macho postures, a type that is self-reflexively performed.

Unsuccessful in her attempts to dissuade Jeff and Wes, Louise accompanies them as they join a pathetic cadre of other riders. Mitchum shares a second scene with Hayward, this time in a travel trailer belonging to another rider, whose wife invites Louise over to take a shower. The trailer in this context reads as the American home made inauthentic, modernized into a consumer product of the postwar family leisure market (a temporary house designed for national tourism, enabled by the rise of the Interstate Highway System and the growth of the automotive industry). Jeff walks into the trailer, suggestively smoking a cigar, but with all of its modern conveniences the trailer ironizes his efforts to return to the Old West. As Louise prepares to shower, wearing only a bathrobe, Jeff flirts in a purely robotic fashion, even though their dialogue is littered with innuendo. Squeezing into the bathroom and towering above her once again, he turns the shower knobs ("Hot, this way. Cold, that way. Anytime your plumbin' don't work, just call McCloud."), and then pours himself a dainty cup of coffee from the percolator in the kitchen.

Despite these light, subtle moments of domestic humor, Jeff's presence casts pallor over the trio's journey, reminding us that the only way out of the rodeo circuit may be in a spiritual, if not literal, death. They witness another rider perish in the arena when he is thrown from his bull and trampled as his wife looks on in horror. Yet, if Jeff represents Wes's dark reflection (or a glimpse into his already used-up future), he also represents his voice of conscience. Wes enjoys the fame and excitement of the rodeo, as well as the drunken parties and female attention of its nightlife, but his inflated ego and brash disregard for his own well-being creates an emotional wedge with Louise.

Toward the end of the film, after Louise and Wes have moved into their own trailer, Jeff sees Louise cooking a pot roast. Again, the almost comical difference in height between Mitchum and Hayward is emphasized, reinforcing Jeff's mythic, bigger-than-life stature in the film and his "puffed-up" performance of self. Louise tells him that they have saved enough money to buy Jeremiah's property, but when Wes arrives to hear the news, he arrogantly balks at her eagerness to go home and leaves instead for a party. Jeff makes himself at home and serves the pot roast, adopting the role of both maternal homemaker (by taking Louise's place in the kitchen) and of man-of-the-house (by usurping Wes at the table as Louise's husband). Angry over Wes's immaturity and selfishness, Louise gets dressed to follow him to the party, while Jeff begins eating. Similar to Jim, Judy, and Plato "playing house," Jeff seeks a fleeting experience of domestic harmony, even if those normative roles must be consciously performed—in a fake home, no less.

When Louise and Jeff try to pull Wes away from the party, Jeff confesses his love for Louise, but she stands by her husband and pleads with Jeff to help save Wes from ending up "crippled," physically, emotionally, and psychologically. Catching them locked in a kiss outside the apartment, Wes accuses Jeff of freeloading off his winnings and trying to sleep with his wife ("All you've been doin' is draggin' your foot in my stirrup!"). Jeff knocks out Wes with a punch to the face, leaving him in the hallway as the party guests surround him. In an apparent effort to prove himself to Wes, the next morning Jeff enters the rodeo and the two men share a brief moment of reconciliation immediately before Jeff's ride. Wes wishes Jeff luck, who responds only with a wink, and he performs magnificently until his foot sticks in his stirrup, recalling Wes's figurative comment the night before and foreshadowing Buzz's demise in *Rebel.* The film ends on Jeff's death, his lung pierced by a broken rib, but it is his death that prevents Wes from suffering the same fate. Passing on his turn, Wes decides to exit the arena with Louise, as another rider takes his place. Whether Jeff had intended to sacrifice himself for Louise's happiness, and to allow Wes the future he always wished for, remains a mystery.

Humphrey Bogart: (In My) Solitude

At the dawn of the 1950s, Ray directed *In a Lonely Place*, starring Humphrey Bogart, arguably (or perhaps inarguably) Hollywood's quintessential urban "tough guy" of the older generation to which Mitchum belonged. A veteran of 1930s gangster films such as *The Petrified Forrest* (1936) and *Dead End* (1937), Bogart was best known for noir films such as *The Maltese Falcon* (1941) and *The Big Sleep* (1946), as well as wartime romantic melodramas such as *Casablanca* (1942) and *To Have and Have Not* (1944). Ray had worked with Bogart prior to *In a Lonely Place*, directing him as the crusading lawyer who defends juvenile delinquent Nick Romano (John Derek)—a precursor to Dean's Jim Stark—in *Knock on Any Door*. The Bogie type was the personification of Hemingway's "grace under pressure."

Following Bogart's death in 1957, film critic André Bazin wrote an article for *Cahiers du cinéma*, in which he called him "the actor/myth of the war and postwar period" (99). Bazin focused on his stardom between 1940 and 1955, and claimed that "to this far reaching modernity which guarantees the profound poetry of the Bogart character and indisputably justifies his entry into legend, there corresponds a more precise modernity within the compass of our generation" (99). For Bazin, Bogart epitomized "the ambiguous hero," announcing "the triumph of interiorization and of ambiguity" in American cinema (100), but he also represented "the immanence of death" (98), "a man defined by fate" (99), and an "existential maturity" (101). Contrary to the "anti-intellectual spontaneity" Bazin saw in Brando and Dean, Bogart was a stoic, characterized in Bazin's terms by "[d]istrust and weariness, wisdom and skepticism" (100).

François Truffaut, Bazin's *Cahiers du cinéma* colleague, wrote a similar appraisal of the actor in 1958, and like Bazin, was particularly fascinated by Bogart's face. "It was Ray who was to make Bogart definitively the appealing hero, much more than an actor, a personality [. . .]," Truffaut wrote (*Films* 294), referring to Bogart as "a modern hero" (*Films* 295). The scar on his upper lip visible in color films (*Films* 295), the unshaven face, half-closed eyes, and furrowed brow (*Films* 294), and the clenched jaw evoking "the smile of death" (*Films* 294) were all elements of what Truffaut saw in Bogart's particular appeal. Elaborating on his physical appearance, Truffaut mused over Bogart's gait, "one hand thrust forward, ready to justify or confound." The typical Bogart gestures and his "jerky pronunciation" were also key to his star image: "He comes to a stop, spreads his legs a bit, unbuttons his jacket, sticks his thumbs inside his belt, and begins to talk" (*Films* 294).

I highlight this cataloging of Bogart's star qualities from these two-period sources as a brief way to indicate what the myth of Bogart meant at *Cahiers du cinéma*. According to these French critics writing after the Occupation, Bogart was a modernist icon because of the way he brought out the existential underpinnings of mass cultural American cinema during wartime and the postwar years. We have seen how Ray was another "modern hero" to them during the same period for similar aesthetic reasons, but the difference is that Bogart was a hero on the screen and in the flesh, who dramatized the importance of individual action and consciousness (i.e., performance decisions) when faced with the void of the unknowable. During the postwar era, however, Bogart's cynical screen persona shifted from populist, antifascist hero to neurotic or psychotic villain in films such as *Dead Reckoning* (1947), *The Treasure of the Sierra Madre* (1948), *The Caine Mutiny* (1954), and *The Desperate Hours* (1955). *In a Lonely Place* presents both the Bogart myth and the deconstruction of that myth. More to the point, Bogart is explicitly the physical analog for Ray in this film, and his performance elevates it from Hollywood murder mystery into an auto-critique of the creative process.

Rather than fundamentally reinventing his star text, this reconfiguration of his virile, hard-boiled image transformed his "toughness" from a function of "an unimpeachable manliness," as Steven Cohan describes in *Masked Men*, to "a mechanism of sexual regulation supporting the authority of postwar hegemonic masculinity" (83). Other "tough" male stars of 1930s and 1940s Hollywood underwent a similar transformation in the 1950s, as they accommodated to middle age, including James Cagney in *White Heat* (1949) and John Wayne in *The Searchers* (1956). In order to ward off the threat of postwar domesticity and conformity, and their spaces of feminization and confinement, male characters in American film noir of the 1950s, for example, acted out their sadistic, masochistic, and fetishistic aggressions that were once only hinted at below the surface (Cohan 97). Masculinist films such as *In a Lonely Place* pathologize men's inability to adjust to life after the war, laying bare the ideological mechanisms of normative masculinity and the violent behavior of the American male. This violence occurs through a homosocial power over men during wartime and a homophobic, misogynistic displacement of the fear of being feminine (Cohan 84). Bogart reveals both facets of this masculine violence as screenwriter Dixon Steele.

Ray was on loan from RKO to direct the film for the independent company Santana Productions, for which Columbia Pictures served as its distributor. As the company's president and cofounder, Bogart also shares authorship of the production. A film noir about Hollywood, it belongs on the same shelf as modernist novels *The Last Tycoon* (1941) by F. Scott Fitzgerald and *The Day of the Locust* (1939) by Nathanael West, and also taps into the zeitgeist of the American film industry during the 1950s. However, an indictment of the motion picture business was not part of Dorothy B. Hughes's project in her original 1947 novel of the same name. Writers Edmund H. North, who penned the treatment, and

Andrew Solt, who was in charge of the script, loosely adapted her thriller about a World War II veteran strangling women in L.A. (told from the killer's point of view), making the misogynistic character a burned-out screenwriter who is just suspected of murder. Only 4 pages of the 140-page shooting script survived without revisions during filming, as Ray improvised changes with his two leads (Eisenschitz 134).[24]

Mirroring Ray's experiences as a disillusioned filmmaker, this foray into the Hollywood Gothic also parallels both the threat of the blacklist and the crumbling marriage that hung over Ray's early career in the studios. Although it never mentions HUAC, it can be read as a response to the culture of political paranoia familiar to both Bogart and Ray, and endemic to Hollywood at large in the 1950s.[25] As a member of the Committee for the First Amendment, Bogart stood up for the Hollywood Ten in Washington, DC, at the 1947 congressional investiga-

Figure 2.4. *In a Lonely Place* (1950): Writers Edmund H. North, who penned the treatment, and Andrew Solt, who was in charge of the script, loosely adapted Dorothy B. Hughes's thriller about a World War II veteran strangling women in L.A. (told from the killer's point-of-view), and made the misogynistic character a burned-out screenwriter (Humphrey Bogart) who is just suspected of murder. (Columbia TriStar Home Entertainment, 2003; digital frame enlargement)

tions, but was then forced to deny any allegiances to the CPUSA when his politics came under scrutiny. As a former member of the CPUSA, Ray was monitored by the FBI from 1941 through the war years, but was protected from the blacklist by Howard Hughes at RKO.

The film costarred Ray's wife, Gloria Grahame, as Dix's suspicious neighbor and lover, Laurel Gray. Ray met Grahame while directing *A Woman's Secret*, but by 1950 their marriage was falling apart. During the shooting of *In a Lonely Place*, Ray slept on the set instead of going home to Grahame at the end of the day. Two years later they divorced after Ray found her in bed with his thirteen-year-old son Tony from his marriage to Jean Evans (McGilligan 207). Grahame told the judge, "My husband hit me twice: once at a party without provocation, once at our home when I locked my bedroom door. He was sullen and morose and he would go into another room when my friends came to the house" (Eisenschitz 192). In 1960, she married Tony. *In a Lonely Place* is therefore not hard to read as a roman à clef, but it is also a demystification of the American domestic ideal of the postwar era. In his BFI monograph on the film, Dana Polan remarks, "In the Hollywood and the U.S. of the late 1940s, marriage and family were not inevitable, were not automatic and natural happy endings" (20). After the war, divorces became as hasty as marriages were during the war, and Polan explains that "men and women frequently found that their partners did not live up to the fantasies of sudden romance" (20).

Both as an unromantic reflection of Hollywood under HUAC and as "scenes from a marriage" in postwar America, the film derives much of its allegorical significance from Bogart's performance and shifting persona as a star. Bogart's performance was a high point for American reviewers at the time, and it helped make *In a Lonely Place* one of Ray's most well-received films (Tinee, "Bogart"; Scheuer, "Hollywood"; "Humphrey's"; and Hopkins). On that rare occasion when Crowther had any complimentary words for a Ray film, he praised the complexity and sensitivity of Bogart's performance. "Mr. Bogart plays the role for all its worth, giving a maniacal fury to his rages and a hard edge to his expressions of sympathy," he conceded, also describing him in "top form" and moving "flawlessly through a script which is almost as flinty as the actor himself" ("Three" 46). Crowther highlighted how Bogart "looms large on the screen" and added that "the actor plays with such terrific drive that one is content not to pick the characterization apart" ("Three" 46). At the end of Crowther's review, Ray only receives a passing mention, as if to imply that *In a Lonely Place* is mainly Bogart's movie. So significant was the film to Bogart's memory that the Humphrey Bogart Estate's independent production company, Santana Films, produced an L.A. neo-noir titled *This Last Lonely Place* (2014), financed by a Kickstarter campaign and made available for streaming or download online.

Somewhere between Dean's excess of melodramatic emotion and Mitchum's impassive disposition, Bogart retains the stoicism of his 1940s roles, but suggests a murderous, self-destructive violence repressed in his earlier screen persona that surges forth after returning home from the war. The film in many ways is about his public character coming unhinged. An alcoholic screenwriter who has not written a hit movie since before the war, blackballed by producers afraid of his reputation for drunken fights, Dix represents the bluntest example of Ray's difficulty in articulation. Refusing to compromise his artistic integrity for Hollywood's crass commercialism, he is a writer who cannot write. What adds another level to the film's self-reflexivity is Ray's reputation as a director who was replaced during shooting, who fought with producers, and who voiced complaints about the differences between his films and their original conceptions and executions (Polan 52).

Psychologically and emotionally scarred from combat and perhaps even sexually wounded from a past love, Dix is a dysfunctional man since he is unable to perform normative masculinity (belying his phallic name). His "impotence," or, at least, his "performance anxiety," inhibits his ability to signify in the new world of the 1950s and results in erratic physical outbursts of violence as the only way to make meaning. "My heroes are no more neurotic than the audience," Ray said in the 1975 documentary *I'm a Stranger Here Myself*, in which he called *In a Lonely Place* a "a very personal film." "Unless you can feel that a hero is just as fucked-up as you are and that you would make the same mistakes that he would make, you can have no satisfaction when he does commit a heroic act." In an interview with Joseph Lederer for *American Film* published the same year, he described the film as "a study of the violence each person has within himself, the seed of his own destruction" (61). We see a glimpse of Dix's isolation and explosive temper in the opening credits sequence as he drives down a busy L.A. street at night, his eyes reflected in the rearview mirror staring straight ahead. The film establishes Dix as nothing but the surface of character (the Bogie type), asking us to wonder what those eyes have seen and what goes on behind them, but it also sets him up as both a voyeuristic masculine subject bearing the gaze and a passive object of investigation (including our own). Dix is never granted control of his own body, identity, or subjectivity, since his power in the narrative and the scopic regime of the mise-en-scène will be constantly destabilized. When he comes to a stop sign, an actress in the neighboring car recognizes him from the last film he wrote for her, announcing his name to us as viewers. The woman's jealous husband insults him, but just before Dix can get out of his car, the couple speeds away.

As if to answer the viewer's inevitable question—"who is Dix Steele?"—he arrives at Paul's Restaurant (a thinly disguised Romanoff's), greeted by a boy asking for an autograph. "Who am I?," Dix asks facetiously, to which the boy replies, "I don't know." The boy's friend chimes in, "Don't bother, he's nobody." "She's right," Dix tells him, signing his name in the autograph book as if to confirm the sentiment and hint at the existential themes to come in the film. Inside Paul's, Dix's loyal agent Mel Lippman informs him of a new opportunity: an adaptation of a trashy romance novel titled *Althea Bruce* ("all you gotta do is follow the book," he assures him).[26] Dix holds contempt for the bankable director assigned to the project, Lloyd Barnes, whom he calls a mere "popcorn salesman," and instead prefers the company of the has-been Shakespearean actor Charlie Waterman. We see the full potential of Dix's temper when a hotshot young producer, nicknamed Junior, snubs Charlie at the bar, and Dix shoves Junior into a table as Mel and Lloyd try to restrain him.[27]

Off the screen, Bogart had his share of violent altercations (he and his third wife Mayo Methot were nicknamed "the Battling Bogarts" for their drunken rows in public), and his performance as Dix calls one strange incident to mind, specifically. A year before the release of *In a Lonely Place*, Bogart and his friend Bill Seeman introduced two three-foot-high plush pandas as their "girlfriends" at the Manhattan nightclub El Morocco, where they bought the pandas drinks. When fashion model Robin Roberts and society girl Peggy Rabe tried to "abduct" Bogart's panda, he reportedly wrestled it away from the women and was bounced from the club. Roberts obtained a summons calling for Bogart's appearance in court charging assault (she alleged that he threw her to the ground, hurting her chest and back), but the complaint was dismissed for lack of evidence ("Bogart Battles" 2; "Bogart Gets Court Call" 2; "Court Throws Out" 3).

The differences between Ray's film and Hughes's novel are made immediately apparent in this first act, to the point that Mel's advice to "follow the book" becomes an ironic inside joke the further the film strays from its source material. Dix asks Mildred Atkinson, the friendly hatcheck girl at Paul's, to summarize the plot of *Althea Bruce* over drinks at his apartment. Another autobiographical dimension to the film is, in fact, Dix's bungalow apartment, which was modeled after Ray's apartment in Villa Primavera (his first apartment in Hollywood) (Eisenschitz 144).

Venturing forth with the project at the expense of his highbrow artistic and intellectual standards, Dix poignantly remarks to the waiter, "There's no sacrifice too great for a chance at immortality."

Mildred enthusiastically recounts the events of the novel to Dix as the camera shoots her from his point of view, but it is Mildred's eventual death that disrupts his visual mastery over his space and forces us to question knowledge gained from identification with Dix. The following morning, Dix's old army buddy Det. Brub Nicolai escorts him to the police station for questioning under Cpt. Lochner when Mildred is found strangled. V. F. Perkins draws parallels between Lochner and the archetype of the studio boss, connecting the cops/detective squad to the film industry establishment/Hollywood front office. The film in this way is a critique of the movie business, Perkins argues, even without "the familiar facades of the Hollywood picture (studios, premieres, previews, etc.)" ("*Lonely*" 223). We believe Dix to be innocent since we saw him pay Mildred's cab fare and send her home, but we also know that Dix may be capable of murder. This suspicion is validated by Lochner's description of Dix's history of violence: brawling in a beer parlor, fracturing a producer's jaw in a fistfight, breaking an ex-girlfriend's nose in a domestic quarrel.

Dix's most violent acts occur off-screen, but his response to Lochner's questioning is characterized less by stoicism (once a marker of virtue, strength, and bravery) than, in his own glib words, a "lack of emotion," which makes the threat of violence as disturbing as anything the film allows us to see. Take, for example, the scene in which Dix sadistically "directs" the possible murder scenario when Brub and his wife Sylvia invite him to their home for dinner. Dix offers to help Brub solve the case by turning to his experience watching Hollywood "whodunits" (screenwriters, he reminds them, "solve every murder in less than two hours"). Facing Dix, Brub and Sylvia sit side-by-side as if they were in a car together driving up Benedict Canyon, where Mildred's murder was committed. Narrating this dark *mise-en-abyme*, Dix gives Brub the following directions: "you put your right arm around her neck. Now, you get to a lonely place in the road and you begin to squeeze. You're an ex-GI, you know judo, you know how to kill a person without using your hands. You're driving the car and you're strangling her. You don't see her bulging eyes or protruding tongue." Brub acts out the part while Dix leans forward grinning maniacally as his narration escalates, taking a perverse, almost orgasmic thrill in his description of the grisly events.

As Dix continues, his face is shown in high-key light, leaving the rest of him in shadows, and by revealing the apparatus, Ray reminds viewers that we are indeed watching a film directed by a person behind the camera. "Go ahead," Dix adds, exposing his latent misogyny and paranoia, "go ahead, Brub. Squeeze harder. You love her, and she's deceived you. You hate her patronizing attitude—she looks down on you, she's impressed with celebrities, she wants to get rid of you. Squeeze harder . . . harder . . . squeeze harder . . . it's wonderful to feel her throat crush under your arm!"

Brub and Lochner undertake an official investigation into Dix as a suspect in the Atkinson case, but the film seems more concerned with the amateur detective work of Laurel, who lives in an apartment across the patio.[28] Not the stereotypical femme fatale of film noir, this beautiful blonde becomes the investigator with whom we are meant to identify, and Dix becomes the mystery to be solved. Dix and Laurel exchange glances through their respective windows the night of Mildred's visit, and when Laurel is called for questioning at Lochner's office, she confirms that she saw Dix saying goodnight to Mildred. There is an obvious attraction between them, and the film (like *On Dangerous Ground*, *Johnny Guitar*, and *Party Girl*) sees redemptive hope for its violent male protagonist in his relationship with a good woman.

At least temporarily, their romance does give Dix the happiness that has eluded him through the years following the war, and he finds the inspiration to write the *Althea Bruce* script. By contrast, Laurel begins to doubt Dix's innocence after Lochner warns her about his violent behavior. When Dix learns that Laurel met with Lochner behind his back, she witnesses firsthand what Lochner described. Furiously speeding down a winding road, Dix crashes into another driver, who shouts insults at him (recalling the opening scene). Dix knocks him to the ground, punching the man in the face repeatedly and then grabbing a rock to slam against his head until Laurel shouts for him to stop. Later, Sylvia encourages Laurel to go away and reflect on her feelings for Dix in light of her suspicions.

The most self-reflexive moment in the film is Dix's marriage proposal, in which he prepares Laurel breakfast when she awakens from a restless sleep. It blends comic pathos with dramatic tension—Dix, thoroughly out-of-place in this environment, straightens a grapefruit knife and then carves the grapefruit in ominous stabbing motions—and once again calls attention to the performances in the film as film performances. Laurel compliments the love scene in Dix's script, and he explains, "A good love scene should be about something else beside love—for instance, this one. Me fixing grapefruit, you sitting over there dopey, half asleep.

Anyone looking at us could tell we were in love." Afraid to do otherwise, she reluctantly accepts his proposal.

Rather than taking the path to enlightenment of, say, Johnny Logan, Dix goes to the darkest place of any of Ray's male protagonists. Confiding in Mel that she does not want to go through with the marriage, Laurel gives him the unfinished *Althea Bruce* script in the hopes that approval from the film's producer will compensate for her rejection. Dix wants to celebrate the engagement and invites Mel and Charlie to join him and Laurel at Paul's that evening. When Dix discovers that Mel took the script to the producer without his permission (another betrayal in his eyes), he gives Mel a backhanded slap across the face, breaking his glasses. Fearing for her safety, Laurel returns to her apartment to pack her bags. Dix follows her home and sees that she has removed her engagement ring, and when he receives a phone call with her flight cancelation, he is sent into a blind rage realizing that she intends to leave him.

The film begins to fulfill its own prophecy as Dix strangles Laurel on her bed, but he is interrupted by a phone call from Brub, informing him that Mildred's fiancée confessed to her murder (the killer, of course, is arbitrary, just as Mildred's killing basically serves as a plot device). Although in the script Dix actually murders Laurel and is arrested, Ray claims to have improvised this more ambiguous ending with Bogart and Grahame (Eisenschitz 144). Laurel watches Dix leave her apartment, walking out onto the patio alone in the dead of night, and she quotes to herself a passage from his script: "I was born when she kissed me, I died when she left me, I lived a few weeks when she loved me." By destroying the love he shared with Laurel, creating the conditions for his own self-destruction, Dix finally achieves a meaningful articulation in those three poetic lines.

The reciprocal legends of Ray and his actors established star/director myths that have become part of the larger myth of anti-authoritarian Hollywood filmmaking. Whereas Ray and Dean were mutually affected by the mass cultural promotion of the Method as a new mode of performance in the 1950s, Ray's work with the older, tougher Bogart and Mitchum channeled the hard-boiled "bad boy" of the 1940s. Modeling problems of self and other, the public and the private, Ray's stature as an "actor's director" unveils the metatheatrical consciousness of modernism, while the star performance texts of Dean, Mitchum, and Bogart speak to the changing attitudes toward masculinity in postwar American culture. In *Rebel*, *The Lusty Men*, and *In a Lonely Place*, the figure of the rebel male is defined by his inability to signify as a normative masculine subject within collapsing structures of articulation, thematizing the literal and metaphorical "interruptions" that reputedly plagued Ray over his career. The next chapter turns to Ray's own performances, both in his self-promotion as a filmmaking professor and as an actor in his final films, through which he created a face for his public image in the 1970s: auteur-as-teacher.

3

Rebirth of the Auteur

Pedagogy, Self-Promotion, and Political Modernism

> I would like to help create a new concept of film as a living, continuously breathing thing, so you see the molecules of thought and emotion and experience working all the time, and in a kind of wonderful disorder that permits the audience to participate in creating its own order and drawing their own conclusions from what they experience. That is what I think we will finally come to. *Sesame Street* on television at times approaches this quality.
>
> —Nicholas Ray, *I Was Interrupted*

Toward a New Auteurism

By 1971, Nicholas Ray, the auteur as we knew him, was dead. Following a successful guest appearance earlier that year at Harpur College of Arts and Sciences, part of the State University of New York at Binghamton, Ray was invited to return as a visiting professor of cinema from September of 1971 to August of 1973. Ray's invitation came from experimental filmmakers Larry Gottheim and Ken Jacobs, the founders of the Harpur film program, and the limited appointment allowed him to direct his final film nearly a decade after he retired from commercial filmmaking. The film was called *We Can't Go Home Again*[1]—a title borrowed from Thomas Wolfe's posthumous novel *You Can't Go Home Again* (1940)—and it was neither a demonstration of ostensibly autonomous authorship made within the industrial demands of the American studio system, nor was it an alliance with Hollywood's hot rebel stars; it was an ambitious new undertaking. "You can only learn filmmaking by making films," Ray would tell his students repeatedly (qtd. in Eisenschitz 430), and together they set out to make *Home*, a film he described as "an adventure in time and space" (Canby, "Nicholas" 22).

Projecting simultaneous and sometimes overlapping Super-8mm, 16mm, 35mm, and video images on a transparent screen (from five projectors, all timed in relation to each other) and then refilming them with a 35 mm camera, the sixty-year-old Ray attempted to modernize the language of cinema through a multiple image process he called "mimage" (S. Ray, "To"; S. Ray, "Out" 21) (see fig. 3.1). Footage shot with Nam

Figure 3.1. *We Can't Go Home Again* (2011): Projecting simultaneous and sometimes overlapping Super-8mm, 16mm, 35mm, and video images on a transparent screen (from five projectors, all timed in relation to each other) and then refilming them with a 35mm camera, the sixty-year-old Ray attempted to modernize the language of cinema through a multiple image process he called "mimage." (Oscilloscope Laboratories, 2012; digital frame enlargement)

June Paik's video synthesizer comprises the most formally inventive sequences in the film, anticipating developments at the intersections of experimental filmmaking and video art. Multiple image techniques have become commonplace in contemporary narrative cinema and news media, but Ray was one of the first filmmakers to put them into effect.[2] Unlike other filmmakers, though, he subverted what Bill Krohn calls "the dream of panoptic vision—a demonic parody of divine omniscience—that has spawned our present day culture of surveillance" (*We*). *Home* premiered at the Cannes International Film Festival in 1973, but Ray continued editing the film until his actual death in 1979.[3] Susan Ray, his widow, completed, reconstructed, and restored the film for a premiere of the new digital master at the 2011 Venice International Film Festival—along with the "making of" documentary *Don't Expect Too Much*—to commemorate the centennial of his birth.[4]

The production of the film was consumed with the spirit of the counterculture, something with which Ray was quite familiar, having begun work on an earlier film about the historic student occupation protests and worker strikes of May '68 in Paris.[5] After living in Europe from 1959 to 1969, Ray came home to make a film about the Chicago Conspiracy Trial, the famous grand jury case in which eight social and political activists were accused of conspiracy to incite riots at the 1968 Democratic National Convention (he hired Susan, then a student at the University of Chicago, to help with the script and run his production office). Ray abandoned both projects.[6]

During his tenure at Harpur College, he recaptured his own left-wing youth from the Depression and his experimental, almost communal work with young actors making *Rebel without a Cause*, while experiencing firsthand this turbulent period of college history. As his former student Tom Farrell[7] recalls:

> We were at the mercy of fate, habitually indulging in sex, drugs, alcohol, and even violence. We lived by night, shooting and editing our bigger than life experiences in a lonely place on dangerous ground. Once, after drinking at a bar, Nick drove home on the back roads in darkness like he was James Dean, when he crashed into a ditch. Miraculously he was unharmed, but he could have been killed. Another time a crazed student on LSD challenged Nick to a fist fight, which had to be stopped . . . (Qtd. in Eisenschitz 442)

In addition to these wild circumstances of the production, Farrell refers to the cultural chaos that surrounded the students in Binghamton, including

"Vietnam war protest, a memorial birthday party for Adolf Hitler, the Attica prison riot, an orgy the night Nixon was reelected, rapes of female hitchhikers, drug raids, police harassment, suicides, and dozens of other insane episodes which determined the film we made" (qtd. in Eisenschitz 442). Footage of the events Ray shot in Chicago made it into *Home*, along with documentary footage of the 1968 Chicago Democratic Convention, speeches by Jane Fonda and Tom Hayden, Richard Nixon's presidential nomination and reelection, and riots and police brutality. "It was not a pleasant time for lonely people," Ray says in the film.

The production was also symptomatic of what D. N. Rodowick calls "the era of political modernism" (*Crisis* vii), which he defines as "the critique of realist form in Hollywood cinema as illusionistic, and the promotion of the semiotic counterstrategies of modernism" (*Crisis* xiv).[8] Ray was not likely conscious of this "ideological turn" in cinema studies, a period Rodowick demarcates from 1968 to 1984. He was more interested in trying to "destroy the rectangular frame" (qtd. in Eisenschitz 433), a goal he maintained for years and inherited from Frank Lloyd Wright, who once declared, "The box is a Fascist symbol, and the architecture of freedom and democracy needed something better than the box" (qtd. in Eisenschitz 433).

The *Cahiers du cinéma* critics had already praised Ray's innovative techniques with color and the CinemaScope frame. Ray was now looking beyond cinema, to Goya's black period, to the Bruegels, to Bosch's *The Garden of Earthly Delights*, and to Velázquez's *Las Meninas*, going so far as to paint a watercolor illustration of his multiple-image vision. Picasso's *Guernica* was a key inspiration and Ray cites it during one of the most dramatically important moments in the film. "Painting in the expressionist school," he asserted, "has been far ahead of us [filmmakers] if you look at the works of Nolde, Kirchner, Kokoschka, Pechstein, Beckmann" (qtd. in S. Ray, "To the Viewer").

The conceptualization of cinema in terms of nonlinearity and abstract, contrapuntal assemblages resonated with the music of Glenn Gould and the art of Robert Rauschenberg, but also with experimental filmmakers such as Stan Brakhage and Jean Rouch, defying any sort of Hollywood understanding of cinema. Ray's great admirer from the 1950s, Jean Luc-Godard, formed the Dziga Vertov Group with other politically progressive filmmakers (taking its name from the renowned Soviet documentarian and film theorist who developed cinéma vérité in 1920s and 1930s). The Dziga Vertov Group worked through similar ideas from 1968 to 1972 (see, for example, *Tout va bien* [1972]). After the group dissolved, Godard continued playing with some of these notions in films such as *Numéro deux* (1975) and *Ici et Ailleurs* (1976).

What Ray's reputation unmasks is how the era of political modernism, of Brechtian aesthetics and the decentralization of the author/artist, ultimately reifies a different type of auteur. The director becomes a figure not deduced by the text, but discursively formed as the structuring absence of the film. Privileging the stated intentions of certain political filmmakers is one way in which this didactic "new auteurism" reinscribes the canonicity and authority of the director. Ray is an example of a director turned into a public figure through self-promotion, who speaks to the reflexive devices that deconstruct the illusionism of industrialized, commercial narrative cinema and its systems of spectator address.

Films activated in this "modernist" framework were held up in opposition to the "realist" productions of Hollywood that adhered to codes of verisimilitude and representation. Questions about the personal vision and signature style of the auteur in film criticism may have epitomized an unapologetically cinephilic mode of writing about movies. While this celebratory approach was eclipsed by more "objectively" theoretical, even cinephobic questions about the politics of representation and interpellation, with its close formal and structural analyses informed by "[t]ext-centered semiology, psychoanalytic accounts of the subject, and Althusserian Marxism" (Rodowick, *Crisis* vii), the auteur did not disappear from film culture. As this chapter shows, Ray's career in the 1970s reminds us how the preeminence of the auteur survives through a series of disciplinary disavowals, repressions, and returns.

Ray's reputation as a modernist filmmaker shaped by *Cahiers du cinéma* in the 1950s was built around his perceived respect for medium-specificity and hyperstylized mise-en-scène (particularly with regards to color and widescreen), as well as his existential worldview in the tradition of modernist authors and artists. However, we must remember that it was also built around his populist image as a rebel, who worked within classical studio and genre systems, but fought with producers and executives to push the boundaries of the medium and attempt to see his personal vision fully articulated. Ray, who never had the autonomy of directors such as Hitchcock or Hawks, once told French filmmaker Barbet Schroeder: "You like these films, but you can't imagine how often they represent only fifty percent of what I wanted to do. You have no idea how I had to fight to achieve that fifty percent" (qtd. in Eisenschitz 314). What made Ray so "modern" for *Cahiers du cinéma* then was his representation of a certain type of Hollywood cinema that could, in turn, modernize French film culture after World War II: products of the American culture industry that could be repurposed to undercut traditional ideologies of artistic value. For cinema studies of the 1970s, the hegemonic institution of Hollywood stood as the antithesis of modernism. On the other hand, "an independent and avant-garde cinema motivated by political concerns" (Rodowick, *Crisis* xiii), of which Ray was now a part, could "practice" film theory by interrogating "which aspects of film form promote identification [. . .], and which break identification [. . .] and thus promote critical awareness in the spectator" (xv). Therefore, Ray emerges as an auteur by any other name, and a new kind of modernist, by performing the role of rebel through a public discourse of pedagogy.

Political modernism was not a theory per se, but (much like *la politique des auteurs*) a discourse with origins in vanguard journals such as *Screen*. In his book *The Crisis of Political Modernism*, Rodowick argues that the 1970s was "a decade in which theoretical work in film studies defined the cutting edge of research in the humanities and in which the field itself became increasingly accepted and recognized as an academic discipline" (vii). A series of theoretical positions influenced by the events of May '68, political modernism sought to address the issue of cinematic identification through a dual focus on form/ideology and form/spectatorship (xv), and, in Rodowick's words, to "broaden how the problem of ideology was addressed" (xiii).

While their critical methodologies were diverse, these film theorists were united by practices of ideological critique, inflected by an often feminist concern with the cinematic apparatus and a foundation in Saussurean linguistics, Althusserian Marxism, and Lacanian psychoanalysis (or some combination of the three). "The aim throughout the 1970s," Rodowick contends, "was to produce a set of concepts that defined the relation between film form and ideology, and in reversing or negating that form, to produce a materialist and nonideological countercinema" (xiv).[9] According to his research, political modernism was "the defining idea [. . .] of 1970s film theory" (viii). Not even the utopian and revolutionary aspirations of auteurism could carry young bohemians through the Sturm und Drang of 1968 in France. In February, Minister for Cultural Affairs André Malraux forced the antibureaucratic cinephile Henri Langlois to step down as director of the Cinémathèque Française, both for his mismanagement and for standing in the way of turning the Cinémathèque into an institution of the government. Godard, Truffaut, and other directors committed to French film culture withdrew their films from the Cinémathèque, led protests, and petitioned Langlois's dismissal. Although Malraux eventually reinstated Langlois, he severely cut funding for the Cinémathèque.

Roland Barthes published "The Death of the Author" in 1967 (in the English-language journal *Aspen* and then in French the following year in *Manteia*), sending shock waves through the humanities with a thesis that overthrew authorial intent and biography as the provenances of textual meaning. At a time in film scholarship when the pleasures of Hollywood and the genius of the auteur were being denied, even *Cahiers du cinéma* more or less followed the dominant trend in the field, despite establishing itself as a forum for challenging prevailing critical assumptions.

With Paris as the world film capital of the 1960s and 1970s, we might suggest that *Cahiers du cinéma* helped set the tone for what was to come. Contrary to historical generalizations about the magazine, its long-standing investment in new cinematic forms and polemical writing always had a political orientation (after all, the postwar acclaim afforded to Ray was nothing less than an antifascist gesture that marshaled an implicit attack on bourgeois artistic standards), but after 1968, its critical project was no longer in the name of the auteur. "By the end of the [1960s]," asks film critic and programmer Gabe Klinger, apropos of Godard, "could anyone reasonably say, without getting laughed out of the room, that Nicholas Ray was the cinema?" (18). The passionate devotion to the poetics and phenomenology of "authored" cinema was superseded by an equally passionate inquiry into the socioeconomic conditions of cultural production, Romantic idealism giving way to neo-Marxist materialism that characterized the repoliticization of *Cahiers du cinéma* for the next five years. Collectively written by the magazine's editors and published in the August 1970 issue, the famous article on John Ford's 1939 classic *Young Mr. Lincoln* (1939) was the first step in this new intellectual direction. Whereas the auteur was once the privileged site of meaning-making in the Hollywood film text, the accent had shifted to the politics of mise-en-scène, and the degree to which studio films deconstructed the ideological and aesthetic practices of Classical Hollywood.

Directors such as Ray had peaked by the 1960s, and in some ways no longer needed to be defended. As Jim Hillier reminds us, "Nicholas Ray [. . .] is now seen to have worked best in conditions of studio-based constraint, his individuality becoming lost in 'super-productions' like *King of Kings* and *55 Days at Peking*." Hillier also goes on to explain that "the 'studio system' had passed definitively, and there was perceived a lack of direction, and a confused sense of what the mass audience—in so far as a mass audience still existed—wanted" ("Introduction: *Cahiers*" 8). In addition to the trauma of May '68, *Cahiers du cinéma* had been reflecting social and political upheavals throughout the 1960s, especially in American culture: the country's economic and military expansion (felt most acutely by the Vietnam War), the effects of transnational conglomerations on media industries (changing the way films were made), and the decline of America's image as a liberal or socially critical nation (an image once propagated by Hollywood). A second wave of anti-Americanism had started to spread among European intellectuals (Hillier, "Introduction: *Cahiers*" 15). Meanwhile, the *nouvelle vague* in French cinema saw Ray's most ardent admirers at *Cahiers du cinéma*—Godard, Truffaut, Rivette, and Rohmer—move away from film criticism to deal with some of these issues in their new work as filmmakers themselves.

The beginning of the 1960s signaled the end of "the last great era of Hollywood filmmaking," with which Ray's films would be identified. Klinger reminds us how the aesthetic quality of Hollywood's output, at least the way critics perceived it, paralleled the new political standards of film criticism. "In less than a decade," he muses, "several of the major Hollywood players would splinter away from studios and form their own companies; new aesthetic and commercial heights would be reached in Europe, South America, and Asia; and more discreetly and less commercially, dazzling works would surface in the avant-garde scene" (G. Klinger 18).

The names associated with political modernism are familiar to cinema studies: Peter Wollen, Laura Mulvey, Christian Metz, Jean-Louis Baudry, Raymond Bellour, Stephen Heath, and Colin MacCabe. One of the most influential pieces of film theory to come out of this period was Jean-Luc Comolli and Jean Narboni's editorial "Cinema/Ideology/Criticism," published in *Cahiers du cinéma* in 1969 and translated in *Screen* in 1971, which classified the relationship between cinema and ideology according seven categories. Investigating to what extent texts can reinforce or transgress dominant ideology, Comolli and Narboni presented a method statement for the analysis of the dominant textual politics of Hollywood and, by extension, an advocacy for a transgressive "countercinema." Barbara Klinger has shown how their model required "the critical identification of a series of 'rebel' texts within the Hollywood empire. These texts, while firmly entrenched within the system, display certain features that are critically deemed as combative to the conventions governing the 'typical' classic text" ("Cinema" 74). Klinger points out that much of the scholarship that followed suit revolved around certain "progressive" genres, such as the family melodrama and film noir of the 1940s and 1950, but she also notes that, for these critics, progressive genres intertwined with progressive auteurs ("Cinema" 75). For example, in his neo-Marxist articles "Distanciation and Douglas Sirk" (*Screen*, 1971) and "Towards an Analysis of the Sirkian System" (*Screen*, 1972/73), Paul Willemen made a frequently cited case for the progressivity of melodrama auteur Douglas Sirk. I would add that these critics could broadly be divided into two theoretical camps: neo-Marxism[10] and feminist psychoanalysis.[11] What they overestimated, Klinger concludes, is how the Classical Hollywood style enables textual ruptures, subversions, and excesses within its very system of signification.

The difference between this strand of political modernism and the auteurist criticism of the 1950s and 1960s is therefore one of degree rather than kind. Whereas the latter mode of critique was driven by an impulse toward canonization of the auteur and the former by an impulse toward deconstruction of the patriarchal-capitalist ideology in which the auteur operated, both imagine Hollywood in deeply formal terms as a cinema of directors. In the case of family melodrama, Ray, Sirk, Vincente Minnelli, and Max Ophuls were highlighted as exemplary directors of the genre in Thomas Elsaesser's influential 1972 *Monogram* article "Tales of Sound and Fury." Films by Ray and Sirk were the subjects of Roger D. McNiven's article on architecture and the family melodrama, "The Middle-Class American Home of the Fifties," published in *Cinema Journal* in 1983, and Ray's films played a key role in Rodowick's own article published in *The Velvet Light Trap* in 1982 on the domestic melodrama of the 1950s, "Madness, Authority, and Ideology."[12]

After the end of the traditional phase of auteurism, we can see how the auteur never really left, but was rather subsumed into theories of the cinematic apparatus and ideological criticism of genre that foregrounded textual politics in a particular way, marrying film style with the material conditions of production and equating countercinematic aesthetics with modernism. Ray, for one, was more visible than ever before, partly because of his new status as a "progressive" director of genre films, but more explicitly because of the reading formations that were facilitated by his new role: auteur-as-teacher.

As an author of the self, rather than of the film text, Ray still anchors the meaning of *Home* in an auteurist presence, literally through the prominent image of himself on the screen.[13] Perhaps even more accurately, he anchors meaning in a presence by his very absence as the film's auteur, following his instructions to view cinema as a collaborative art form that mined the culture for its raw material. Thus, what political modernism enabled was a demystification of the auteur that ultimately resulted in a "transference" of the auteur theory. Auteurs were still very much part of the critical discourse on cinema in the 1970s, and of the film collectives that sprung up at the time.

When Ray first appeared on the Binghamton campus as a guest lecturer, Gottheim projected *They Live by Night* several times amid the Harpur Film Society's usual underground program (Gottheim 90). In fact, Ray's political modernism did more to bolster the work he completed in Hollywood, while *Home*, as Gabe Klinger puts it, "is truly one of the loneliest films" (20), and it is precisely this quality that makes it so significant to Ray's reputation as a *poète maudit*. Klinger accounts for the film's "loneliness" in the way that "champions of Ray's Hollywood phase have never challenged themselves to see beyond its inherent flaws (the technical sloppiness, the fact that it was never finished, etc.). Similarly, the avant-garde community [. . .] has always approached it with indifference, never quite willing to place it alongside the multi-screen experiments of Warhol, Harry Smith, and Godard" (19–20).

The contemporary equation between Ray and the medium of cinema remains both his blessing and his curse. When Ray's films screened at the New York City Public Theater in 1981, Andrew Sarris looked back on "the visual explosion that was Nicholas Ray throughout the '50s" ("Acid" 43). "Perhaps I need more time in which to exorcise my disturbing impressions of the man," he acknowledged, "before I can come more fully to terms with his movies. It may also be that there is a built-in limitation to a filmmaker who is so intuitively 'cinematic' " ("Acid" 43). In a more recent editorial written for the release of *Home*, Gabe Klinger refers to Ray as an "eternal auteurist pet project" (18). Klinger reflects, "Iterations of Jean-Luc Godard's poetic formulation that Ray is the cinema have appeared and likely will continue to appear wherever and whenever the director of *They Live by Night* and *Rebel without a Cause* is remembered. Without much reflection, the phrase has been absorbed as a sort of impassioned cinephilic mantra" (18).

Just as Jon Halliday gave critics a political lens with which to interpret the films of Douglas Sirk in his published interviews with the director, *Sirk on Sirk* (1972), Ray embraced his reputation by enacting an auteurist ethos in which his ideas about filmmaking were made public and in which he could "play" himself in a film. Paradoxically, he also effaced his own auteurism by collaborating with his students on a politically modernist and anti-Hollywood production (a film "by Us," according to the credits). Gottheim remembers that while Ray was a controversial member of the Harpur faculty, "using everything he could get his hands on for his project" (93), his students looked up to him as a film guru of sorts, and his "own living persona would itself be a performance to pull people magnetically into his own aura in order for them to finally become more of themselves, as well as creatures of his own imagination" (95).

Ray again adopted a pedagogical persona, as the mentor to German auteur Wim Wenders in *Lightning over Water*, his other major project of the era released in 1980, a year after his death. Like *Home*, *Lightning* was a pseudo-documentary and an autobiographical experiment, and Ray's self-promotion for both films—as well as his roles in them—simultaneously verify and negate his auteurist image. The years Ray spent making *Home* and *Lightning* on the backdrop of the seismic shift in cinema studies gave critics a new avenue to approach his career that had been previously inaccessible. Audiences literally had a face to the name, as well as the spoken words of the author. But Ray's sudden renaissance in the 1970s did not correct the record by sealing his films with a final signified as modernist texts in a new public and political consciousness. Instead, Ray was a reminder of the potential for filmmakers, audiences, critics, and teachers in a cinema culture where those viewing positions are not mutually exclusive.

Rodowick argues that criticism is a political act and, although we may be creating a reading unintended by the filmmaker by constructing meaning from a discursive matrix in which the film is embedded, we can also "create new positions or perspectives of reading" (*Crisis* xii). Reading is not simply a process of decoding a text from its network of possible meanings to which it has already been inscribed, but, as Rodowick explains, "a performative act, and an active construction of meaning" (*Crisis* xviii). If Ray is a performer, as a self-fashioned auteur and an anti-academic theorist positing new intellectual and affective ways of directing and encountering cinema, then he also invites his readers to perform with him as collaborators. Much like his actors and his students, we find meanings through our unique individual experiences with his films. In this way, the image of Ray as pedagogue "teaches" us how to watch his films through an auteurist reading strategy that also yields dynamic, pluralistic, and contextual possibilities of rereading and meaning-making.

Auteur as Teacher, or: Authoring a Public Self

Ray was not a cinephile himself, as we learned from the previous chapter, but he was in love with cinema as a medium and he believed in its radical possibilities. Susan Ray remarks that he consciously saw film as "a means of approaching a greater reality" ("Out" 23), and this philosophical commitment gives him serious credibility among the auteurists and cinephiles who love his films. She tells us, "To him the celluloid strip was no mere piece of plastic. Through the mediation of the camera, the celluloid strip registered life. Thus it became a thing of infinite potential, as it 'recognize[d] neither time nor space, only the limits of man's imagination.' He called film 'the cathedral of the arts' " ("Out" 23).

In addition to his ideas about cinema, he also lends himself to auteurist appreciation and cinephilic idolatry by fashioning himself as a rebel filmmaker, both in physical appearance and personal affect, outspoken about his antagonistic relationship with the industrial restrictions of Hollywood. Dana Polan observes the following in his monograph on *In a Lonely Place*:

> Ray's comportment helped in the construction of him as an auteur. Beyond the fact that he was a hard-living rebel, he also cultivated an image as intellectual artist, as a thinker. On the one hand, he talked to the Europeans of authors they knew (on several occasions Ray talked of making a film of the life of the poet Rimbaud) and of themes dear to their cultural tastes, such as the existential crisis of the individual. [. . .] On the other hand, the very fact that Ray talked with the critics, that with intelligence he made explicit his artistic goals and desires, allowed them to feel that he was not so far from themselves. (52–53).

The most idiosyncratic details—his shock of white hair, his eye patch, his craggy face, and emaciated, almost ghoulish look later in life—tell a war story to his audience. Sarris described seeing the six-foot-tall filmmaker "in his ravaged flesh," as if "he had burned himself up on the screen" ("Acid" 43), while his biographer Patrick McGilligan remarks:

> For the sixties radicals, the eye patch helped confirm Ray as one of them: an adventurer, an outlaw, a buccaneer. For film aficionados, it evoked an elite club of one-eyed directors with similar patches [. . .]. Ray's looks had always been a deceptive part of his appeal. For a man who cut a romantic, bigger-than-life figure—though "with a crucifixion in his face," as Melville described Ahab—the eye patch was the perfect adornment, the advertisement of a flaw (466).

How Ray lost his eye is a bit of a mystery, but Ray claims to have fallen asleep at the editing table one night in Chicago at the end of January in 1970, and woke up with an embolism (McGilligan 465). If we believe his legend, and there is a part of us that wants to, the eye patch also signifies his self-destructive dedication to his art.

When Ray first came to Binghamton for his guest lecture, he decided to turn his visit into an intensive workshop with little actual lecturing involved, and this approach became his only real pedagogical "method" when he returned as a professor. Ray told the story this way: "The hell with the lecture! I made the kids hold the camera, handle videotape, set lights, operate sound—*do* things. The session began at two that afternoon and ended at six the next morning" (Lederer 62). As he began the production of *Home*, he rented a farmhouse—the same one seen in the film—and opened it for students to live with him as long as they pleased. Some would stay anywhere from a night to a week at a time.[14]

The project started as a possible ten- to fifteen-minute short to be screened on campus, but it turned into a feature film when Ray said he and his students realized that they "were touching at the texture of life. We had been shooting ad-lib, and acting out the things that students had confidence enough to bring in to me. One day it seemed to me that we had the potential for a film" (Goodwin and Wise 20). After the first three months of shooting, students culled together from Ray's three classes had rotated different jobs on the production and settled into more specialized roles. "From the beginning," Ray announced, "my objective at Harpur was to develop the best film team that ever existed" (Lederer 63). Other than Camus's *Myth of Sisyphus* and Bergson's *Essay on Laughter*, which he assigned to his students, there was no philosophy for Ray's teaching per se (Eisenschitz 430).

The opening monologue in *Home* eschews a conventional introduction to the director, presuming a familiarity with his classic films, while still trying to erase the traces of an auteurist or art world celebrity. Ray's narration seems to want to speak for the voice of the older generation whose guilt he assumes, as well as the voice of the counterculture that was being silenced. As Ray stated in an interview, "My generation has been the biggest betrayers of any generation we've ever known. The betrayals that I engage in (in the movie) are like asking your kid to jump into your arms and then pulling your arms away, the kind of betrayals that lie behind the wars, the assassinations, the Watergates" (Goodwin and Wise 20). The sympathies Ray expresses for his young characters puts *Home* on an unexpected continuum with *They Live by Night*, *Knock on Any Door*, *Rebel*, and *The True Story of Jesse James* (see fig. 3.2).

Heard over a cluster of images that form a collage of Chicago in 1969, Ray's cigarette-burned voice both severs him from the elitism of the Hollywood studio auteur and grounds the film in his auteurist vision

Figure 3.2. *The True Story of Jesse James* (1957): The sympathies Ray expresses for his young characters puts *We Can't Go Home Again* on an unexpected continuum with *They Live by Night*, *Knock on Any Door*, *Rebel*, and *The True Story of Jesse James*. (Twentieth Century Fox Home Entertainment, 2006; digital frame enlargement)

through self-attribution: "I had read of a festival of life being called in Chicago, Illinois. I remembered that in the late nineteenth-century, a governor of Illinois had refused to allow a major political party to hold its convention on the grounds that such a demonstration might incite riots and violence. Within three hours after being inside that city, I had been maced and my camera had been smashed." He goes on to talk about the (now seven) defendants at the Chicago Conspiracy Trial and the murder of Fred Hampton, the deputy chairman of the Black Panther Party chapter in Illinois, whom we see speaking in documentary footage, powerfully capturing the zeitgeist of the late 1960s.[15]

The dizzying barrage of images not only makes for an authentic period piece, but also an indictment of Ray's own generation for failing to live up to the promise of the American Dream and its democratic ideals on which the country was founded. "What really made me wonder was, where is everybody?" he asks, suggesting that the progressive mission of the American counterculture, to uphold social justice and world peace, civil rights and liberties, and equal opportunity for all to succeed, had also failed. In the midst of a fracturing in the counterculture, the assassinations of Robert Kennedy and Martin Luther King, Jr. in 1968 gave the New Left little hope for the future of the country. Militant organizations such as the Black Panther Party and the Weather Underground, the latter of which formed in 1969, turned to more revolutionary forms of social action to achieve the goals of the left. The "summer of love" was officially over.

This prologue abruptly shifts to a more playful tone as Ray seems aware of his own reputation and exploits it for dramatic effect. A bearded student tells the camera that he wants to look like Charlton Heston in Cecil B. De Mille's *The Ten Commandments* (1956), an icon of MacMahonist cinephilia out of which Ray's reputation grew in France, who starred in Ray's last commercial film, *55 Days at Peking*. Another student describes the first traumatic experience she can recall, the Bay of Pigs Invasion. Old Hollywood masculinity and Cold War conflict are the two most impressionable forces on these young people, the ideal new audience for Ray. "Fortunately, I was offered a job in an upstate New York university," he informs us, ". . . hell, I decided I'd buy a crooked cane, grow a goatee, wear a crooked smile, and impress them with my rhetoric, rebellion, and ponderosity."

In these first few sequences, the film sets up the internal logic and hierarchy of power in *Home*, one last gasp from the shattered remnants of America's counterculture, explicitly seeking to find a democratized political address, but implicitly looking to the figure of the auteur as an organizing principle or, at the very least, as a spiritual, guiding light through darkness. Ray is a teacher, of course, but also a surrogate father to his student filmmakers, evoking his relationship with Dean in the production of *Rebel* and the alternative families that often develop in his films (Jim, Judy, and Plato in *Rebel*; the rodeo cowboys in *The Lusty Men*; the gangs in *They Live by Night* and *Johnny Guitar*; etc.).

The title appears on the screen over touching images of Ray and his students at work together, and the blues song "Bless the Family" performed by Suzy Williams, with piano accompaniment by composer Stormin' Norman Zamcheck, harkens back to these familial bonds from Ray's filmography: "God bless the family that sings together / A song bursts from their throats / Booming out, some rooted sorrow / They'll strain at every note / And these sad notes keep hope alive / And help this fragile love survive / Bless the family that lives and dies together / Mm-hmm, mm-hmm / Together, together." Williams continues, building to a mournful cry of protest that ignites what we can loosely call the main narrative of the film: "Oh, bless the family that loves / Bring them some happiness / And shelter from loneliness / Oh, oh, oh, oh."

To be clear, Ray was no poseur in this new environment; as an American auteur, he was a veteran of the Classical Hollywood system, but his work on the "Chicago Seven" film also made him an honorary member of the counterculture, giving him ground-level experience with the changing tides in American politics. While Ray was living in Europe, his remove from the filmmaking establishment also helped preserve his image as a serious and misunderstood artist rather than a commercial entertainer, casting him as a part of Hollywood's "Lost Generation" comprised of expatriate auteurs, such as Orson Welles, and victims of the blacklist, such as Joseph Losey and Jules Dassin.

Vincent Canby of the *New York Times* described Ray's appearance at Cannes in 1969 as "a tourist in an exotic but slightly hostile land. He may be familiar with the terrain but he cannot be a part of it, even though he may be something of an attraction himself" ("Fine" D1). Refusing to stay at the Majestic Hotel on the Croisette because it was "too expensive," Ray planned to spend only a few hours in Cannes to end his multiple-picture deal with Yugoslavia's Alva Films (which began in 1965), as studio politics prevented any films from getting made. One of Ray's films for Alva was to be *The Doctor and the Devils*, an adaptation of the Dylan Thomas script with Gore Vidal about the notorious nineteenth-century "body snatchers" Burke and Hare.[16] Despite Ray's fall from the graces of Hollywood, he was not humble about his career, boasting, "I started out as an actor, so did Elia Kazan. That's why we're two of the greatest movie directors in the world" (18).

Ray discussed with Canby his various activities since *55 Days at Peking*, including opening a restaurant in Madrid and living on the Baltic island of Sylt. After collapsing on the set of *55 Days* from exhaustion (not a heart attack as producer Samuel Bronston's press agents claimed), Andrew Marton and Guy Green were hired to complete the film. From that point on, Ray was thought of in the industry as a "dying man." However, he confirmed that he has "never worked harder in his life," writing scripts, traveling, and visiting friends and colleagues. "I want to make pictures," he told Canby, "not deals, but most of this business is just making deals." Referring to his work for Bronston on *King of Kings*, in which he just "wanted to do a simple story of Jesus Christ with no mystique," Ray said it was Bronston who raised the budget to an $8 million deal with MGM. In order to get away from the meddling of producer Paul Graetz on *Bitter Victory*, Ray admitted he gambled away all his money playing chemin de fer. "I've known that I was an artist since I was 45—it was a nice surprise. An artist always has to expose himself when he works . . . ," he declared, adding that only his death will cut off his creative productivity: "My epitaph will read, 'I was interrupted.' " Having completed the editing on an unfinished film about the " 'uncomfortableness' of being a teenager" titled *What?*, shot by Ray's son Timothy and his school roommate on a 16 mm camera Ray gave them, he boldly positioned himself outside the bounds of Hollywood. "They have some fantastic footage," he bragged, "including one of the most lyrical, poetic expressions of masturbation I've ever seen" ("Fine" 18).[17]

Chicago may have been the closest place to a home in which Ray ever worked. In the 1930s, the city was the Midwest Mecca for modern art, writing, architecture, and jazz (recall that he studied under Thornton Wilder at the University of Chicago in 1931). One of the first *and* last commercial films Ray directed, *Knock on Any Door* and *Party Girl*, respectively, were both set in Chicago. When he returned in 1969, those days were a faint memory and the city was now one of the country's hotbeds of violent political unrest.

The new film critic for the *Chicago Sun-Times*, Roger Ebert, interviewed Ray about his plans for the "Chicago Seven" movie, but the interview (like Canby's) was more of a platform for Ray's public image as Hollywood's persona non grata, contemptuous of the commercialism that defines the industry. For the first time, American moviegoers saw Ray as a hard-bitten and world-weary artist, still charged with a political aesthetic that had never been properly appreciated, waiting to flourish with the right independent project. Until John Sturges adapted Hemingway's *The Old Man and the Sea* (1952) with Spencer Tracy in 1958, Ray hoped to make that film with Humphrey Bogart (Ebert N14), but he was now exhausting all his efforts on his film about the "Chicago Seven."

Ray wanted to shoot on a replica of the courtroom in a Chicago studio, with the defendants playing themselves and the dialogue drawn from the trial transcript, which prompted a rumor that Judge Julius Hoffman denied bail to prevent the defendants from acting in the film. According to Ray, Hoffman said that "anyone connected with the film in an executive capacity would be liable for contempt of court," to which Ray replied, "Well I didn't give a damn about that. I knew I could show the movie anywhere else in the world, and not show it in America until that was cleared up."

The 16mm footage Ray shot during defendants Abbie Hoffman and Rennie Davis's trip to Washington, DC invited comparisons both to highbrow auteurs and Hollywood's rebel stars. Ebert referred to a "long, Godardian sequence in the airplane, where Abbie and Rennie talked and kidded each other while a girl in the window seat pretended to be asleep." On the other hand, Ray likened Yippie leader Abbie Hoffman to Robert Mitchum, another "born provocateur." While filming *The Lusty Men*, Mitchum would expose his bare stomach between takes to get a rise out of Susan Hayward, just as Hoffman lifted his shirt imitating "the L.B.J. gall bladder pose." Ray's living conditions as he began working in Chicago were not far off from one of his transient characters, and also reflected his almost myopic fixation on his art. "He is living at the moment in an apartment furnished with the things you absolutely can't do without," Ebert wrote, "like a mattress (on the floor), a projector, a screen, an icebox with beer in it, a transcript of the trial" (N14).

Part of Ray's reputation as a rebellious independent, built around the "Chicago Seven" film, stems from the sense of political commitment as a director that Hollywood never fully allowed him. But it was also a result of the film's own reputation as a risky project doomed to be unfinished from the start. Although Ray promised that the film would get made, and that it would be the best film he had directed, he could never get the financial support needed since there was a possibility it could never be sold to television.

Chicago millionaire Michael Butler, a theatrical producer best known for bringing the hippie rock musical *Hair* to Broadway, agreed to act as a liaison for backers to raise half a million dollars (Ray would go on to make a cameo as the General in Butler's 1979 film version, directed by Miloš Forman). Butler's assistants reported that he was "unable" to raise the money, and Butler then turned to the founder and editor-in-chief of *Playboy* magazine, Hugh Hefner, who had a filmmaker contact willing to fund the film if he saw the ending of the script first. With the trial still in progress, Ray had no ending, and his "three pornographers," as he called them all, backed out: Butler, Hefner, and finally Grove Press, which had been involved in its own court cases over the publications of D. H. Lawrence's *Lady Chatterley's Lover* (1928, Grove edition in 1959), Henry Miller's *Tropic of Cancer* (1934, Grove edition in 1961), and William S. Burroughs's *Naked Lunch* (1959, Grove edition in 1962) (Ebert N14).[18]

Abbie Hoffman told the press that he was codirecting the film with Ray and his fellow defendant Jerry Rubin, and that "because we're not allowed to make seditious speeches," the film would be titled *The Seditious Movie* (Sarris, "Seditious" 55). In addition to starring "sympathetic" celebrities (including Dustin Hoffman on the heels of the counterculture hit *Midnight Cowboy* [1969]), he said the film would also star the seven defendants along with their lawyers as themselves.[19] The prosecutor and assistant prosecutor were offered money to do the same. As to whether such a "seditious" film could change the minds of American audiences, Andrew Sarris remained skeptical, remarking woefully in the *Village Voice*, "Reliable observers tell me that Southern audiences give the murderous rednecks in *Easy Rider* [1969] standing ovations for blowing up the nonconformist bikers" ("Seditious" 55). Dennis Hopper, the director and costar of *Easy Rider* who first met Ray among the cast of *Rebel*, even visited Binghamton to see Ray back behind the camera. The actor-director was fresh off his latest film *The Last Movie* (1971), which he also cowrote with *Rebel* screenwriter Stewart Stern.

At the risk of overstating Ray's case, we must keep in mind that the self-promotion of film directors is not a unique phenomenon. In his book *Hitchcock: The Making of a Reputation*, Robert Kapsis points out that examples of directorial self-promotion can be found as early as the silent era, including those by Fritz Lang, F. W. Murnau, Abel Gance, and Sergei Eisenstein in Europe, and Cecil B. DeMille and D. W. Griffith in Hollywood.[20] Such promotions were standard advertising practices in the European and American film industries (16). Both in Britain and America, Hitchcock's efforts were novel in that he was one of the few directors successful at self-promotion (17), taking advantage of advanced notices, press releases, staged interviews, and the new medium of television. Hitchcock even reportedly authored newspaper and magazine articles instructing audiences on what to expect from his films (36). As we learned in chapter 1, Ray was never shy about self-promotion, granting interviews in the 1950s and early 1960s with European film magazines such as *Cahiers du cinéma*, *Movie*, and *Sight and Sound*. Ray also communicated with outlets of the industry trade press such as the *Daily Variety* and *The Hollywood Reporter*.[21]

While his tactics were not as elaborate or as mainstream as Hitchcock's, whose public, multimedia celebrity gives him the honor of being the first director to become a television star, Ray was equally strategic. What makes him an unusual case for Hollywood directors is his associations with highbrow tastemakers (e.g., Canby, who had just taken over Bosley Crowther's prestigious position at the *Times* as chief film critic, and Ebert, who was five years away from winning the first Pulitzer Prize for film criticism) and urban, artistically minded publications (e.g., the *New York Times*, the *Village Voice*). This kind of elite journalistic endorsement gave him a previously unseen visibility among a cinema-savvy intelligentsia in his native land after he was no longer making commercial films.

Ray's self-promotion thus established both a highbrow and retroactive reading formation that could be easily translated into the discourses of countercultural rebellion and political modernism, priming a new generation to appreciate not only Ray's "Chicago Seven" film (which was folded into *Home*), but also his work in Hollywood. While Ray taught at Harpur, he would use the films he made in Hollywood to investigate with his students the impact of cinema on the unconscious. In addition to subjecting his students to the Lüscher test, a practice in color psychology, he had them study the color experimentations in his films (Eisenschitz 434).

Some of the most famous films Ray directed are cited early in *Home*, situating this decidedly anti-Hollywood production within Ray's auteurist body of work from Hollywood. One of Ray's students, Richie Bock, does a backward somersault into his office and sits on the floor, asking, "Hey, are you the new professor of cinema around here? Aren't you too old to be a new professor?"[22] Another student, Ned Weisman, follows up to ask, "Didn't you, uh, direct that Eskimo movie with Anthony Quinn?" "And *Rebel without a Cause*," he continues, "you directed that also?" When Ray replies, "Yeah, did you like it?" Ned responds coolly, "It was okay." Leslie Levinson, a student who will become one of the film's most important characters, echoes the chorus of questions: "You were the guy that did, uh, *They Live by Night*, right?" Ray says, "Yeah, you know quite a bit about film, don't you?" "*Johnny Guitar*?" Richie asks, and when Ray confirms, he quips back, "Then what the hell you doing here, man?"

An image from *Johnny Guitar* appears above Ray in his office with the students—the death of the Dancin' Kid (Scott Brady) in the climactic shoot-out with Emma (Mercedes McCambridge)—creating a then-and-now comparison between the Ray of Hollywood in the 1950s and the Ray of Harpur in the 1970s. "Now, look, we don't want to have anything to do with Hollywood, man. I wanna do my own thing," Richie tells Ray, walking out of his office. Leslie seems more interested ("Maybe sometime you can tell me more about Marilyn [Monroe] and Jane [Russell]"), and Ray nicknames her Lola Montès after the eponymous character from Ophüls's final film. Ray's first interaction with his students shows the audience that the film they are about to experience is most definitely not a Hollywood film, but that they still cannot underestimate how the rebellious aura of Ray's Hollywood auteurism indirectly constructs their relationship with the film and to Ray.

Home is by no means a love letter to academia or even the Harpur film program ("education was very big business," Ray tells the viewer cynically). If anything, it suggests that radical thought and action are only possible by working within the institution of higher education to push the boundaries of pedagogy, much the way Ray was thought of working within the institution of Hollywood. Ray is no less an outsider at Harpur than he was in Hollywood, and he prefers the company of his students in the film over his fellow university faculty. The communal working conditions of Frank Lloyd Wright's Taliesin Fellowship and the Theatre of Action would provide mere warm-up acts for the production of *Home*, his ultimate foray into collaborative creative expression.

When Canby visited Ray in Binghamton during September of 1972 for a *New York Times* column, he still could not resist writing about Ray as a Hollywood auteur, echoing the students in that early scene in the film. "Here, for the past year," Canby editorialized, "the man who directed such Hollywood movies as *In a Lonely Place*, *The Lusty Men*, and *Johnny Guitar*—phenomena that are as much a part of America of the 1950s as Eisenhower, the Korean War, loafers, and James Dean—has been teaching a film by making a film" ("Nicholas" D1). Canby reported on the leaking screening room in the basement of the Lecture Hall at Harpur College, where, crowded among Ray's students as he viewed footage from *Home*, one of the projectors broke down every three to four minutes (the 35 mm projector was not used, for fear that it would blow a fuse).

The space also functioned as an editing room, classroom, storage room, set, and party scene (we are told that a spilled washbasin at a party on the floor above caused the leak in the ceiling the night before). Although Ray was a long way away from the Hollywood studios, Canby attested that he "still looks, behaves, and thinks like a man on a set" ("Nicholas" D1), and the headline—"Nicholas Ray: Still a Rebel with a Cause"—makes that continuity between Hollywood and Binghamton explicit. For Canby, the film "recalls the controlled melodramatic density and sheer technique of *They Live by Night* and *Rebel without a Cause*." Referring to *The Lusty Men*, he also noted, "There's a very funny scene of Ray directing a fist fight between a student and himself as if it were a scene with Robert Mitchum and Arthur Kennedy." Canby added that one of the female students has "the round, beautiful, sullen-sexy face of the young Gloria Grahame" ("Nicholas" 22).

Tom Farrell wrote in *Sight & Sound* about his experiences making *Home* with Ray. "The film was about the withdrawal from conflict in the streets to face the conflict within ourselves," he assessed, "and Nick's self-portrait in it is rooted in the gifted, neurotic characters from the films he had directed earlier: Bogart playing in *In a Lonely Place*, James Mason in *Bigger Than* Life, Richard Burton in *Bitter Victory*, Robert Ryan in *On Dangerous Ground*." Farrell described *Home* as a remake of *Rebel* "for the postwar generation that woke up in 1968," reflecting that the 1960s was the climax of the latent rebellion in the 1950s. Before Ray screened the film at Cannes, he and six students even worked on the editing and sound mixing in his Chateau Marmont bungalow, where he lived during the making of *Rebel* ("*We*" 92). Ray's Hollywood past makes his work in the political avant-garde of the 1970s legible through claims to biographical and auteurist coherence despite a seemingly disparate career. At the same time, Ray's self-reinvention as an avant-gardist rewrites the classicism of his Hollywood past as part of the same modernist project.

The stories about the making of *Home* are not dissimilar from the stories about Ray's career in Hollywood or in the theater. One student described getting to know Ray at Harpur, evoking, perhaps unintentionally, the ways in which Ray began directing *The Lusty Men*: "Nick arrived with a few pages of written script and handed them to us. He talked with all of us, found out our backgrounds and interests, got in our heads" (Lederer 63). The makeshift conditions of the production were not something with which Ray contended in the studios—there were no lights and lamps among Harpur's film equipment, the sync sound cable broke down often, and the Arriflex camera was repeatedly sent to the factory for repairs. But Ray was used to relying on technical improvisation. "During the Depression," he reminded the press, "I lit a show with miners' lamps and used a hay wagon for a stage" (Lederer 64).

Whether the film's authorship is attributed to Ray or "Us," Ray is clearly the star of the film and he determines the film's dialectics of meaning. By playing himself (a director), he is the autonomous author of the film; by playing a teacher invested in American counterculture, he redefines his role as a political body. This new definition of the director can also extend back across Ray's entire body of work. Ray's first assignment to his students is to "find a boy-girl story" at the demonstrations for the inmates of Attica, who in September of 1971 revolted and held the prison hostage, demanding the rights and living conditions to which they felt they were entitled. Compared to his recent experiences in Chicago, Ray jokes, "this was like a picnic on the lawn." A young man meets Leslie, and the couple is shown in one frame, juxtaposed against the police violently subduing the crowds in other frames, all of which is accompanied by an impassioned speech from an African American protester.

Of course, the film is not *their* story, but it is the story of young people just like them: Richie, who is uncomfortable with his girlfriend Jill sleeping with other men over her summer travels; Leslie, who agrees to masturbate in front of a Binghamton store owner for $1,200; and Tom, who thinks he is falling in love with Leslie, but says he does not get along with Jewish girls. Yet, it is Ray who commands all of our attention. Beyond these vague sketches, Ray's students are generally interchangeable, representing the countercultural youth in broad, abstract terms, whereas Ray is more of a character, albeit a character drawn according to modernist notions of self-reflexivity, instability, fragmentation, and contradiction. "In fact," Ray said in an interview, "I tried to write myself out of it altogether. But by the time we got to a point where it looked like we had a film, the character was too organic a part of it" (Lederer 63).

The characters in *Home* are "real people," but are not psychologically realist or "three dimensional" figures. Although their stories elicit empathy and emotional involvement, the ensemble cast and multiplicity of voices often makes it difficult to discern exactly whose story the film intends to tell. Peter Wollen has compared Godard to Ezra Pound and James Joyce, for whom "meaning can no longer be said to express the intention of the author or to be a representation of the world, but must like the discourse of the unconscious be understood by a different kind of decipherment" (*Paris* 87). The same could be said about Ray in this film.

Home uses traditional cinéma vérité shots, presumably improvised, of Ray teaching his students, granting the viewer a fly-on-the-wall perspective observing the director and his students at work. For example, we see Leslie, an aspiring dancer, leading an outdoor class session on performance exercises, while another student steadily films them stretching and moving their bodies (Ray participates right along with the group). In another scene, Ray hunches tiredly over his Steenbeck, looking at footage of political speeches by Jane Fonda and Tom Hayden, as Richie stands attentively behind him with a student cinematographer and sound recordist, Steve Maurer. Ray asks Steve for a cigarette and clumsily sticks it in his mouth end-first; Steve quickly extends his lighter to the right of Ray, while Tom hurries on Ray's left to reverse the dangling cigarette, both students eager to assist their somewhat befuddled mentor who has obviously won them over.

In other scenes, Ray calls attention to his authorial identity by playing the role of a father confessor and a catalyst in the drama of his students' lives. Leslie shares her devastating story about her attempt to prostitute herself to a capitalist "pig" in order to make money to help complete the film. "I really felt good you know," she tells a shocked Ray, "I really felt good. For the first time in my life I felt as though I had no problems, you know what I mean? I felt one, I felt at peace with who I was." During a break, Ray is approached by a shy student named David, who proudly tells him he lost eight pounds in less than three months at a Duke University camp, but admits that he still feels a paranoid need to guard and defend himself, often through humor, the way he did when he was overweight. Tom, the student with whom the film spends the most time, confides in Ray about his ambivalent relationship with his father. The son of a conservative Catholic police detective on the New York City homicide squad, Tom has become estranged from his father due to their political disagreements. He tells Ray that he contemplated joining the priesthood just to leave home or committing suicide with his father's gun.

As Tom and Ray walk on campus together, Tom wearing a long-sleeved red T-shirt and Ray dressed in a red sport coat reminiscent of Dean in *Rebel*, Ray opens up about his insecurities as a teacher by telling Tom the absurd fable of the wise man and the Sphinx:

> Once there was a wise man who traveled to every other wise man he knew throughout the world, who had a reputation for wisdom and sagacity, and he said, "Tell me something that you have learned that will help me pass on to other people something that will help them, guide them in their lives." And he left every single one of them satisfied. And he walked and walked and walked until he got to the Sphinx in Egypt, and said, "Hey Sphinx! Hey Sphinx," and the Sphinx hadn't talked for 4,000 years. "Hey Sphinx, would you open your mouth and tell me one single thing that I can tell man that will help him, guide him through his life?" For the first time in 5,000 years [*sic*], the Sphinx opened her mouth and said, "Don't expect too much. Don't expect too much from a teacher."

Tom throws fake punches to the right side of his teacher's face to see if Ray, who has temporarily discarded his eye patch, is actually blind in his right eye. A deep connection is established between the two men that transcends a traditional pedagogical relationship: Ray says he lost his eye at the Chicago Conspiracy Trial, and Tom says he has been blind in the same eye since an accident with a bow and arrow when he was thirteen.

In this nakedly honest scene, we realize that the aging Ray is as confused as his young students, lost in the generation gap, and that the making of *Home* is a painful quest for both teacher and student to find meaning in themselves and the seemingly meaningless world around them. At the risk of putting too fine a point on it, the production is as much a struggle to find a new mode of communication as it is to find a new mode of perception in order to face existential uncertainty.

❧

Ray's figure looms so large that he is sorely missed when he is not onscreen. Despite his compelling presence, however, his role has more to do with distanciation than identification. *Home* does not present a linear plot, but a series of vignettes, or, more accurately, digressions and interruptions reflected through a *mise-en-abyme* that come to dominate the film. Attempts to summarize the film in narrative terms seem inadequate, as its organization seems based on affective connections rather than traditional structures of cinematic rhetoric, and the film defies generic categorization of any recognizable kind. The brief script outline, which Ray drafted with Susan, focused on "the vulnerability of a new professor—an amateur in teaching, just as his students were amateurs in film" (Lederer 62). Perhaps a more precise way to describe *Home* is the "making of" this very film.

Densely self-reflexive and intertextual, *Home* constantly lays bare its own mode of production, destroying not only the rectangular frame through Ray's "mimage" process, but also destroying Hollywood's system of narrative transitivity (derived from continuity-based editing, cinematography, and mise-en-scène). The film violates the invisibility and transparency we would expect from a Hollywood production, built on the illusion of unity and seamlessness, and it deliberately confuses everyday life perceptions of space and time. Multiple images also create multiple diegetic spaces. The heterogeneity of *Home* enables a composite, contradictory system of signification, while foreclosing a coherent subject position for the spectator. If there is any goal-oriented action to speak of, it is the making of the film itself. Since the film was never technically completed, it remains profoundly open-ended, foregoing the harmonious closure of classical storytelling. The result achieves a sensation of both heightened reality and estrangement, challenging the spectator to think about, question, and possibly resist the film text. This provocation purges the aesthetics of commercial entertainment through a confrontational spectator address, while fully realizing the always modernist trajectory of Ray's cinema.

As the film's auteur, or structuring author, and, simultaneously, its anti-auteur or agent of deconstruction, Ray is responsible for many of these formal destabilizations. In his memoirs, he wrote, "The professor-director concentrated on de-imagizing himself as a Hollywood director successfully enough to gain the confidence of his students" (*Interrupted* 204). This production awakened the political consciousness of his students, who had "retired from the conflicts of the late '60s," Ray reflected, "and submerged themselves in what they thought was a sage and serene womb, where no outside voices could be heard, least of all that of a Hollywood director" (204).

Ray described the film not as a documentary, but as "a documentation," or, "a feature-length color film of the history of our youth during the past few years" (204). Moreover, the experience of the film unsettles the implied spectator out of his or her complicity with the conservative textual politics of the Classical Hollywood style in which he or she is sutured. For instance, Leslie's confession to Ray about her prostitution experience at first appears as though we are witnessing a behind-the-scenes interaction between director and actor, teacher and student, but the film disrupts the documentary realism of their private conversation as if to remind the spectator of the manipulative artifice of cinematic realities. Claims to "truth" and "reality" in cinema, the film wants to argue, are aesthetically constructed and ideologically determined.

When Leslie spies a man on the set she has not seen before, Ray tells her that he invited a journalist from *Harper's*, Bill Lederer, to help the crew with some of their work that night. Leslie introduces herself to Bill, who identifies himself as Joe, and whose voice has obviously been dubbed by Ray. The partial loss of the original sound motivated the decision to dub Ray's voice (Krohn, *We*), but the mismatching of voice and speaker gives an aural dimension to one of the film's central themes, that both reality and identity are deceptive and always in flux. Bill/Joe is working on a sound board and admits with embarrassment that he is a professional writer, not a professional sound man. "You were splendid in the last scene," he tells her, praising her "immediacy" and "spontaneity," but apologizing for not getting the microphone levels right. "There are no rehearsals here," she responds, "not in this film we're making. We don't work like that." Collapsing the boundaries between the film and the film-within-the-film, this scene puts Leslie's earlier exchange with Ray in the realm of fiction ("You were splendid in the last scene"), while her exchange with Bill/Joe is presented as reality, even though it is clearly falsified by Ray's dubbing.

After taking "bad speed" later in the film, Leslie tearfully relays to Ray how she asked a wanted drug dealer to give her syphilis. Feeling both guilty and humiliated, she realizes, "I'm always doing this to myself. Always!" Ray senses that she is desperately in search of an intimate connection, but crippled by issues of self-worth (when Leslie demands that Ray, as her teacher, figures out how to help her, he laments, "who can teach?"). In one of the most surprising moments in the film, he covers his good eye with a second eye patch and instructs two other students to pelt Leslie with juicy red tomatoes as she screams, "I'm always ugly! I can't help it!" and "You get outta here!" We hear a cacophony of electronic noises as flashes of *Guernica* appear alongside Leslie, intercut with shots of Ray making machine-gun gestures with his hands and his students performing a play in which they appear to be fired on at another moment in time. Additional images are shown during this bizarre montage, including Turkey (Ben Cooper) from *Johnny Guitar* (another one of Ray's innocent young casualties of modernity) and a student wearing a bandaged face mask, holding a baby doll up to the camera.

First the compassionate father and teacher eager to help Leslie, Ray then becomes the "betrayer," a personification of what his generation represents to him: judgmental and intolerant, blind to the problems of society, and uncaring toward the alienated youth looking to the adult world for answers. In another metafilmic twist, the sequence is revealed to be staged for the camera, foregrounding the mechanical apparatus of filmmaking. A student inarticulately justifies to the cast and crew what we have seen: "we gotta hit her with tomatoes to prove, you know, like the scene we're trying to make here." When a student asks Leslie whether what they just shot was "real," she wipes off tomato chunks and assures him, "Yeah, except for the tomatoes," further blurring the lines between fiction and "reality." Richie begins to shoot another take, and a second version of this scene unfolds.

One of the most difficult and heartbreaking scenes in the film occurs when Tom returns to Binghamton from his trips to the 1972 presidential conventions in Miami. Over shots of the Democratic National Convention in July, including appearances by Allen Ginsberg, Tom's commentary describes the hostile atmosphere to the viewer: "people walking around, yelling at each other, raising their voices—very few of them said 'hello' to me—with the slight hum of Allen Ginsberg once in a while. There were people representing every different kind of group, from the Jesus freaks to S.D.S. There were even evangelists on the campsite. Abbie Hoffman is right. Politics is leveled." Woody Guthrie's folk song, "Goin' Down the Road and Feeling Bad" plays on the soundtrack. Although it is not shown in the film, Tom was attacked by right-wing thugs en route to the Republican National Convention in August, his beard marking him as a "hippie" (Eisenschitz 438).

Demoralized by what he witnessed from both political parties and shaken from his assault, Tom proceeds to shave his beard in front of the mirror, a symbolic and ritualistic gesture of personal and political defeat through a physical transformation of his identity. Beside the close-up shot of Tom's face are slow-motion images of newspaper headlines ("Nixon Wins") and Richard Nixon celebrating his nomination. Tom pants and sobs uncontrollably, to the point of accidentally cutting his skin, frustrated by what he perceives as a futile effort on the part of the left to enact progressive social change. As he begins a monologue about his relationship with his father, we hear Ray off-screen feeding him lines. Suddenly, it becomes apparent that Ray is directing Tom, which not only records this momentous event in Tom's life on film, but allows Tom to reach a greater truth about himself through an act of performance. Ray encourages Tom to improvise and expose his emotions in their rawest state, pleading, "Just talk to me, Tom" and "Make me believe you." Both the film and film-within-a-film are paradoxically one and the same here, fusing personal and political crisis, the lives of Ray's students and the years following 1968 in America, as well as reality and cinematic fiction.

Tom is particularly proud of his father for talking people out of committing suicide (recall that Tom contemplated committing suicide with his father's gun), making Ray's fatal attempt to prevent Tom's suicide at the end of the film that much more poignant. Immediately following Tom's monologue in the mirror, Ray retreats to the barn behind his farmhouse, disillusioned, and ties a noose with which to hang himself, but does not go through with the suicide (leaving the noose behind him). This scene puts an earlier episode in the film into context, in which Ray is hit by a car and killed while hitchhiking at Christmastime, dressed as Santa Claus. Strips of celluloid fall to the ground along with pieces of his costume—a dark joke on Godard's quote, "the cinema is Nicholas Ray." Whether this uncanny anticipation of Ray's death is his premonition, one of his students' prophetic nightmares, or the film's own vision of its inevitable outcome remains ambiguous.

Toward the end of the film, Ray sees Tom heading for the barn and fears *he* will commit suicide, but when Ray climbs to the hayloft to retrieve the noose, he accidentally hangs himself with it. The American Gothic mise-en-scène calls to mind the wintry, Upstate New York setting of *On Dangerous Ground*, in which a young fugitive reveals his dark secret to an older police detective in a barn. Looking down at Richie and Leslie, who have just witnessed the sacrificial event, Ray utters the words, "I have been interrupted." For one of Ray's bitterest films, the ending offers an earnest appeal wrought with liberal idealism, hinting that the real rebellion is yet to come and requires mutual understanding and communication. As Tom sleeps in a corner of the barn, like Plato in the mansion at the end of *Rebel*, Ray instructs Richie and Leslie, "Let him sleep for a short time. Not too long a time, just long enough to get back his dream. The floodgates are opening. The water is rushing, like the people against the dams . . . and the goddamns. But waken him in time. Take care of each other; it is your only chance for survival. All else is vanity . . . and let the rest of us swing." Ray's postmortem speech is one of the many unrealities in *Home*, something only possible in the movies, and yet the film ironically refuses to acknowledge it as faked.

The soundtrack reprises "Bless the Family" and images from the outside world, including Nixon's inauguration, envelop Tom's childlike face in a social mosaic. This literalization of Barthes's metaphor—the death of the author—on the one hand relinquishes responsibility from the author to the reader as a producer of meaning (represented by Ray's students and their potential for change as artist-activists). On the other hand, the ending gives Ray a privileged position in the text: he is both the author who taught us how to read and a martyr for his cause.

After the 1973 Cannes premiere, *Home* was screened in other such hip venues as the Cinémathèque Française the same year and, in 1974, the Andy Warhol Factory and the First Avenue Screening Room in New York City. Ray also spoke at universities and archives hosting retrospectives of his films, including Berkeley's Pacific Film Archive in 1974. He continued to appear as an auteur-cum-pedagogue in various interviews. Joseph Lederer met Ray in Manhattan and drove him back to Binghamton for an *American Film* interview published in 1975.[23] At the time of the interview, he was looking for a backer to finance the completion of *Home*.[24] Also in search of a distributor, he screened a rough cut for David Picker, president of United Artists (Ray's friend Dore Schary, former studio chief at RKO and MGM, was in attendance, as well). Ray and his students had shot twenty-five hours of footage by this point.

From one of the highest paid directors in the world on *55 Days at Peking* to an unemployable relic of the Hollywood studio era, living in oblivion, he reinforced to Lederer the earlier image he had shown to Canby and Ebert. However, he also talked a great deal about the making of *Home*, proclaiming, "film can't be taught academically, it has to be an experience" (62). Lederer mentioned that on top of the film's $10,000 grant, Ray "has put at least eighty-five percent of his university salary into the film, along with everything he's been able to borrow and hustle" (64). The students, whose late hours five nights a week gave rise to their nickname "Creatures of the Night," also commented on Ray's unorthodox approach to teaching. "As a teaching method," one student maintained, "it's fantastic. It takes you out of the classroom, out of theories—actually takes you back to the Renaissance where apprentices, working with a master, learn by doing" (63). Another student was quoted a year into production saying, "To this day, we don't know how this picture is going to end—or begin!" (64).

In 1974, Michael Goodwin and Naomi Wise conducted a lengthy interview with Ray in New York City, while he was preparing *Home* for an investor's screening, building Ray's reputation with retroactive analyses of his films via the auteur himself. The interview was published in 1977 in the now defunct *Take One*, the first major Canadian film magazine, which was founded by graduates of the McGill University Film Society. Ray had just begun several new projects, although none would come to fruition. *City Blues* (aka, *Murphy*) was to be a pornographic courtroom drama starring Norman Mailer, Rip Torn, and porn actress Marilyn Chambers, who achieved considerable notoriety with her X-rated hit *Behind the Green Door* (1972). V. F. Perkins, Ray's biggest advocate from *Movie*, planned to cowrite a thriller with him called *The Truth*. The founder of Alcoholics Anonymous, William Griffith Wilson, was the subject of a prospective film that especially interested Ray, *The Story of Bill W.* Finally, Zoetrope Studios approached Ray to direct an adaptation of Edward J. Moore's two-character Off-Broadway play *The Sea Horse*.

Goodwin and Wise's interview was a full-blown celebration of Ray's modernism, wherein they placed him in the category of "Experimentalists," directors who broke new structural and ideological ground, pushing the boundaries of film art, as opposed to the "Classicists," in which they included John Ford, Howard Hawks, and Raoul Walsh. "Ray is a thoroughly modern filmmaker," they argued, "perhaps the greatest of the native American existentialists" (7). Championing his "courage to experiment" and his "willingness to risk failure" (7), Goodwin and Wise also commend his desire to reach a mass audience even at the vanguard of cinema, making him a model for innovators in media and the other arts (8).

One of the major claims in their interview was that "Nicholas Ray is even more interesting than his movies—but it is only through his movies that we can truly see him" (7). Ray went on to explain how in both *Home* and his Hollywood films he tried to deploy these "experimental" techniques. In *Johnny Guitar*, for example, he said he "set out to break every goddamn rule there was to break in a western" (11), and in *The True Story of Jesse James*, he wanted the film to be a staged ballad about the displacement of postwar youth, shot in areas of light with no exteriors (14). *Party Girl* was an opportunity for what he described as "experimenting with color" (18). He referred to the lack of plot in *Rebel* (20) and the "avant-garde" ending of *Knock on Any Door* (10), in which his juvenile delinquent antihero is executed despite the efforts of his attorney. This ending, he boasted, "wasn't the kind of ending that ties up a movie in a nice pink ribbon" (10). Ray's Hollywood films were all over a decade old by the mid-1970s, but they were never fully appreciated in America until after he left the industry. Here was his opportunity to model for his audiences (much like he did for his students) the way to approach and understand his body of work, as prescient films that paved the way for his contemporary independent endeavors. "I never think of a film as doing anything except providing a heightened sense of being," he told Goodwin and Wise (10).

Having moved back to New York City in 1974 and joined Alcoholics Anonymous in 1976, he accepted teaching positions at the Lee Strasberg

Institute and the New York University Tisch School of the Arts in 1977. When Cliff Jahr interviewed Ray for *Camera Three* on CBS the same year, he went as far as to act out the improvised scene in *Rebel* that takes place in the Starks's living room after the "chickie run." "I really think directors who have not had the experience with acting are crippled to a degree," he declared on the episode, discussing his father-son relationship with Dean and the value of improvisation for him as a director. Ray added, "The director has to help an actor contribute, you know? That's one of his functions." Commenting on his use of the camera, he explained how he places it in the position of an actor to anchor a character's point of view, intensifying conflict and allowing the camera itself to "act." On the subject of his methodologies, he described his extensive research for his films, such as his contact with the Hollywood High Gang while making *Rebel* (Hollywood High's Frank Mazzola acted as his liaison and also played a member of Buzz's gang in the film).[25] Ray also spoke to his major themes, emphasizing his sympathies for outcasts.

Over the course of these interviews and public appearances, Ray essentially picked up where *Cahiers du cinéma* left off in the beginning of the 1960s, showing American audiences what they may have missed or perhaps not entirely comprehend, but also providing them with the tools for analysis. Framed by *Home*, his auteurism was also mapped onto a different political project (and a different modernist discourse) associated with post-1968 ideological and theoretical concerns. Ray could be both a singular rebel artist *and* a member of American counterculture working to liberate art from classical conceptions of autonomous authorship and formal construction. The next feature-length film he undertook was more aesthetically accessible than *Home*, and did not tackle the same sort of incendiary political content. As another modernist self-portrait, however, it makes "the death of the author" its principle subject, advancing further into the ambiguous territory between fiction and reality. Ray became the author of his own death, and by allowing him to live through his art, cinema became the only medium for him capable of transcending death. A new teacher-student collaboration was born, only this time it was with another well-known director of the 1970s: Wim Wenders.

Last Rites

In 1977, Ray was diagnosed with lung cancer, which eventually metastasized to his brain and caused his death, even after three operations. Preoccupied either with his own mortality or the ontology of the director (or both), Ray returned to "the death of the author" in literal and figurative terms twice more after *Home*. "I love living dearly, but I'm involved in dying," he cried during a low point prior to its premiere at Cannes (qtd. in Farrell, "*We*" 93). After the premiere, Henri Langlois put him in touch with Dutch painter Max Fischer, who was making an anthology film titled *Wet Dreams*, comprised of erotic fantasies contributed by artists, writers, and filmmakers (including Dusan Makavejev, credited as Sam Rotterdam). *Wet Dreams* was released in 1974, and the segment Ray directed, "The Janitor" (Dream 12), ran the longest, at thirteen minutes.

Starring as an eccentric janitor, who sweeps up the floor of a film set, and as the janitor's double, a hypocritical preacher in a film projecting on a screen above him, Ray appears in both roles with his trademark eye patch and missing tooth. In a perverse parody of Ray's teaching persona, the preacher instigates an orgy with his fire-and-brimstone sermon and allows three female parishioners—including his young daughter—to fellate him. The janitor shoots his own image with a shotgun, sickened by what he sees, killing his dark Other reflected by (or displaced onto) the film as he watches the screen burn in flames. Impressed by Ray's virile performance in the oral sex sequence, Fischer alleged, "He had an erection the whole time!" (qtd. in Eisenschitz 452).

While Ray taught at the Lee Strasberg Institute he directed a second short, which brought him back to collaborating with his students. The improvised, 16 mm film was called *Marco*, adapted from the first three pages of Curtis Bill Pepper's 1977 novel of the same name.[26] It consists of only two sequences. A group of criminals (played by Ray's students) file into a police station, and two detectives interrogate the last person to arrive, a distraught man named Marco (Claudio Mazzatenta). Jim's emotional breakdown at the police station in *Rebel* comes to mind as a precedent for the film, as Marco confesses to the murder of his son. The experiment was partly an extension of an unfinished film project Ray began with three of his acting students called *Macho Gaspacho*, which was to be a collection of a dozen scenes that encapsulated an Institute workshop for actors and directors. Both "The Janitor" and *Marco* remain curious oddities, but it was Ray's final film, *Lightning over Water*, that allowed him to build more elaborately on some of the complex ideas he introduced in *Home*.

The worst thing that ever happened to Ray, wrote Canby in his *New York Times* review of the film, "was when in the late 1950s, he began to hear himself acclaimed as 'an artist,' and attempted to live up to the reputation that had been imposed on him, initially by European critics and filmmakers" (13). As Ray continued editing *Home* toward the end of the 1970s, his legacy was supported by fans, students, critical devotees, and filmmakers he influenced, the closest of whom was his friend Wim Wenders, the German New Wave auteur who directed Ray as an art forger in his 1977 thriller *The American Friend*. "The more [Ray] talked about his 'art,' the less sense he made of it, as well as of his own life," added Canby, "and the more he depended on groups of always ready, solemnly respectful admirers." Canby explained that Ray's public character at this time, "the artist who was too big and bold to be confined within the Hollywood system," was actually enabled by the Hollywood system from which Ray claimed to rebel. Contrary to the standard auteurist account, Canby insisted that Ray's films were not simply infused with his singular creative genius, but that "the very distinctive personal qualities that Ray exhibited in his films were as much a result of the restrictions imposed in him as of his own distinctive art" (13).

The project behind *Lightning* seems to be Ray's attempt to come to terms with his reputation before he dies, interrogating what it means to be "an artist," while at the same time participating in his own artistic memorialization. Ray called *Lightning* a film "about a man who wants to bring himself all together before he dies . . . a regaining of self-esteem [for] a once highly successful man." This elliptical description occurs in the film itself, one of the many ways in which Ray comments on his own authorship and performance, and also one of the many ways in which the film comments on its own making. Of course, its problems of authorship are difficult since both Ray and Wenders are credited as writers and directors, and they are both the stars of the film. It would be fair to say that although the original idea belonged to Ray, he and Wenders developed the project together, and since Ray was too ill to direct, *Lightning* is ultimately Wenders's film (Andrew 158). Ray died before the editing could be completed. Hence, more than most films, it is one that was created in the editing room (Geist, "*Lightning*" 48). *Lightning* was presented as "Nick's Film," which was in fact the subtitle of the version that premiered at Cannes in 1980.

The version screened at Cannes and the version subsequently released in theaters that year were considerably different.[27] Edited by Peter Przygodda, who edited all of Wenders's previous films, the first version contained lengthier speeches and a formal style more inclined toward extreme discontinuity. Wenders recut the film with Chris Sievernich, one of the film's producers, following Przygodda's chronology and image selection. In addition to trimming the running time from 116 to 91 minutes, Wenders added his voice-over narration and excerpts from Ray's diary to explain the action, while streamlining and clarifying the narrative for a more generally comprehensible film (Geist, "*Lightning*" 48). "We constantly made the effort to make it a fiction film, or at least make it believable as fiction," Wenders said, maintaining that his and Ray's visions were lost in the confusing first cut (qtd. in Farrell, "Nick" 67).

When Wenders completed the second cut, he felt he had a new film altogether. He concluded, "What I found was the closest thing to the reality that had taken us forward, that had liberated us, and at the same time had limited us so ruthlessly" (qtd. in Farrell, "Nick" 67). *Lightning* attracted attention from high places, including the Bundes National Film Award in West Germany and a large book of color illustrations from Blue Angel Press (with an introduction by Bernardo Bertolucci and a German-English biography of Ray). However, it also generated controversy over what was sometimes perceived as Wenders's morbidly voyeuristic and morally irresponsible depiction of Ray's death.

On a two-week leave from the preproduction work for his first American film, *Hammett* (1982), a fictionalized film about Dashiell Hammett, produced by Francis Ford Coppola, Wenders visited Ray in his SoHo loft on Spring Street, where he and Susan had been living since 1974. *Lightning* chronicles Ray and Wenders's attempt to make a film together, which at first sounds like it will reimagine Ray's character from *The American Friend*. In their story, a sixty-year-old artist named Nick, whose career has faded after early success, learns he is dying of cancer and decides to steal his own paintings from museums, replacing them with forgeries in an attempt to "regain his own identity as fully as he can before he dies."[28]

This artist is obviously a thinly disguised Nicholas Ray, even down to his loft in New York City, where the character has been living with his lover for five years ("he is forty years her senior"). Ray and Wenders quickly give up this idea—the roman à clef is so transparent, after all—and instead make *Lightning* a recursive documentary on the very film we are watching (part cinéma vérité, part essay film, part home movie, part surrealist exercise in automatic writing). "Well, I have one action, which is to regain my self-image and my image in the rest of the world," Ray tells Wenders, referring to himself now as an actor, not only a character.

Alternating between 35 mm footage shot by Wenders's crew and Betacam video shot by Ray's former student Tom Farrell, *Lightning* purports to contrast its staged, fictionalized material (a first level of reality recorded on film) with rough "outtake" footage of the technicians at work, the production equipment, and Wenders directing (a second level of reality captured on video). Almost as soon as *Lightning* establishes this relationship, it collapses the borders between fictional and nonfictional representation, and the viewer is left wondering to what degree anything on the screen is real and true. In *The Films of Nicholas Ray*, Geoff Andrew rightly argues that *Lightning* is about "the problem of representation through cinema" (160), but it is also about the urgency of filmmaking and the mediated experience of cinema. "The making of the movie was more important than the outcome," Wenders has said (qtd. in Farrell, "Nick" 67). For example, in a scene shot in 35 mm, Ray asks Wenders to repeat one of his lines, and in another 35 mm scene, Wenders returns to the loft to find his crew setting up to film Ray, who has disappeared. The best laid plans of writing scripts and scheduling shoots, the directors seem to argue, are destined to go awry when the drama of real life intervenes to play a role in the film.

Lightning also runs the gamut of self-reflexive techniques: Wenders's then wife Ronee Blakley sings the title song in an extra-diegetic musical performance; images of Ray are superimposed over a camera "shooting" the viewer, and therefore facing Wenders's camera; handwritten text from Ray's diary is laid over a shot of Wenders reading the diary ("To experience death without dying seemed like a natural goal for me") and again over an aerial shot of New York City; Ray directly addresses the viewer and demands that the camera operator "cut" just before he dies. The last shot, taken from a helicopter that reminds the viewer of Ray's opening credits shot in *They Live by Night*, shows Chinese junk (or sailing ship) on the East River carrying an urn of Ray's ashes. After a freeze frame and a fade to black-and-white, more text from Ray's diary appears onscreen.

References to Ray's directorial past appear throughout *Lightning*: Ray's red nightshirt links him to Dean in *Rebel*; a *Party Girl* poster adorns his apartment; *The Lusty Men* screens at Vassar College; and Ray holds a private screening of *Home* with Wenders, Susan, and Tom. *Lightning* also cleverly cites *The American Friend*. The piercing chords on the soundtrack are borrowed from this earlier film, as is the first shot of a stranger from Germany exiting a taxi and paying a visit to Ray in his Lower Manhattan loft. This time, the stranger is not Tom Ripley (Dennis Hopper), but Wenders himself, and his voice-over narration suggests that what we are about to see is indeed real (beginning on April 7, 1979, to be exact). Wenders ascends the staircase and introduces *his* American friend to the viewer:

> Nicholas Ray, director of *Rebel without a Cause*, *Johnny Guitar*, and a few other movies that have their solid place in the history of cinema. I had climbed up these stairs for the first time about two years ago when Nick had agreed to play a

> part in a film of mine, *The American Friend.* The part hadn't been in the script, so we wrote it together, played a lot of backgammon, and became good friends.

Ray, however, has deteriorated since we last saw him—frail, cachectic, and balding—coughing up phlegm and howling in pain as he awakens in bed.

By mirroring the opening scenes of *Lightning* and *The American Friend*, Wenders rewrites himself into his own fiction and at the same time extracts Ray from it into the intransigent reality of imminent death. Even as Wenders grows concerned that he is taking advantage of Ray's illness and suffering, he clearly looks up to his older friend as an artistic model. Tom follows Ray around with a Sony Betamax loaned from Coppola's Zoetrope Studios and still views him as very much a paternal figure. At one point, Tom and Wenders argue over whether Ray is a surrogate father to them, a sentiment with which Wenders does not agree. Whatever Wenders's feelings on the matter, his relationship with Ray on-screen reads according to a father-son dynamic (Tom stands-in as Wenders's brother and competitor for Ray's affections).[29]

In other ways, Ray reprises his role as a teacher in *Home* for his role in *Lightning*. When Vassar College invites him to give a lecture after a screening of *The Lusty Men*, he explicitly returns to this pedagogical mode. Wenders and Tom join Susan to accompany him in order to record the event. The audience watches the beginning of Ray's 1952 classic and, as film plays on the diegetic theater screen, *The Lusty Men* fills the frame of *Lightning*. We see Jeff McCloud (Robert Mitchum) limping across the deserted rodeo arena and visiting his childhood home to find tokens of his youth hidden under the house. "It's more about coming home than anything I've ever seen," Wenders tells Ray admiringly.

Ray uses his lecture to foreground the continuities between his 1970s career in experimental filmmaking and his 1950s career in Hollywood. Comparing *The Lusty Men* to *Lightning*, he discusses the ongoing role of improvisation in his directing of actors. A member of the audience asks for Ray's opinion about working with representations of reality, and Ray responds by stressing the fine line between reality and fantasy, which are both socially constructed. Wenders and Tom record the lecture and watch it again on video later that evening, somewhat bewildered by the film they are in the process of making—and the film in which they have found themselves—but nonetheless fascinated by its subject. The implications of Ray's thesis unfold as *Lightning* increasingly loses its footing in documentary realism the closer we come to Ray's death.

Visions of the Chinese junk interrupt the film's story in the present tense, similar to the way in which *Home* prefigures Ray's death in the fantasy Christmas sequence. The first time we see the ship is during and immediately after the opening credits. On the deck of the ship sits the urn of Ray's ashes, as well as a Mitchell camera slowly rotating to point at the viewer, both as a gesture of confrontation and an invitation to participate in the fiction. The second interruption is more obtrusive and occurs later in the film. Ray rehearses actor Gerry Bamman at the Lee Strasberg Institute for a stage adaptation of Franz Kafka's "A Report to an Academy" (1917), and as Gerry's monologue escalates dramatically, an abrupt cutaway takes us to the East River, where a helicopter shot gradually moves toward the ship.

From the deck, we then see the helicopter that enabled the previous shot. A Moviola is suddenly revealed with celluloid strips blowing in the wind, symbolizing Ray's life in cinema, and once again Wenders's camera focuses on the Mitchell, this time shooting through its viewfinder to make visible the film's multiple levels of mediation. When the film cuts back to the rehearsal, Wenders's camera situates the viewer in Bamman's point-of-view as the performer, watching Ray and the audience applaud wildly (Tom and crewmembers are seen recording). The sequence ends from the audience's point-of-view with a shot of Bamman and the onstage camera returning the gaze.

More stylized sequences draw from the artifice of staged fiction to complicate the ostensible documentary realism. Wrestling with his obligations to the film as an artist, and to Ray as a friend, Wenders dreams that he is sitting up in a hospital bed to find Tom creepily videotaping him (a manifestation of Wenders's guilt over his questionable ethics and his anxiety over what lies ahead). Tom then proceeds to strangle Wenders, and before he awakens in his "real" bed, he imagines his crew on video, "always watching, silently, each one with his or her own thoughts or fears about what we were doing and where we were going." Wenders's nightmare also foreshadows Ray's real-life hospitalization, which Tom captures with the Betamax in one of the most uncomfortable sequences in the film (Ray hears on the news that John Wayne, whom he directed in *Flying Leathernecks*, was coincidentally in the hospital at the same time).

Just as the modernist aesthetics of *Home* can be traced to abstract painting, the liveness and immediacy of the performances in *Lightning* have origins in modernist performance art and happenings. Ivone Margulies analyzes the film's "authenticating effects of real time representation" and "the fluctuation between realism and actuality" in relation to the experimentations of body and performance art in the 1960s and 1970s (Fluxus

Group, John Cage, Allen Kaprow, Chris Burden, Vito Acconci, etc.). The long takes of Ray's near-death performance in *Lightning* are uncomfortable in large part because, as Margulies discusses, "the literal actual event is presented as indistinguishable from representation" (56). In contrast to the experimental video art of the 1970s, in which video technology provided a screened or mediated presence that was therefore temporally displaced, *Lightning* presumes to work in "*real time representation*" (56). Margulies explains, "Extended duration tests the limits of the bodies of performer and spectator. Their endurance serves as proof of the actuality of their mutual presence" (56). Following her argument, the cinematic father of *Lightning* may be Andy Warhol rather than Nicholas Ray.

Nowhere is this aesthetic more apparent than in the penultimate sequence in the film. Recalling Wenders's staged nightmare and Ray's real hospitalization, this sequence conflates those two episodes in an indeterminate narrative space between fiction and reality. Ronee Blakley rehearses a weird scene with Ray from a modern day version of *King Lear*, Ray playing a bedridden Lear and Ronee in the role of Cordelia, which Wenders and his crew shoot on the set of an all-white hospital suite (see fig. 3.3). "But once more," Wenders says in voice-over, "our

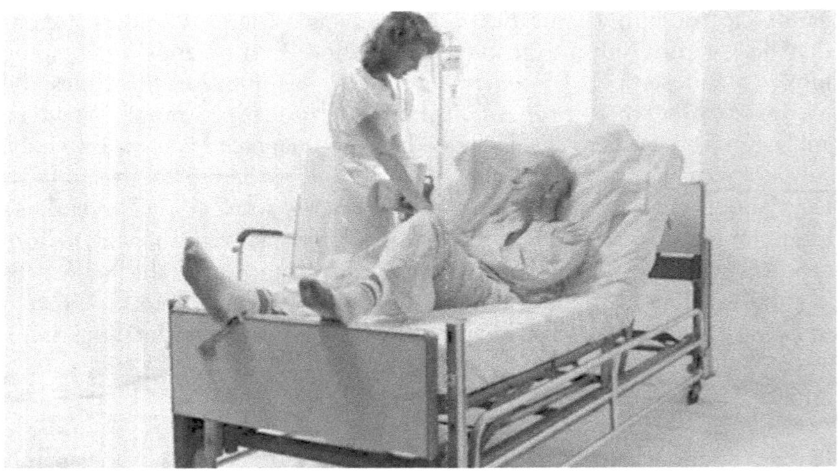

Figure 3.3. *Lightning over Water* (1980): Ronee Blakley rehearses a weird scene with Ray from a modern-day version of *King Lear*, Ray playing a bedridden Lear and Blakley in the role of Cordelia, which Wim Wenders and his crew shoot on the set of an all-white hospital suite. (Anchor Bay Entertainment, 2003; digital frame enlargement)

reality was stronger than the fiction we wanted to turn it into. It was going to be the last time." Wenders watches the rehearsal progress and falls asleep just as Ray/Lear explains to Ronee/Cordelia that "telling the truth becomes very dull, except sometimes not. Sometimes telling the truth becomes very exciting because you never expect to tell it." Waking from the dream, Wenders now finds himself in the hospital bed—an unexpected, heightened reality achieved through fiction—and Ray sits next to him wearing his eye patch.

Shot in a straight-on medium close-up, Ray addresses both Wenders and, apparently, the audience. Ray is utterly nonsensical, humming, coughing, and drooling. He pinches Wenders, spits, pretends to vomit, sings to himself off-key, curses, and finally tells him, "You're making me sick to my stomach, you realize that? You are. I don't know why." This abject performance of death is a complete breakdown in codes of realist film acting and coherency of character, and through aesthetics of shock and disgust, it also destroys the image of glamour, desire, and pleasure associated with Hollywood film stardom and entertainment. We want to look away, but the camera lingers on Ray's withered face, "delaying the cut," to use Margulies's language of performance space. "I have to go now," Ray says, adding, "okay, okay, I'm finished." Directing him off camera, Wenders asks Ray to "say cut," and Ray looks into the camera and goads the operator (Edward Lachman) to cut. When Wenders interjects with "don't cut," Ray confidently reclaims his role as director one final time, to direct his own death, and yells in defiance, "Cut!"

Readers of *I Was Interrupted* will recall that "action" was always paramount in Ray's direction of actors, and this idea only gained importance for Ray after directing himself in this film. Ray wrote, "action is the most helpful, most meaningful tool I can find in the vocabulary of this profession" (209).[30] The *Cahiers du cinéma* critics understood Ray's authorship through its physicality, an immediate and heedless action aesthetic within his mise-en-scène that included gestures of performance, accidents or mistakes in staging or editing, dynamism of camera movement, and excesses of color and décor, as well as the panoramic view of violent spaces that CinemaScope facilitated.

For Ray, action had more to do with the unspoken psychology of actor and character that motivated the drama of a particular scene. The rhetorical questions that he and his actors tried to answer were: "What is the scene about? [. . .] What is the character about? What does the character want?" (210). Although Ray's goal is ambiguous to be sure—"to regain his own identity as fully as he can before he dies"—this line of action is one more way in which he establishes continuity rather than a disconnection between his work on *Lightning* and his work in Hollywood.

A few days after shooting wrapped on *Lightning* in May, Ray appeared at the Museum of Modern Art's exhibition of *They Live by Night* and *On Dangerous Ground*, a celebration of his career that also prematurely commemorated his life. Ray died on Father's Day, June 16, 1979, five days after the death of another cinematic father figure, John Wayne.

Following the negative press the film received at Cannes, reviews of the recut *Lightning* were mixed. Canby dismissed it in the *New York Times* as "wretched and empty," an "almost unwatchable film" that turns "a real death into a ceremony that honors nothing except, possibly, the mistaken notion that the camera ennobles everything it records" ("Last" 13). In her review for *Film Quarterly*, Kathy Geist took an oppositional interpretation by reading the film as a personal statement on Ray's "quest for self-realization" of a piece within his and Wenders's respective oeuvres.[31] According to Geist, "The search for home for these two is connected to the search for identity which underlies all of Wenders's feature films and dominated Ray's life" ("*Lightning*" 50). Ray's real death was important for Geist thematically because, as she submitted, death is "objectively the most intransigent reality" and is "subjectively unreal because totally unknown" ("*Lightning*" 48). Despite the shifts in "objective" and "subjective" realities, it is Ray's death that in the end determined the film.

On the fence of the critical debate, Richard Combs in *Sight & Sound* referred to Ray and Wenders's objectives with the film as "disturbing" and "distasteful" (96). Combs felt that the film sought to excuse Wenders's determined exploitation the terminally ill Ray by fulfilling Ray's equally determined wish to put himself on the screen before he expired. As he proposed, "Wenders, in search of direction, wants Ray to lead him, to take over the film; he casts himself, in effect, as the bewildered young protagonist of a Ray movie who despairs of parental understanding and guidance" (97). For all of his reservations, though, Combs also saw Wenders as an unlikely hero. "Admitting his own uncertainty about how to make a film with the dying Ray," he meditated, "Wenders seems almost to want to bequeath the film to him, to have it become his last work, an encapsulation perhaps of the unwieldy *We Can't Go Home Again*" (97).

Members of the production were outspoken about their experiences of making the film. Independent filmmaker Jon Jost, who stayed with Ray in SoHo and was recruited to help raise funds during preproduction, wrote in *Sight & Sound* that he was asked to leave when Susan accused him of "being disruptive" and "spreading 'negative vibrations.'" "My feeling was that the surge of film people, with their own energies and interests, was taking over," he asserted, "and that unless extreme care was taken to see Nick for what he was, a terribly sick and desperate man, it would only come to tragedy" (95). Writing for the now defunct cinema studies journal *Wide Angle*, Tom Farrell published an alternative take, which preserved Ray's auteurist heritage and appeals to his reputation as an actor's director, defending Ray as a self-conscious artist rather than the victim of a grotesque practice in cinephilia. Farrell wrote, "Nick Ray demonstrated acting as a psychoanalytical adventure to superimpose himself on a character. By exhibiting his proximity to death, Nick's acting was organic; it was genuine behavior" ("Nick Ray's" 67).

Lightning finally resolves its ambivalence about itself in the last sequence, Ray's wake, which attempts to justify Wenders's motivations. More than validating Ray's cooperation with the project, it gives him the final authorial attribution. The film is no longer Wenders's homage to Ray, but Ray's epilogue to his legendary career that he accomplished by dying. We return to the Chinese junk on the East River, not unlike the one on which Ray supposedly lived while filming *55 Days at Peking*. Now, as Ray "takes the slow boat to China," the ship is filled with crew members reminiscing about Ray with Wenders and Tom, and trying to make sense of the film we have just watched. "He would have died sooner if it wasn't for this film," Tom insists, as if the film kept Ray alive and he, in turn, kept the film alive. One of the crew members remarks that "dying was his last directorial assertion."

Lines from Ray's diary (spoken by Wenders in voice-over) appear over a frozen helicopter shot of the junk fading to black-and-white: "I looked into my face and what did I see? No granite rock of identity. Faded blue, drawn skin, and wrinkled lips. And sadness. And the wildest urge to recognize and accept the face of my mother." This poetic, bittersweet epitaph suggests that the film was a mirror by which Ray successfully regained a metaphysical sense of himself as a human being, seeing through the European critical acclaim in the 1950s and 1960s, the American cult following in the 1970s, and the biographical legends that formed an impossible self-image of a rebel artist. "I know myself, but that is all," one imagines Ray crying at the end of his life, invoking Fitzgerald's immortal words at the end of *This Side of Paradise* (1920).

Conversely, for the viewer, *Lightning* leaves one with little sense of who Ray actually was since the film is still very much part of the myth-making process. For as much as the cinema community knew about Ray in 1979, the film must have raised more questions than it provided answers about Ray, the man. How did the director of *Rebel without a Cause*, one of Hollywood's most successful films of the 1950s, lose nearly everything he had, falling from a Chateau Marmont bungalow with studio resources at his fingertips to a SoHo loft with barely enough funds to complete his last film? How did this once great auteur end up in films that few critics knew how to decode?

Jonathan Rosenbaum, one of the first American critics to discover Ray, set out to shed light on the life of the recently deceased filmmaker in a 1981 story for *American Film*, appropriately titled "Looking for Nicholas Ray." "For better or worse," he opened, "the life of Nicholas Ray has become the stuff of legends. Ray has been sentimentalized, analyzed, worshipped, dismissed, and debated for what he was and did to such a degree that it has been difficult to hold him in focus" (55). In addition to reflecting on his own meetings with Ray, first in Paris in 1973 and again in 1977 at the Spring Street Bar, a block away from his SoHo loft, Rosenbaum interviewed the various people who knew Ray at the end of his life.

Tom Luddy of the Pacific Film Archive described how Ray stayed in Berkeley well after his retrospective, apparently with nowhere else to go, and used Coppola's San Francisco editing rooms for *The Conversation* (1974) to continue cutting *Home* (sleeping in the Zoetrope screening rooms during the day, editing from midnight to eight in the morning). After accumulating expenses from setting off burglar alarms, making long-distance phone calls, and finally breaking the editing machine, Ray had to leave Zoetrope and temporarily moved into the San Francisco–based film collective Cine Manifest (thanks to Luddy's connections), and then to a Sausalito clothing factory. Around the same time Wenders was editing *The American Friend*, he told Rosenbaum that he was revolted both by the "amateurish aspect" and "sense of destruction" in *Home*. However, he confessed that after seeing the film six or seven times (and eventually on a new print), he came to appreciate it, calling it "brilliant" and "mind-blowing" (56, 72).

Others saw Ray as self-protective, noncommittal, and generally difficult during this last stage of his career. Tom Farrell spoke to Rosenbaum and credited Wenders for *Lightning*, without whom Ray would never have allowed it to be seen. According to Farrell, Ray "was deathly afraid of exposing himself," as much as he believed it was the artist's duty to expose himself, and he would create excuses or withdraw to avoid finishing work (73). Chris Sievernich concluded that Ray's difficulties in the United States stemmed from his "endless, riotous discussions" with his producers. "I think, in Europe," he speculated, "there's somehow more generosity towards the freaky artist, the drunken artist, the crazy artist. In America there's a tendency for a person to be clean and straight and have a straight sense of business" (73). Although Ray "lived on his projects" and had the ability to develop and expand creative ideas, Sievernich went on to admit, he lacked "the follow-through energy" to see them to completion. "I think he enjoyed tremendously being the rebel," he added (75). The chair of the NYU Tisch School of the Arts graduate program, László Benedek, Ray's old friend who directed *The Wild One* (1953), referred to Ray simply as "difficult," a reputation that was no different in the late 1970s than it was in late 1940s. Benedek explained that Ray "didn't take orders willingly from the production department. But as long as these people made money, one could get away with that" (73).

While Rosenbaum's article remains one of the most illuminating pieces of journalism ever written on Ray, it does not provide answers to the questions raised in the wake of *Home* and *Lightning* (Rosenbaum seems more interested in what a thoughtful evocation of the auteur might reveal than a comprehensive investigation). In death, Ray was even more revered, more well-known, and, above all, a subject of intrigue now permanently out of reach. "A hero to some, a pariah to others," to quote Rosenbaum's pithiest and most salient passage, "Ray sought and relished the role of outlaw, of maverick. He created an outsize portrait of himself during his final years that perhaps no film of his, finished or otherwise, could have expressed or contained" (55). From a contemporary perspective on Ray's reputation, Rosenbaum's article is therefore is rich historical evidence of the ways in which Ray, the man, became indistinguishable from Ray, the myth.

Those who knew Ray offered opinions about his intentions and methods, accounting for the unpredictable ebbs and flows of his career. Those who admired him espoused interpretations of his body of work that his public image corroborated. In addition, Ray's self-proclaimed status as a rebellious experimenter gave his Hollywood films a belated appreciation among American cinephile cults and bridged his employment in the classical studio system with his late career independent ventures.

Ray worked to efface his authorship in the 1970s through collaborations, through dramatizations of his own death, and through an avant-garde mode that worked to undo classical structures of cinematic rhetoric and the institutionalization of the director as the locus of cinematic meaning. However, as we have seen, Ray's self-promotion and public discourse of pedagogy gave him more visibility as a director in the United States than he ever had as a director in Hollywood, remythologizing his role as a rebel auteur. Rather than bearing witness to the death of directorial authority in this radical period of cinema studies,

Ray's critics, students, and colleagues helped in that process, ironically made possible by the anti-auteurist aesthetics and discourses of political modernism. The next chapter looks at how Ray's legacy was sustained from the 1960s to the 1980s by other rebel auteurs. A new generation of directors influenced by Ray filtered practices of modernist art cinema through their nostalgia for Classical Hollywood auteurism, wherein Ray functioned as a common point of reference as an author of coolness.

4

Generations of Rebels

Influence, Legacy, and Modernist Art Cinemas

The closer I get to my ending, the closer I get to re-writing my beginning.

—Nicholas Ray, *Lightning over Water*

The Birth of the Cool and the Journey to Hip

THIS FINAL CHAPTER IS NOT ABOUT Nicholas Ray, but about three contemporary auteurs he influenced: Jean-Luc Godard, Wim Wenders, and Jim Jarmusch. Robert Kapsis demonstrates through his study of Alfred Hitchcock that the reputations of film directors as great artists are established by sponsors (i.e., critics and scholars), publicity, and self-promotion, which we have seen place Ray within different contexts of modernism. Yet, Kapsis adds that these reputations are also maintained over time by the legacies of film directors in their afterlives, as well as their impact on contemporary developments and trends in film. By way of art historian George Kubler, he insists that an individual artist's lifework is conceptualized and judged within historical traditions (e.g., the thriller and Alfred Hitchcock) that link their primary works in a succession of replications (e.g., the thriller, Hitchcock, and later Brian De Palma) (188–190). With this time-of-entry perspective on a film director's reputation, understanding Ray's place in the histories of modernism benefits from a look ahead of Ray at more recent filmmakers—all of whom are still working—that have been interpreted and evaluated under standards for modernist aesthetics.

Comprising a heterogeneous mix of what is broadly called international modernist art cinema, Godard, Wenders, and Jarmusch were members of the French New Wave in the 1960s, New German Cinema in the 1970s, and (with roots in the New York Underground) American Independent Cinema in the 1980s, respectively. As three of Ray's most outspoken admirers, these iconoclastic filmmakers have all alluded to his inspiration on their early careers, setting off comparisons to Ray in their critical receptions.[1] The Introduction to this book refers to some of the major elements of modernist film style in postwar art cinema.[2] However, the analysis that follows is not based on material evidence that demonstrates a continuity of historical poetics beginning with Ray, but a broad constellation of intertextual citations across films directed by Godard, Wenders, and Jarmusch.[3]

We can see Ray's legacy as a Hollywood rebel by looking at the ways in which he serves as a model for these three figures, who themselves sought to challenge the formal conventions and industrial practices of classical cinema as rebel auteurs and earned cultural capital as modernists. Ray's direct(or) influence remains part of a storehouse of references for a generation of art filmmakers, who fashioned authorial images through vanguard movements in cinema culture and a retro cool factor. The modernisms of Godard, Wenders, and Jarmusch overlap, but are also distinct. Each filmmaker touches on a different "aesthetic of cool" associated with Ray that is refracted by their individual contexts of modernism. Collectively, they exhibit nostalgia for the kind of American auteurism Ray epitomizes among cinephiles through these culturally agreed on codes of coolness.

Whether explicitly (as in the case of Godard and Wenders) or more obliquely (as in the case of Jarmusch), Ray's films authenticate a privileged cinematic knowledge, a hip awareness of film history—and one's place within it—that pays homage to the role of the artist as the cine-historical world-maker. Following this particular understanding, the role of the artist is not only indebted to modernist notions of autonomy, medium-specificity, and rebellion from artistic tradition, but to the masculine conception of rebel-as-hipster.

In this way, Ray personifies the cool ethos of American enlightenment and individualism that remains symptomatic of the modern era and developed through different cultural formations: an emotional style or personal attitude of cynical, bohemian removal as the U.S. became a world power; a racialized liminality of identity after World War II; and Southern California's innovations in art and media at midcentury. Reputedly the quintessential outsider director in Hollywood who challenged the studio system, and whose films concerned outsiders resisting the norms of American society, Ray both resonated with these discourses and gave them a certain international visibility. By citing Ray, or, more accurately, the discourses of a modern American cool that his films promoted, subsequent auteurs trading on hip affects created a palimpsest of rebellious film authorship.

Despite the varied definitions and manifestations of "cool" throughout history, in his book *American Cool* Peter N. Stearns arrives at one of the most far-reaching sociological accounts of what the term implies and encompasses. Deployed as a colloquialism for "an air of disengagement, of nonchalance," the term connotes a positive, even admired aura of restraint, composure, and self-control. "Cool has become an emotional mantle," Stearns explains, "sheltering the whole personality from embarrassing excess" (1). A twentieth-century phenomenon, "cool" more specifically refers to an emotional change signaled by new social needs during the transition from the Victorian to the modern period. Whereas passion and sentimentality—deep feelings of jealousy, love, grief, anger, and guilt—characterized the intense emotional culture of the late nineteenth-century, by the 1920s the U.S. white middle-class had curbed those feelings and shifted toward a more low-key, informal expression of emotion. This "cooler" performance of self brought a more emotionally distant style of behavior to new social functions in the contexts of family, sexuality, media and technology, economics, consumerism, and labor in the first decades of the twentieth-century.

The terms *cool* and *hip* are related, but not synonymous. As John Leland defines it his book *Hip: The History*, "cool" is a "balance in an individual" or "stability in a group" (57), but he linguistically distinguishes "hip" as that "which denotes a state of enlightenment or awareness" (58). To put another way, hip is the mental and emotional interiority or cultural process behind the protective mask of cool. "In its thoughtful repose," he clarifies, "cool begins the journey to hip" (58). Leland defines "hipsters" in the 1910s and 1920s as young Americans who were "smart, urban, literate and disaffected, colonizing marginal neighborhoods and using popular culture to accomplish what they couldn't through other means" (61). Although hipness was associated with an authenticity of the individual, it developed in cliques, and one of the first groups of hipsters in the twentieth century was the "Lost Generation" (a phrase coined by Gertrude Stein and popularized by Ernest Hemingway). After World War I, white modernist authors such as Stein and Hemingway, as well as F. Scott Fitzgerald, John Dos Passos, T. S. Eliot, and other disillusioned expatriates, lived in Paris on limited funds, drank and wrote late into the night, and mingled with local artists. Providing a new voice for the Jazz Age, they responded to the horrors of war and the banalities of industrialization by rejecting Victorian literary traditions and experimenting with language and form. Another group, the Harlem Renaissance, included African American writers who migrated from the South to New York City. Langston Hughes, Zora Neale Hurston, Jean Toomer, and Claude McKay were among the literary exemplar of this politically progressive movement in black cultural expression, which fought against racism, supported integration, and worked toward the construction of a new black identity in the arts and in American society.

The 1930s and 1940s continued the journey to hip with the hard-boiled detective of American crime fiction. "Pulps" were cheap, serialized magazines and paperback books printed on rough, unfinished paper with lurid covers, and consumed by working-class men. This popular countertradition to modernism gave American authors such as Dashiell Hammett and Raymond Chandler a literary venue for their Southern California private-eye heroes (e.g., Hammett introduced Sam Spade and the Continental Op in the pulp magazine par excellence *Black Mask*). Hard-cover crime novels were also supported by middle-class book clubs, such as Chandler's *The Big Sleep*, which featured his investigator Philip Marlowe, and was first published by Knopf in 1939. Leland pronounces, "The literature these men produced was a West Coast answer to the Lost Generation and the Greenwich Village moderns: harsh, profane, alienated and geographically dystopian. The pulp hero, the first hip icon that did not rely on East Coast bohemia or intelligentsia, drew on the character of the western outlaw, but without the tragic fatalism" (97–98). Spade and Marlowe only reach the false promise of the West, where claims to progress and opportunity are mocked by the corrupting influences of industrialization, consumer capitalism, and technological developments endemic to the modern urban spaces of San Francisco and Los Angeles. But as neither part of law-abiding society nor the criminal class, they are able to navigate both spheres.

A product of post–World War I disillusionment, the hard-boiled detective may provide the reader with a moral compass through his pride, honesty, and sense of character, but he is also prone to violence and dispassionate revenge. The hard-boiled author therefore does not play out detective stories with the hip detachment of the Jazz Age, what Leland calls a displacement of "destructive and inarticulate" rage. Rather, Hammett and Chandler "brought rage closer to the surface," containing emotion instead of altogether masking it (91). In this way the hard-boiled school can be seen as a bridge between the socially acceptable emotionalism of the Victorian era and the cooled, existentially tinged modernism of midcentury.

America's cool culture and hip character are also tied to ideas about race. Norman Mailer's controversial 1957 article published in the magazine *Dissent* posited the hipster as an American existentialist male, "who knows that if our collective condition is to live with instant death [. . .] then the only life-giving answer is to accept the terms of death, to live with death as immediate danger, to divorce oneself from society, to exist without roots, to set out on that uncharted journey into the rebellious imperatives of the self" (212). For Mailer, it was the postwar figure of the cosmopolitan African American that represented the intellectual adventurer, whose unconventional action showed courage in the face of the threats of death pervading the Atomic Age, reintroducing emotion as a return of the repressed, but with intelligence.[4]

Living between totalitarianism and democracy, learning from the 1920s, the Great Depression, and World War II, and navigating the subculture of jazz and its larger avant-garde scene, the African American modeled a philosophy of defiance among the powerless that, according to Mailer, white "hipsters" strove to emulate. To be hip meant to stave off the conformity of the corporatist, white middle-class society of the Eisenhower years. Mailer referred to the hipster less as a social rebel than as a "philosophical psychopath" (216), who works to create a "new nervous system" for himself, while others are psychoanalytically trained to diminish their "most interesting qualities and vices" so that they remain "less bad, less good, less bright, less willful, less destructive, less creative" (218–19). Although he makes no mention of Ray's films in this article, Mailer does cite Robert Lindner's case history *Rebel without a Cause: The Hypnoanalysis of a Criminal Psychopath*, which gave Ray the title of his 1955 film and which was to serve as its source material.

The characters in Ray's *Rebel* are more neurotic than psychopathic, but films such as *In a Lonely Place*, *On Dangerous Ground*, and *Bigger Than Life* are a different story (see fig. 4.1). We have seen how the violence and alienation of Humphrey Bogart's cynical character in *In a Lonely Place*,

Figure 4.1. *On Dangerous Ground* (1952): The characters in Ray's *Rebel without a Cause* are more neurotic than psychopathic, but films such as *In a Lonely Place*, *On Dangerous Ground*, and *Bigger Than Life* are a different story. (Warner Home Video, 2006; digital frame enlargement)

Dix Steele, partly follows from his refusal to compromise his artistic integrity as a screenwriter for the industrial demands of the Hollywood studio system. This refusal, in turn, leads to his self-destructive, antisocial search for an alternative mode of articulation within that system. Dix has not written a hit film since before the war, as a smarmy director reminds him, but the loneliness to which the title refers comes from his narcissistic withdrawal, his retreat into himself. By disengaging from the business of "popcorn salesmen," and, ultimately, from the world around him, Dix rebels against the institution of Hollywood even at the cost of his ability to form meaningful relationships—a bit of the tragic fatalism inherited from the Western outlaw.

In *On Dangerous Ground*, self-loathing police detective Jim Wilson reckons with his masculine insecurities and repressions, unable to trust anyone, let alone himself. Wilson feels absolute disdain for criminals, evident by his sadistic abuses of power, and yet he remains dubious about what his toughness accomplishes any longer (on a case hunting cop killers, he angrily compares his job to handling "garbage"). Embittered by the social prejudices toward the police force, he also maintains contempt for his department's soft-pedaling and bureaucratic procedures that impede the carriage of justice (the gluttonous chief reprimands him at a restaurant over an elaborate lunch of meat and potatoes). While Wilson is one of Ray's more conservative "rebels"—one might go as far as to say a fascist—he willfully abandons the social conventions of family and protocol, opting for a life of anger and solitude to uphold his own personal code of law and order.

The monomaniacal protagonist of *Bigger Than Life*, Ed Avery, is similar to Wilson, but as an intellectual schoolteacher living in the suburbs, his rebellion derives from the "petty domesticity" to which he feels forced to resign. Under the influence of cortisone, Ed devises a "revolutionary" practice of teaching, the details of which are never made entirely clear to the audience, and he believes it will lead to a new type of television programming for adults. Ed berates his students at a PTA meeting and forces his son to adhere to regimented math and football exercises at home, but as critics Éric Rohmer, François Truffaut, and Robin Wood pointed out, the cortisone simply raised to the surface Ed's resentment toward his "dull" bourgeois life and his desire to escape the trappings of mediocrity he perceives in his family (see chapter 1).

If this "new nervous system" (and its failings) make up one side of rebellion in Ray's male melodramas and noir films, bohemian creativity makes up the other side in his juvenile delinquency films. Ray formed a network of hip associations by the end of his career: the Café Society crowd of Greenwich Village and culture of jazz, blues, and folk music in the 1930s; French cinephilia, existentialism, and Method acting in the 1950s; and the underground film community in the 1970s. Stars James Dean, Robert Mitchum, and Humphrey Bogart, whom we know all worked with Ray, were spotlighted in the 2014 exhibit *American Cool* at the National Portrait Gallery in Washington, DC. However, it is Ray's rootless young male characters, children of the Lost Generation and older brothers of the Beats, who have most overtly given Ray his hip and cool credibility: Jim and Plato in *Rebel*, Bowie Bowers in *They Live by Night*, Nick Romano in *Knock on Any Door*, and Jesse James in *The True Story of Jesse James*.

Jim and Plato are both middle-class teenagers and therefore rebel from inside the status quo rather than from outside of it. Further, the hysterical performances of Dean and Mineo might not exactly qualify as "cool" if we understand the term to refer to a degree of emotional suppression. As outlaws according to gender and sex, though, Jim and Plato strike their hip stances by not conforming to the normative standards of masculine identity. Jim's very lack of control over his own body (he is always on the verge of being torn apart) and Plato's gay awakening (he finds himself sexually attracted to Jim) inhibit them from signifying as stable, coherent subjects in the traditional world of the film. Throughout *Rebel*, Ray seems to be dissecting what it means to be cool in highly self-aware ways. On the other hand, Bowie, Nick, and Jesse are outlaws according to class, and are thus excluded from society. Ironically, they are forced to become criminals because hegemonic structures of power have denied them access to the requirements for living in a privileged middle-class society (capital, family, property ownership, etc.).

The marginal positions of Ray's characters code them as invisible Others, and while Jim's visibility is restored at the end of *Rebel*, Plato, Bowie, Nick, and Jesse are each rendered invisible when they are killed off at the end of their respective films. Until those moments of narrative closure in which order is reinstated, they temporarily pass for members of middle-class society (e.g., Bowie's attempt to live "just like other people" and Jesse's efforts to begin a new life with his family under the false identity Thomas Howard) and go into hiding to avoid arrest or violent confrontation (e.g., Jim, Judy, and Plato "playing house" at the abandoned mansion). Or, they remain altogether unseen by that society (e.g., Nick on "Skid Row"). Once they are publically exposed, their visibility precipitates their demise: Bowie is shot by the police in front of his pregnant wife's motel cabin, Nick is found guilty for killing a police officer and is sent to the electric chair, Plato is shot by the police on the steps of the Griffith Observatory, and Jesse is shot in the back by the "coward" Robert Ford, who wants to go down in history as the man who assassinated the infamous bandit.

Ray's films adapted these racial discourses of "psychopathy" and marginality for a white, middle-class audience, similar to how the Beats appropriated African American "bebop" as music for hip young white men (see fig. 4.2). African-American musical performers Marie Bryant and Hedda Brooks appear in *They Live by Night* and *In a Lonely Place*, respectively, as if to remind us of another invisible world that exists just beyond Ray's central characters. Indeed, the rallying cry to "Live fast, die young, and have a good-looking corpse" was not a Ray original, but a line from the best-selling 1947 novel *Knock on Any Door* by Chicago's forgotten African American author Willard Motley, whose sequel, *Let No Man Write My Epitaph* (1958), inspired a 1960 film directed by Philip Leacock and starring James Darren as Nick Romano, Jr.[5]

Figure 4.2. *Knock on Any Door* (1949): Ray's films adapted racial discourses of "psychopathy" and marginality for a white, middle-class audience, similar to how the Beats appropriated African American "bebop" as music for hip young white men. (Warner Home Video, 2013; digital frame enlargement)

Part of Mailer's analysis is a response to the ways in which white hipsters tried to act like the bebop players, who invented the criteria for what was considered cool in the postwar era. The origins of "the cool" lie in bebop, which Frank Tirro defines in his book *Jazz: A History* as a style that arose in the early 1940s. Bebop, he explains, was "characterized by asymmetrical phrases, ornate melodic lines with much solo improvisation, complex rhythmic patterns, and more novel and dissonant harmonies than those used in the swing style of the preceding decade" (Appendices 169). Bebop legends such as Miles Davis, John Coltrane, Thelonious Monk, Charles Mingus, Charlie Parker, Dizzy Gillespie, Bud Powell, Max Roach, and Dexter Gordan intended to elevate jazz from dance music as entertainment to a serious art form.

The jazz "hipster" came out of this black avant-garde subculture, embodying bebop artists' scorn for their public, their employers, and their fellow musicians (jazz or otherwise) who could not keep up with their technical demands or who proved incompetent by their standards of the form. During solos, bebop musicians were known to play with their backs to the audience and then immediately walk off the stage, leaving the rest of their group still playing (Tirro 290). By the early 1950s, bebop had developed into "cool jazz" through the incorporation of a new timbral quality found in the saxophone and the minimization of overtones and vibrato (Tirro, Appendices 170). Tracks on Davis's groundbreaking 1957 Capitol Records album *Birth of the Cool*, compiled from three recording sessions between 1949 and 1950, inaugurated this new sound, although saxophonist Lester Young has been credited with popularizing the term *cool* within the black hipster idiolect.

During the 1940s and 1950s, white American writers such as Jack Kerouac, Allen Ginsberg, Neal Cassady, and William Burroughs took on an nebulous philosophical practice that drew from the psychology of bebop, from what it symbolized as the experimental music of outsiders and artistic rebels, transforming the hipster into the "Beat" (as in beatific). Writers of the "Beat Generation," a phrase Kerouac coined in 1948, were romantic outcasts who dropped out of dominant, commonplace society and the mytho-historical-ideological narrative of the American Dream. As writer and activist Marty Jezer argues in his cultural history *The Dark Ages: Life in the United States, 1945–1960*, the Beats did not criticize or despair over society, nor did they punish themselves for not fitting in. They also did not prescribe to an ideological movement, but looked "to create new space and new lives" (254), and strove to find "a way of being without attempting to explain why" (255). According to their philosophy, the Beats lived only in the present and did not acknowledge reality. Instead, they partook of drugs, flouted the conventions of monogamous, heterosexual relationships, and valued the emotion behind words rather than the words themselves. If words could only express illusions, the Beats found existential truth in the uninhibited, improvisational sound of a bebop solo, and endeavored to find a literary equivalent (255).

The capital of cool toward the end of the 1950s was the West Coast, where not only cool jazz, but also art, architecture, design, cinema, and popular music flourished as Southern California became the hub of midcentury American modernism.[6] In the catalog accompanying her extraordinarily ambitious 2007 exhibit at the Orange County Museum of Modern Art, *Birth of the Cool: California Art, Design, and Culture at Midcentury*, Elizabeth Armstrong writes that the work in this cultural moment was produced through "the distinctive fusion of high modernism and an aesthetic of cool that we now project onto this progressive time and place" (25). Cool was "a cerebral mix of seeming detachment and effortlessness" (56), she notes, and it was the ethos of the hipster. At this point, the hipster signified both "the mellow, laid-back sound of West Coast jazz" (25), as well as the metropolitan "Beatnik," the Beat stereotype popularized by American media, both of which seemed cut off from traditional, small-town American domesticity. The relationship between modernism and an aesthetic of cool was also firmly established here, in which a purity of style (hard-edged, sleek, and streamlined), as Armstrong describes, gets read as an "an out-of-the-box cachet that has become a shorthand for beauty, sophistication, and aspiration" (56).

This smooth, elegant sensibility circulated widely in commercial movies of the 1950s. Avant-garde filmmaker John Whitney, a pioneer of computer animation, contributed to United Productions of America (UPA), the studio responsible for the *Mister Magoo* series (coincidentally, Jim Backus, who played Jim's father in *Rebel*, provided the voice to the character). Whitney collaborated with graphic designer Saul Bass on the title sequence for Alfred Hitchcock's *Vertigo* (1958), with its famous color spiral motif. The photographs of midcentury modernist houses by Julius Shulman captured "the élan of Hollywood movies," observes Armstrong, as they were known for "their cinematic framing, minimal décor, and fashionable inhabitants" (37). A Shulman photograph was not unlike a shot of the villain's posh Mount Rushmore home in Hitchcock's *North by Northwest* (1959), modeled after the architectural style of Ray's former mentor Frank Lloyd Wright.

Among the first modern jazz scores for films were also written at this time, including Elmer Bernstein's score for *The Man with the Golden Arm* (1955), featuring Shorty Rogers and His Giants, and Duke Ellington's score for *Anatomy of a Murder* (1959), both films directed by Otto Preminger, who rivaled Hitchcock in his 1950s directorial celebrity (Bass, incidentally, designed the titles and posters for these two films and for *North by Northwest*). One of the most popular jazz men of the era, the young and handsome Chet Baker, whose trumpet and vocals exuded the cool of West Coast modernism, earned comparisons to none other than James Dean. In short, Hollywood films both reflected and shaped American modernism outside of cinema in the 1950s, but Ray contributed the young, American, and self-consciously artistic character to that cinema, personified by Dean, Sal Mineo, John Derek, Robert Wagner, and Jeffrey Hunter.

The following decade witnessed an increasing commercialization of cool and institutionalization of modernism. What was once understood as a subcultural philosophy and artistic practice of black avant-gardists had been depoliticized and commodified into a mainstream performance style for the white middle-class, specifically for men, who continued to serve as the gatekeepers of cool. James Dean was cool because of his swagger and sensitivity, and his red jacket, white T-shirt, and blue jeans ensemble could be sold to teenagers who wanted to look like him (indeed, a cottage industry of Dean T-shirts, posters, and collectables still grows strong in the contemporary marketplace). When the 4K digital restoration of *Rebel* played at the 2014 Berlin International Film Festival, part of a larger film restoration project between Gucci and the Film Foundation that Martin Scorsese founded, the chief marketing officer for Gucci mused how the film still inspires fashion designers: "It's sort of a fashion moment, isn't it, the whole film?" (Stone).

The marketing of *Rebel* had already advertised its star—even in his postmortem publicity—as too cool to comb his hair or button his shirts. Dean was promoted in black clothes, leather jackets, and deliberately mismatched casual and formal attire, leaning against walls, and looking slyly over his shoulder at the spectator or gazing into the distance deep in thought. Somehow he managed to appear both relaxed and intense at the same time, and by keeping his cool, never too far on either of those extremes, he could more persuasively pass off his sexy, mysterious, and brooding image as a natural state of being. Grace, poise, and confidence were the ingredients of cool, which projected both a moderate and a cavalier approach to life, and with the rise of postwar consumer culture, one could buy such a look (or at least pay to see it enacted onscreen).

In addition to teen movies and rock-and-roll, advertising co-opted rebel youth cultures and corporately sponsored an image of hip consumerism. Journalist Thomas Frank reveals in his book *The Conquest of Cool* that counterculture is "an enduring commercial myth" and hip is "ubiquitous as a commercial style" (32). Americans were taught that buying certain commodities over others, such as a Volkswagen Beetle instead of a family station wagon, was the proper (i.e., enlightened) way to rebel against a "square," conformist society. Therefore, Frank affirms, hip is "a staple of advertising that promises to deliver the consumer from the dreary nightmare of square consumerism" (32). As we have learned, Ray's films too were situated within larger discourses of modernism and mass culture (the widescreen and color genre pictures of 1950s Hollywood, Method acting and film stardom, and the self-promotion of directorial celebrity), allowing various user groups (critics, actors, and the director himself) to express modernist forms and ideas through an industrial systems of production and consumption.

Ray worked in Hollywood while the pop images and sounds of West Coast modernism were in the air, and although he may not have consciously tapped into this art-historical phenomenon, his films were produced in the same cultural context and share some of the same appeal as the Beats, the musicians of the bebop and cool jazz schools, and visual artists such as Whitney, Bass, and Shulman. Southern California was the hip place to be at midcentury, and as Ray has come to stand as a metonym for Hollywood rebellion in the 1950s, by extension he is a metonym for the coolness of American modernism. Our conception of Ray as a rebel auteur is largely imagined retroactively and projected onto the 1950s, in the same way an aesthetic of cool is mapped onto the larger creative practices on the West Coast. But as we will see, those lines converge through a construction of the rebel hipster-artist vis-à-vis the nostalgia of retro-auteurist filmmakers.

Jean-Luc Godard: Opening the Cinémathèque Vault

First of all, Godard looked cool. The blazer and Wayfarer sunglasses combination has become a recognizable "Godardian" look. Anna Karina, his beautiful, ultra-chic muse who starred in eight of his films and to whom he was married from 1961 to 1967, made him look even cooler. However, Godard's encyclopedic knowledge of cinema, amassed during his twenties as a critic at *Cahiers du cinéma* and demonstrated through reference and citation, put on full display his level of hip awareness and intellectual authority. It was a kind of allusionary, intertextual cine-cool.

A close viewer of Godard's first seven years as a filmmaker will find numerous references to *Johnny Guitar*, for instance: the "Tell me lies" sequence in *La Petit Soldat* (1963) is a callback to the "Lie to me" sequence with Sterling Hayden and Joan Crawford; in *Pierrot le fou* (1965), Pierrot sends his maid to see *Johnny Guitar* because he thinks it will be "good for her education"; in *La Chinoise* (1967), university student Henri is expelled from his group of revolutionaries for defending *Johnny Guitar*; and in *Weekend* (1967), "Johnny Guitar" is the codename for one of the guerrilla fighters. *Contempt* (1963) contains one of my favorite references to Ray, as screenwriter Paul Javal, played by Michel Piccoli, tells his wife Camille, played by Brigitte Bardot, that he wants to go see *Bigger Than Life*, a film he takes credit for writing.

Of course, Ray was only one of many sources of quotation in Godard's cinema: Fritz Lang and Samuel Fuller make cameo appearances in *Contempt* and *Pierrot le fou*, respectively; Karina's character in *Vivre sa vie* (1962) attends a screening of Carl Theodor Dreyer's *The*

Passion of Joan of Arc (1928); and FBI agent Lemmy Caution returns to the screen in the science fiction noir *Alphaville* (1965) (this hard-boiled character, created by British author Peter Cheyney, was popularized by a series of French films starring Eddie Constantine, most of which Bernard Borderie directed). *Made in U.S.A.* (1966), Godard's ode to American crime fiction, was dedicated to Ray and Fuller: "To Nick and Samuel, who raised me to respect image and sound." This list only begins to disentangle Godard's web of cinematic discourse.

The original trailer for Godard's picaresque crime film *Breathless* (1960), his first feature, literally names a handful of its cinematic citations: Claude Autant-Lara's *Devil in the Flesh* (1947), Jules Dassin's *Rififi* (1955), Roger Vadim's. . . . *And God Created Woman* (1956), and Howard Hawks's *Scarface* (1932). Godard dedicated the film to Monogram Pictures, one of Hollywood's minor studios on "Poverty Row" that specialized in B-rate crime pictures in the 1940s and 1950s, and later said he mistakenly thought he made a realistic film like Richard Quine's noir film *Pushover* (1954) (*Godard* 175). *Breathless* seems more obviously a riff on the *l'amour fou* plots of Ray's *They Live by Night* and Lang's *You Only Live Once* (1937).[7] The film, in turn, made Godard's reputation as a modern art film auteur and "young turk" of the postwar cineaste set, raised by Henri Langlois at the Cinémathèque Française.

Hollywood cinema and American popular culture fascinated Godard throughout the 1960s, but as he became increasingly suspicious of mainstream narrative forms (along with the capitalist machinery of commercial cinema), over the course of the decade his films gradually shifted their attention from Coca-Cola to Marx, culminating in "the end of cinema" with *Weekend* in 1967. The next phase of Godard's career moved him into the political avant-garde with the Dziga Vertov Group and subsequent essay films derived from Brechtian aesthetics. More than any other title of his oeuvre, *Breathless* best represents the mass cultural modernism of the first years of the *nouvelle vague* and Godard's earlier unabashed passion for the more populist topics in which Ray was invested (rebellious young delinquents, love-on-the-lam, the modernity of the city).

Nowhere are these tendencies more apparent than in the film's fugitive antihero Michel Poiccard, who puffs on cigarettes, wears a suit and a fedora, keeps his sunglasses on indoors, and idolizes one of Ray's favorite actors, Humphrey Bogart. On the run from the law after stealing an American car and shooting a police officer, he hides out in Paris with his pretty American girlfriend, Patricia, a student at the Sorbonne and an aspiring journalist who sells the *New York Herald Tribune* along the Champs-Élysées. Jean Seberg plays Patricia, showing off the same blond pixie cut she immortalized in Otto Preminger's recent Hollywood films set in France, *Saint Joan* (1957) and *Bonjour Tristesse* (1958). Later in the film, she will escape from the police into a screening of Preminger's *Whirlpool* (1949) at the Cinema MacMahon. As if to solidify its French-American relationships, the film takes place against the backdrop of President Dwight D. Eisenhower's 1959 trip to Paris to visit the Tomb of the Unknown Soldier under the Arc de Triomphe with General Charles de Gaulle.

To be clear, *Breathless* was not modeled after Classical Hollywood cinema per se, but merely borrowed certain elements (star images, generic conventions, and subjects like girls and guns) to serve a postwar modernist cinema that was coming into the fore in France. Louis Malle had just won the coveted Louis Delluc Prize for the Miles Davis–scored noir film *Elevator to the Gallows* (1958), joining a new group of French auteurs that included Jean Cocteau, Robert Bresson, Jacques Tati, and Henri-Georges Clouzot, all of whom not only won the Delluc Prize, but who also paved the way for the *nouvelle vague*. The major turning point came with a series of first feature films. From the Right Bank, Claude Chabrol's *Le Beau Serge* was released in 1958 and François Truffaut's *The 400 Blows* was released in 1959, the latter of which won Truffaut the Cannes Film Festival Award for Best Director. Having also written for *Cahiers du cinéma*, both directors followed in the footsteps of Italian neorealist auteurs (among the darlings of the magazine were Luchino Visconti, Roberto Rossellini, and Vittorio De Sica), who employed long takes and location shooting, as well as loose structures of narrative causality surrounding psychologically ambiguous or ambivalent characters. The disavowal of artifice was equated with a disavowal of fascist and bourgeois taste politics.

From the Left Bank, Alain Resnais's *Hiroshima, Mon Amour* was released in 1959. Resnais and screenwriter Marguerite Duras made use of flashbacks and nonlinear storytelling to depict the end of a love affair between a French woman and a Japanese man, who, in a thirty-six-hour conversation, meditate on the bombing of Hiroshima and on the nature of memory and history at large. The film earned immediate international acclaim, and was the subject of a roundtable discussion with the *Cahiers du cinéma* editorial board, in which Éric Rohmer called Resnais "the first modern film-maker of sound film" (61). Comparing him to the art world's Picasso and to literature's Faulkner and Dos Passos, Rohmer declared, "There has not yet been any profoundly modern cinema that attempts to do what cubism did in painting and the American novel in literature, in other words a kind of reconstitution of reality out of a kind of splintering which could have seemed quite arbitrary to the uninitiated" (Domarchi et al. 61). Regardless of the filmmaker's approach in the *nouvelle vague*, this diverse movement was united in its mission to overturn the country's square "Tradition of Quality," a hegemonic period of classical cinema dominated by bloated period films and literary adaptations made by directors who lacked a signature style or personal vision. Long gone were the days of Poetic Realism, which gave France its beloved films of Jean Renoir and Marcel Carné.

Within this context, as a filmmaker Godard resumed his role as a critic, turning film itself into an essayistic vehicle for film criticism. Partial to the episodic storytelling, long takes, and location shooting of his colleagues and their neorealist predecessors, he was also one of the most precocious, eccentric, and formally radical members of the *nouvelle vague*. Less committed to a coherent program for art cinema than to his own personal idiosyncrasies, Godard mixed genres and styles (e.g., science fiction and film noir in *Alphaville*), crossed existentialist philosophy and Marxist politics with popular culture (e.g., the comic strip panels intercut with Marxist-Leninist diatribes in *La Chinoise*), and played with self-reflexive techniques (e.g., direct address, jump cuts, freeze frames, etc.) that fragment classical perceptions of space and time preserved by continuity editing. The freewheeling structure and dynamic mise-en-scène of an early Godard film often spoke to his continued interest in the energetic, youth-oriented mass culture of postwar America, which he could repurpose from products of commercial industries into the seeds of rebellion sewn by a new language of cinema.

This form of intertextuality does not work in the same way as blank parody. Peter Wollen acknowledges that while Godard's Americanist "mixture of modernism with B-movies" may account for part of his appeal in the 1960s, his work was also strongly influenced by French theoretical concerns. On the one hand, there was what Wollen calls "'life-style modernism,' which combined a journalistic sense of the topical with a more sociologically oriented mode of investigation and an attachment to the 'critique of everyday life,' to use Henri Lefebvre's phrase" (*Paris* 77). On the other hand, Godard's early films were self-conscious not just about their function as political critique or urban anthropology, but as works of modern art. If art was a cultural heritage for Godard, it also "required the reinscription and destruction of that heritage." His films "oscillate between a critique of consumerism and mass culture and a delighted fascination with it" (*Paris* 78). After all, art was intimately part of consumerism and everyday life, and mined that cultural landscape. In many ways, Godard's early films had more in common with Pop Art, which was bourgeoning in the mid-1950s, than with films by his French contemporaries. One need only consult Andy Warhol's paintings of Coke bottles and Campbell's Soup cans, or his renderings of American celebrities such as Marilyn Monroe and Elvis Presley.

Unlike Hitchcock's relationship to De Palma, Ray was less the subject of sustained stylistic imitation for Godard than an important reference point in a larger repertoire of artistic and cultural sources. Hollywood exported the raw material for rebellion in French film culture, and we have learned how the *Cahiers du cinéma* critics held up Ray's films as the liberating potential of cinema, a modernism for the masses attributable to a single author/artist. Ray was a cultural hero among those critics, and as a director Godard paid homage to his films with references to titles, characters, scenes, or story lines. Yet, it was less about copying Ray's techniques in individual films than about emulating his ambition to articulate an individual worldview under restrictive institutional conditions. Becoming an auteur was a way to carry on that legacy.

Breathless may not have been the first film of the *nouvelle vague*, but it was the first film to announce the major players of the *nouvelle vague* as a bold, auteurist filmmaking collective. The result was a critical and commercial success. Godard directed the film, Truffaut wrote the story, and Chabrol served as the technical advisor. Jean-Pierre Melville, an adjunct member of the *nouvelle vague* who directed gangster films such as *Bob le flambeur* (1956) and whose career began a decade earlier, makes a cameo as the pompous writer Parvulesco. Actor Jean-Paul Belmondo, who plays Michel, had already starred in Chabrol's *À double tour* (1959), and would go on to make additional films with Chabrol (*Dr. Popaul* [1972]), Godard (*A Woman Is a Woman* [1961]; *Pierrot le fou*), Resnais (*Stavinski* [1974]), Melville (*Léon Morin, Priest* [1961]; *Le Doulos* [1962]; *L'aîné des Ferchaux* [1963]), and Truffaut (*Mississippi Mermaid* [1969]). Godard himself shows up briefly as a bystander who snitches on Michel to the police (in a nod to silent cinema, an iris closes their exchange).[8] Establishing a self-contained diegetic universe for the *nouvelle vague*, Godard cleverly links *Breathless* to earlier French films. Michel's alias is Laszlo Kovacs,[9] the same name as his character from *À double tour*, and he hears that "Bob, le flambeur" (Bob, the gambler) is in jail. *Hiroshima, Mon Amour* is playing at a Champs-Élysées theater, and in one shot we see the poster and title on the marquee.

Godard filmed quickly on a shoestring budget with a silent 35 mm Arriflex camera, took advantage of natural lighting, dubbed the sound in postproduction, and had his cinematographer Raoul Coutard push him around in a wheelchair for traveling shots. For all of the spontaneity in his directorial style and his self-professed "anything goes" approach to the film (*Godard* 173), Godard's intertextual references are in fact quite systematic. Consider the way in which he develops Michel's character. Martial Solal's moody jazz score opens the film, which fades in on a pin-up drawing on the cover of a French tabloid. "So I'm a son of a bitch," says the man holding the paper, lowering it to reveal his face. The downturned fedora and cigarette dangling from his mouth are the semiotic codes of the American tough guy, and the vulgar language he uses throughout the film is an attempt to inhabit completely this macho Hollywood star type.

In his book *The Films of Jean-Luc Godard*, David Sterritt makes the case that one of Godard's working methods is "cultural kleptomania," or "to show how both of his main characters draw key aspects of their seem-

Figure 4.3. *Breathless* (1960): Rubbing his thumb across his lips, a gesture he repeats multiple times, Michel (Jean-Paul Belmondo) performs a self based in particular on the grimacing Bogie persona. (Fox Lorber, 2001; digital frame enlargement)

ingly anarchic personalities from the culture in which they live." Michel, in *Breathless*, he continues, "is an actor without a theater—or with one, if we remember that all the world's a stage, especially in a modern city overflowing with potential spectators" (57). Rubbing his thumb across his lips, a gesture he repeats multiple times, he performs a self based in particular on the grimacing Bogie persona (see fig. 4.3). More broadly, he demonstrates a compulsion to assume masks. One of Michel's most peculiar habits is making three nonsense faces to himself—opening his mouth wide, stretching it sideways, and pursing his lips with a furrowed brow. He even teaches these expressions to Patricia (exaggerations of the expressive pantomime in silent cinema).

When Michel later happens upon a movie theater showing Bogart's last film, the boxing picture *The Harder They Fall* (1956) directed by Mark Robson, he pauses to admire the poster and then looks reverently at the publicity photos of the star, rubbing his lips again as if to cement the connection with Bogart's tic for audiences outside of the know. In other words, to be hip was to be a cinephile. Bogart was already a cult figure at this point, and his cool image that Michel cultivates is the mannered identity he wants to project publically.

The 1950s MacMahonist action movies Godard cites are more than movies by which Michel defines himself, though. Films are the only apparent signposts that map the course of Michel's future, constructing an identity for him. Michel walks past a poster of Robert Aldrich's World War II film *Ten Seconds to Hell* (1959), starring tough guys Jeff Chandler and Jack Palance, the latter of whom went on to costar in *Contempt*. The film's title appears onscreen approximately ten seconds before Michel witnesses a hit-and-run accident that he nearly avoids (the anonymous victim was played by *Cahiers du cinéma* critic Jacques Rivette, who was in the process of making his own first film, *Paris Belongs to Us*, released the following year).

Glancing down at his newspaper, Michel sees that his fingerprints have been identified in the killing of the police officer, and he realizes that the law is no doubt after him. While the police pursue both Michel and Patricia, they decide, of course, to stop and see a movie together: Budd Boetticher's *Westbound* (1959), a Randolph Scott Western.[10] The Boetticher film reminds us how Godard has updated the nineteenth-century trope of the American outlaw to a modern Parisian thief. Filtered through Michel's fetish for American movies, Godard's imagination of the outlaw is produced through a simultaneous re-mystification of the frontier figure and a deconstruction of Western narratives and mass culture.

On a second viewing of *Breathless*, *The Harder They Fall* foreshadows the great "fall" Michel takes when Patricia informs on him to the police and he is finally gunned-down and killed on the streets of Paris. The scene evokes the climactic death of gangster Roy "Mad Dog" Earle, Bogart's first role as a star, in Raoul Walsh's *High Sierra* (1941). Just as Marie (Ida Lupino) asks, "Mister, what does it mean . . . when a man 'crashes out'?" Patricia, in reference to Michel's dying words, asks, "what is a 'dégueulasse'?" (French for "scumbag" or "bitch"). Marie was loyal to Roy until the end, but Patricia's mysterious betrayal is more consistent with Seberg's character Cécile in *Bonjour Tristesse*. Godard was so taken with her performance in the Preminger film that he envisioned Patricia as a continuation of Cécile three years later (*Godard* 173).

Apart from mentioning that he assisted on a Cinecittà production, Michel is almost exclusively aligned with mass culture,[11] whereas Patricia collapses the boundaries between mass culture and high art, endowing the film with its real voice and point-of-view even though we spend more time with Michel. She listens to Bach, Mozart, and Chopin, while Michel's previous girlfriend, a wannabe actress who works at a television station, likes Paul Anka and frequents a discotheque. As a cipher, Patricia is the more thoroughly Godardian character.

One of the lengthiest scenes in the film occurs in Patricia's apartment, the sort of bedroom scene that would have been cut from a Classical Hollywood crime film for its sexual suggestiveness and also for halting the progression of plot. The camera highlights numerous reproductions of modern paintings as the couple converses during this *temps mort*. Posters of *Jacqueline avec des fleurs* (1954) and *L'ancienne année* (1953), both by Pablo Picasso, adorn Patricia's walls, as does a postcard of his *Les Amants* (1923). We also see a poster of Paul Klee's *Timid Brute* (1938) and a postcard of his *Kettle Drummer* (1940) at other moments. Godard even pays tribute to Pierre-Auguste Renoir and Samuel Fuller in the same shot as Patricia rolls her new poster of Renoir's *Head of a Young Girl* (1894) and looks through it at Michel, a visual quotation of the gun-barrel point-of-view shot in Fuller's Western *Forty Guns* (1957).

Although Patricia mentions Dylan Thomas's 1940 short story collection *Portrait of the Artist as a Young Dog* and reads from William Faulkner's 1939 novel *The Wild Palms* (aka, *If I Forget Thee, Jerusalem*), she is not above popular magazines such as *Life*, which we glimpse earlier in the film, or *Silver Screen*, a copy of which sits on her nightstand bearing the face of Rock Hudson. The most surprising title in her collection is the catalog *Photography of the Female Figure* (1957) by photographer and ex-pinup model Bunny Yeager, who helped discover 1950s Playmates

Bettie Page and Lisa Winters, and who went on to photograph "Bond girl" Ursula Andress on the beach for her *Dr. No* (1962) publicity shoot. Michel thumbs through the art photos of nude women and the camera lingers on the pages.

There is also a photo of Patricia/Seberg on the wall, about which one would not likely think twice were it not for its resemblance to a real publicity photo, and for Godard's penchant for blurring reality and art. The other women in Michel's life have vainly decorated their living spaces with professional photographs of themselves, both his previous girlfriend and the model in whose home he eventually hides with Patricia. Never having spoken of acting or modeling, Patricia would be unlikely to display such a photograph of herself—and yet Godard makes a point to include a shot of it. Given his adoration of Seberg's role in *Bonjour Tristesse*, I think the reference here is to Seberg, not to Patricia, foregrounding the film's layers of mediation. Life imitates art, and vice versa (Belmondo playing Michel playing Bogart, Seberg playing Patricia playing Seberg).

This metaperformance comes full-circle when Patricia sees Michel die on the street and he makes his three faces at her, after which she turns to the camera and mimics his Bogart gesture as if to relinquish her performance of self for his. In his book *The Films of Jean-Luc Godard*, Wheeler Winston Dixon discusses the absurd randomness of this ending, remarking how the meaningless and inconsequentiality of Michel's death reflects that of his life (17). Eschewing psychological realism, Godard preferred "characters whose entire existence lies in a series of gestures, motions, appearances, and escapes," Dixon points out, "all to disguise the essentially phantom nature of their ephemeral existence" (24). It is not Bogart whom the film ultimately calls to mind, but Cécile from *Bonjour Tristesse*, a film that also ends with Seberg's sad, enigmatic look into the camera.

The motives behind Patricia's betrayal are mostly ambiguous, and this resistance to narrative closure is indeed a hallmark of modernist art cinemas. Michel is a self-absorbed dropout, whose adolescent misogyny and life of petty crime is obviously incompatible with Patricia's life as an independent woman, who desires a relationship predicated on love and commitment rather than just sex. Patricia is pregnant from an earlier encounter with Michel and contemplates an abortion in order to pursue her career in Paris, but Michel wants her to run away with him to that Cinema City, Rome. She asks if they could be like Shakespeare's Romeo and Juliet, a couple who loves each other, but, tragically, who has no future, while Michel believes that an *amour fou* scenario from Hollywood is a viable option. Both Patricia and Michel are more attracted to an illusion of love, which they have received from "high" and "low" culture, respectively. Despite falling for Michel's charms and his whimsical lifestyle, Patricia informs on Michel to prove—to him as much as to herself—that she does not love him.[12]

If we read Patricia as a continuation of the teenage femme fatale Cécile (or, rather, Patricia as a role performed by Cécile), the final shot opens another dimension to her character. In Preminger's tragic Electra melodrama, Cécile is the spoiled daughter of a wealthy, widowed playboy (David Niven) living on the Riviera. Angered by her father's relationship with a woman (Deborah Kerr) with whom she must compete for his attention, and who threatens to draw their carefree, hedonistic life to a close, Cécile conspires to thwart their engagement. The plans spiral out-of-control and lead to the woman's suicide, wracking Cécile with a heavy guilt that ends her innocent and decadent youth. Three years later, as a student living alone in Paris and still ambivalent about men other than her father, Cécile has presumably begun a new life as Patricia. Yet, her impulsive and somewhat inexplicable decision has resulted in another tragedy, pulling her back into a cycle of inevitable destruction from which she cannot escape.

Godard's shot compositions nevertheless emphasize the couple's genuine feelings for each other, and I cannot help but think of Ray's romantic, soft-focus close-ups of Farley Granger and Cathy O'Donnell in *They Live by Night* whenever I see the film. Sitting in the theater watching *Westbound*, Michel and Patricia gaze into each other's eyes and then kiss. The close-ups of their profiles against a black background mirrors the opening shot of Bowie and Keechie in *They Live by Night*, their faces slowly coming together from opposite sides of the screen. Ray's subtitles tell us, "This boy . . . and this girl . . . were never properly introduced to the world we live in . . . to tell their story." During their conversation in Patricia's apartment, Godard zooms out from an extreme-close-up to a close-up of Michel and Patricia kissing against the wall. Later, he shoots them lying on the bed together in medium-shot, Michel's face resting on Patricia, and the film then cuts to a close-up of a kiss as their faces fill the screen.

Both of these shots are reminiscent of the celebrated two-shot close-up in *They Live by Night* (an inspiration for its posters, lobby cards, and publicity photos), in which Bowie and Keechie recline in front of the fireplace of their honeymoon cabin. Keechie's face lies horizontally across the screen, and Bowie props his head up above her in the palm of his hand. The couples stare into space, contemplating their future, before leaning into each other for a kiss. *They Live by Night* acts as shorthand for the cinephiles viewing *Breathless*, who are able to decode Michel and Patricia in relation to Bowie and Keechie; the characters may be quite different, but their idealized relationship is the same.

The parade of Classical Hollywood recollections in the film is part of the way in which Godard comprehends modernism. A good amount of scholarly material has already dealt with Godard's modernist aesthetics, defined by reflexivity, abstraction, and subjectivity. For example, in his book *Screening Modernism* András Bálint Kovács locates Godard within the cinematic trend of "Romantic Modernism" from 1959 to 1961, "a critique of conventional forms of cinematic representation, and a desire to reinvent art cinema according to a personal, subjective experience" (349).[13] How do we account for his investment in classicisms, though? Kovács clarifies that "classical" and "modern" were not necessarily value judgments for the *nouvelle vague* wherein the former was abandoned for the latter. Godard and his compatriots instead "looked for traditions that were worthy enough to be continued," and "singled out certain tendencies and auteurs they accepted as their precursors or mentors and rejected others as outmoded" (35). Therefore, the modernism with which Godard has been credited, and his belief in cinema as a modern technological art form, should not overshadow his unironic attachment to artistic, literary, and cinematic traditions.

Gabriel Rockhill provocatively suggests that most understandings of Godard's modernism are inadequate in that they frame his innovations and experimentations as breaks from tradition that totally abolish classical conventions. Like literary modernists such as Eliot and Baudelaire, Godard was an archeologist of the past, whose "modernism" presented a new relationship with the past through new modes of historical engagement. Rockhill contends:

> Modernity, understood according to the dual imperative outlined by Baudelaire and performatively appropriated by Eliot, is not a rejection of the past in the name of the new. It is the recognition of the historicity of art and the attempt to propose a novel configuration of the relationship between the present and the past, the temporal and the atemporal, that avoids enthroning one at the expense of the other. (120)

Godard's historiographies of cinema, both as a critic and as a filmmaker, do not consider the classical and the modern to be mutually exclusive, but rather as interconnected.

Think of the English teacher's lesson in Godard's *Band of Outsiders* (1964) that begins with the premise "*classique = moderne*" and invokes Eliot: "Everything that is new is automatically traditional." Rockhill asserts, "Instead of being a childishly paternal rebel who is supposedly 'without a cause,' Godard is a rebel in search of a cause, in pursuit of the invisible sources that animate things" (111). When a young woman selling copies of *Cahiers du cinéma* on the streets asks whether Michel supports youth, he replies, "I like the old." The joke is that Godard was still writing for the magazine at the time and was responsible for its new *politiques* aimed at young Parisian cinephiles, but he is also introducing a view of modernity that preoccupied him throughout his career: revolution in the arts is only possible with an acute awareness and even respect for the historical traditions under which art is created.

The modernism Godard brought to the *nouvelle vague* in the 1960s is therefore dependent on the "old," on Ray, Lang, Preminger, and the auteurism they exemplified in the 1940s and 1950s as modern directors of a classical style. Godard once said about directing *Breathless*, "What I wanted was to take a conventional story and remake, but differently, everything the cinema had done. I also wanted to give the feeling that the techniques of film-making had just been discovered or experienced for the first time" (*Godard* 173). As if directing a cinémathèque of repertoire programs, Godard staged a theoretical investigation into the future of cinema by archiving its past, a project that was hip to the formal and ideological work of the medium, which also constructed a reading strategy that rewarded audiences for being hip to Godard's intertextual matrix.

Wim Wenders: A Cowboy in Hamburg

We have seen how Wenders's admiration for Ray went as far as making a film with, and about, the dying Hollywood director. However, perhaps less obviously than Godard, Wenders's whole career shows the impact that old Hollywood had on his filmmaking style and subjects.

Allusions to classical films and auteurs are abounding. Wenders cited Hitchcock as an influence on *The Goalkeeper's Fear of the Penalty* (1972), a film about a goalkeeper who, after he is kicked out of a soccer game for committing a foul, spends the night with a movie theater cashier and murders her the next morning (251). John Ford's *Young Mr. Lincoln* (1939) is seen playing on a television in *Alice in the Cities* (1974), which focuses on a German writer struggling to finish an article about the U.S. *Kings of the Road* (1976), the Walker Evans–inspired conclusion to Wenders's "road movie trilogy" preceded by *Alice in the Cities* and *The Wrong Move* (1975), follows two traveling mechanics who repair projection equipment at rural movie theaters. It even re-creates the scene from *The Lusty Men* in which Jeff returns to his childhood home to find mementos from his youth still hidden under the house. An homage to Hollywood films from the 1940s and 1950s, *The State of Things* (1982) concerns a German director who travels to L.A. to find his missing producer when his film crew runs out of money in Portugal (Samuel Fuller and Roger Corman both appear). Even in the philosophical fantasy *Wings of Desire* (1987), which Wenders dedicated to international art cinema auteurs Yasujirō Ozu, François Truffaut, and Andrei Tarkovsky, there is a subplot involving American actor Peter Falk shooting a film in Berlin about its Nazi history (Falk plays an angel who gave up his immortality to live as a human being).

The first film Wenders made in Hollywood, commissioned by producer Francis Ford Coppola, was a neo-noir about Dashiell Hammett based not on the author's life, but on a 1975 novel by Joe Gores.[14] *Hammett* (1982) lovingly reconstructs the iconography of Classical Hollywood film noir, complete with the lonely apartments and dangerous city streets through which Ray traveled in his films. The oddest science fiction noir this side of Godard's *Alphaville*, *Until the End of the World* (1991) was more directly made in the Ray tradition as an outlaw couple road film, although Wenders took the title from the last line spoken in *King of Kings*. Wenders shot parts of his film about Hollywood, *The End of Violence* (1997), at one of Ray's most recognizable locales, the Griffith Observatory, where a computer scientist named Ray (Gabriel Byrne) spies on L.A. denizens with hidden cameras. "Now they have a gigantic bronze statue of James Dean there and the plaque doesn't even mention Nick," Wenders lamented, "although he discovered Dean and virtually discovered the place" (*The End of Violence* Press Release). Samuel Fuller, Wenders's other hero, has a small part in the film.

The Western genre is perhaps the clearest example of the ways in which Hollywood shaped Wenders. *Paris, Texas* (1984) and especially *Don't Come Knocking* (2005), his road films of the American Southwest written by Sam Shepard, could both be visually and thematically interpreted as modern-day Westerns.[15] Wenders wrote that he saw "about forty or fifty old American Westerns" (9) in Munich over the span of a few weeks in June of 1969, including *Johnny Guitar*, Otto Preminger's *River of No Return* (1954), Delmer Daves's *3:10 to Yuma* (1957), Arthur Penn's *The Left-Handed Gun* (1958), and various films by Anthony Mann, recording his impressions of the actors and landscapes. Recall that in *Lightning over Water*, Wenders told Ray that *The Lusty Men* is "more about coming home than anything I've ever seen," and in March of 1983 he penned an illuminating meditation on the film.

By this point, the male psyche and the construction of masculinity had become recurring issues in Wenders's films, which often told stories about male friendship and solidarity, and the disconnection between men and women, so it is no wonder he was intrigued by Ray's representations of gender. "Nicholas Ray has done more to question 'men' than any other American director," he declared, "confronting them with women who haven't defined themselves solely in terms of men, but have built up their own identity based around themselves" (118). Wenders went on to discuss how the men in the film are really cow*boys*, and the adults are the women who take care of them. The subject of *The Lusty Men*, the rodeo, is central to the history American entertainment, a rural amusement that dramatized the settling of the West, but Wenders also saw the film as an expression Ray's interlocking and paradoxical themes: the American dream to have a home of one's own and the inevitability of change that makes going home an impossible journey. Praising Ray's work with his actors and Lee Garmes's cinematography, Wenders underscored the film's fatal tensions between "growing old and wanting to stay young," between "wanting to be at home and yet belonging in the wilds" (120). According to Wenders, *The Lusty Men* was in many ways a documentary about America in the 1950s. Godard had claimed that if cinema did not exist, Ray would have been the filmmaker to invent it. For Wenders, Ray *did* invent cinema (122), and Wenders took to heart Ray's nostalgic thesis that "we can't go home again." Both his films and his directorial mythos inherited that sentiment (Wenders has stated, "I spend more time on the road than I do at home" [436]).

Unlike the members of the *nouvelle vague*, the New German Cinema directors did not talk about aesthetics together, nor did they seek to hone a style as a collective. They did not attempt to improve, join, or replace the film industry, either. Wenders explains, "we saw our activity as an alternative to it. No models, no tradition, no one whose place we wanted to usurp" (250). This new generation of independent filmmakers started the Filmverlag der Autoren as a kind of cooperative that gave them the autonomous system of production they craved and the means to finance and distribute their films. Joining Wenders were Werner Herzog and Rainer Werner Fassbinder.

The New German Cinema is commonly thought of as an avant-garde reaction to the country's films and filmmakers that came before it: a national cinema renaissance inaugurated by a new wave of auteurs, upholding the goals of the Oberhausener Manifesto (signed in 1962 by a group of filmmakers at the International Short Film Festival Oberhausen) that called for independence from industrial-economic control and the creation of an anticonventional film language. As Thomas Elsaesser shows in his comprehensive book *New German Cinema*, the self-legitimating movement was more precisely a historical confluence of industrial factors in which these filmmakers tried to pursue sources of funding, including government sponsorship and broadcast television partnerships, and their aesthetic and production practices tried to define a particular audience. What united these auteurs (along with German writers of the era) was less the prescription to the avant-garde dogma that persists in their reputations as romantic individualists and more the appropriation of the American culture. Wenders built a transnational lineage to Ray and Fuller, Fassbinder to Douglas Sirk, Peter Handke to Raymond Chandler, Rolf Dieter Brinkman to Andy Warhol, and so on.

Take, for example, Wenders's great respect for American artist Edward Hopper, whose paintings such as *Nighthawks* (1942) conveyed a cinematic vision of America's urban geography—one of suited men in all-night diners and dark, transient spaces of alienation—that could also be found in Hollywood gangster films and film noir. Hopper's desolate land- and cityscapes shared more in common with Pop Art and its everyday view of American modernity than with the dominant high modernist trends of Cubism and Abstract Expressionism. Themes of loss and existential isolation are prominent in Wenders's films, which specialize in the type of melancholy dreamers who could have wandered out of one of Hopper's paintings. Wenders, a former painter himself, studied Hopper for *The American Friend* (Elsaesser, *New* 257), and in a self-reflexive move, his film within the film, *The End of Violence*, actually reenacts *Nighthawks*.

According to Gerd Gemünden in his book on the Americanization of contemporary German and Austrian culture, *Framed Visions*, the popular American Imaginary allowed postwar German filmmakers and writers to reenvision their own cultural traditions and repress the historical traumas of their fascist past. Gemünden argues, "Hopper's paintings stylize loneliness to such a proportion that they no longer merely reflect its social or political roots but turn loneliness into a myth. It is this mythological aspect of Hopper's art—so prevalent also in Hollywood cinema, hard-boiled detective fiction, and even Pop art, where it is playfully subverted—that appeals directly to a German sensibility" (15). After the wartime embargoes were over, West Germany, like France, was flooded with American films. Similar to the ways in which *Cahiers du cinéma* used American mass culture after World War II, writers and filmmakers of the New German Cinema era saw in American industry and technology a potential for modernization and democratization, and could ally itself with the country that liberated them from fascism.[16]

Wenders was among many Germans who were raised with American mass culture in the 1950s (movies and rock-and-roll, in particular), which enabled them to rebel against a traditional German culture that was forced on them in their youth by an older, conservative generation. Young artists and intellectuals in Germany may have been concerned over America's cultural imperialism, capitalism, and global colonization, but they were eager to embrace an alternative to the hegemonic taste politics they associated with fascism. As this generation grew up in the late 1960s, the image of "freedom" they had mapped onto the United States was tainted by the Vietnam War. Paradoxically, American culture also gave them the very tools they needed to critique American culture, while at the same time working to reconcile their own national, cultural, and psychological histories.

Part of this awareness of American cinema owes to the fact that Hollywood was their major competitor in film production, holding an iron-clad grip over the European marketplace. This postwar crisis of German identity manifested itself in an anxiety of influence. Gemünden theorizes Germany's relationship with the United States in gendered Oedipal terms: "Having lost their German fathers in the war—either literally or figuratively, since they lost their integrity and credibility fighting in Hitler's Army—Americans provided ersatz fathers" (32). The only way to rid one's Oedipal father, of course, is to kill him. Wenders "directed" Ray's death in *Lightning over Water*, a symbolic Oedipal murder, but a film such as *The American Friend* (also with Ray) thematizes in a less literal drama the transnational love/hate relationship Gemünden identifies.

In *Breathless*, Godard transplants his characters into Ray's universe, while in *The American Friend*, writer-director Wenders transplants Ray into his universe. Godard's method is best summed-up as "cultural kleptomania," while Wenders's method might be called "cultural schizophrenia" (Gemünden 159). Based on Patricia Highsmith's novel *Ripley's Game* (1974), the third installment in her popular series of thrillers that Wenders avidly read, *The American Friend* stars Dennis Hopper as Highsmith's American expatriate Tom Ripley, a career criminal who ropes a terminally ill painting framer and restorer, Jonathan Zimmermann (Bruno Gantz), into an assassination plot. Hopper had made his screen debut in *Rebel without a Cause* and acted in films throughout the 1950s and 1960s, but he gained a foothold in the counterculture as a director and star with *Easy Rider* (1969), the now classic biker film he scripted with Terry Southern and his co-tar Peter Fonda (Wenders wrote a glowing review of the film after attending a screening at Columbia Pictures in 1969). Other directors turn up in *The American Friend*, including Fuller and French director Gérard Blain (who played a James Dean-type in Chabrol's *Le Beau Serge*). Wenders wrote that he cast them all in the roles of criminals "because [directors are] the only rascals I know, and the ones who make life-and-death decisions as airily as the Mafia" (178).[17]

The opening scene reunites Hopper, the actor, and Ray, the director, who embrace as if to forgive each other for their differences (namely over Natalie Wood) during the making of *Rebel*. Kissing Ray on the cheek, Hopper jokingly asks, "How's your wife?" Ray plays a reclusive painter named Andrew Pogash Derwatt, who is believed to be dead and lives in anonymity in a New York City loft (see fig. 4.4). Derwatt forges his own paintings and Ripley takes them to auctions, and they split the profit from the bidding.[18]

The film grants Ray yet another opportunity to promote his image in the 1970s as a rogue artist, whom at one point the industry thought was dying. By 1977, when he was living in a New York City loft for real, he was figuratively dead to Hollywood and had to rely on friends to get his

Figure 4.4. *The American Friend*: Ray plays a reclusive painter named Andrew Pogash Derwatt, who is believed to be dead and lives in anonymity in a New York City loft. (Anchor Bay Entertainment, 2002; digital frame enlargement)

films to a public (just after he died, Wenders performed this service with *Lightning over Water*). Later in the film, Derwatt wears Ray's trademark eye patch, and Ray even pokes fun at his image in this meeting between Derwatt and Ripley. When Ripley assures Derwatt that he has "got a good eye" (for forgeries), Derwatt replies (in reference to the painting), "Take care of it. A new one's hard to buy." Ripley is more of a typical Ray character than Derwatt, who has resigned himself to damnation (he contemplates hanging a sign outside his window that reads, "Deliver Me from Evil"), but like a Ray character, Derwatt feels the need to assert his identity. "You son of a bitch, my name is Pogash!" he tells Ripley when he arrives at his apartment, and in a different scene he says to him, "You're right, I'm dead and doing very well. Andrew Pogash Derwatt. I *am* alive."

A dislocated cowboy who can't go home again, Ripley dresses like Robert Mitchum in *The Lusty Men*—cowboy hat, boots, denim ware, and all—and lives in a colonial mansion in Hamburg filled with the detritus of Americana. "There's nothing to fear but fear itself. I know less and less about . . . who I am . . . or who anybody else is," he says into a tape recorder, and then proceeds to sing "The Ballad of Easy Rider," a song written and performed by Roger McGuinn for the *Easy Rider* soundtrack. Ripley is Kane without Rosebud, and his pop-infused Xanadu surrounds him with a past collected entirely from myth: he owns a Wurlitzer juke box and a Coca-Cola machine, he smokes Marlboro cigarettes and drives a vintage white Thunderbird, and he drinks beer and eats bowls of Kellogg's Corn Flakes on his pool table, over which hangs a Canada Dry sign that bathes his game room in an eerie neon-green glow. When Derwatt questions his conspicuous hat, Ripley responds, "What's wrong with a cowboy in Hamburg?" and later he wears a T-shirt with a Native American logo (playing both cowboy and Indian). Most of his things are wrapped in plastic since his house is under renovation, but it looks as though he either never completely moved in or is never there. The home is the junk heap of history wherein identity is a manufactured illusion. An atmosphere of imminent death hovers around Ripley as he is caught between Derwatt, a man pretending to be dead, and Jonathan, a dying man.

Jonathan lives in his own historical dustbin as a picture framer (read: director) and collector of early cinematic technologies. Although he is keen on 1960s British rock-and-roll (he sings along to "Too Much on My Mind" by the Kinks while playing their record *Face to Face* on his turntable, and also listens to "Nothin' in the World Can Stop Me Worryin' 'Bout that Girl"), the film primarily anchors him in the history of cinema. Around his home, we see a zoetrope, a Taxiphote stereoscopic viewer, and a lampshade illustrated with a moving steam train that almost creates a magic lantern effect. His son plays with a Maltese cross, the intermittent mechanism by which celluloid passes through a projector and is held in place. Ripley and Jonathan exchange handheld optical toys as gifts or peace offerings: the childlike Jonathan gives Ripley a portrait that animates a man's smiling face, and the earthier Ripley gives Jonathan a viewing device with slides of nude women. For these reasons, Wenders saw himself in Jonathan (258), but both of the characters could be read as extensions of the director.

At an early stage in his career, Wenders showed interest in some of the same techniques as his contemporaries in modernist art cinema. In their book *The Films of Wim Wenders*, Robert Kolker and Peter Beicken define cinematic modernism as a process of selection and adaptation that guides the determination of which artistic practices are still viable and which should be left behind. According to Kolker and Beicken, modernism is a "movement in which (among other things) a new generation of artists consciously seeks legitimacy by developing new expressive forms both against and from the past" (29). While he may not have been as formally radical as Godard, Wenders's narrativity speaks to a modernist mode of spectator address. Kolker and Beicken find that his films "downplay action and narrative direction in order to make room for images that present the visual field as a staging place for the imagination of the viewer" (21).[19] What makes the New German Cinema a problematic example of modernism for the authors is that it had intervened in a moment of "historical amnesia" (29); it had no tradition of image and narrative from which to rebel (no Tradition of Quality like the *nouvelle vague*), and therefore shouldered the responsibility of establishing a past and present. The artifacts of American mass culture afforded Wenders that grounding he lacked in the way that Ripley and Jonathan have built homes out of memorabilia, the relics and antiques that signify historical reality amid their counterfeit surroundings.

❧

The impetus behind Jonathan and Ripley's relationship is their roles on the fringes of the art world, Jonathan as a failed painter who frames pictures in Hamburg (the unfulfilled artisan), and Ripley as a faux investor (the would-be capitalist), who tells Jonathan, "I've always wanted to be able to make something with my hands." They meet at an auction where Ripley sells one of Derwatt's forgeries, and Jonathan, suspecting the painting is a fake, refuses to shake his hand when they are introduced ("I've heard of you," he remarks abruptly, implying that he is aware of Ripley's disreputable background). Insulted by the slight, and afraid Jonathan might expose him as a fraud, Ripley involves Jonathan in a new scheme after learning that Jonathan is dying of an unnamed blood disease for which there is no cure.

A shadowy criminal figure, Raoul Minot (Blain), decides to call in a favor and ask Ripley to rub out an American Mafioso. Ripley wants no part in murder, so instead of pulling the trigger himself, he "frames" Jonathan from behind the scenes into executing the deed. Once Ripley conspires with Minot to spread a rumor that Jonathan's illness has worsened, going so far as to falsify medical evidence, Jonathan is convinced he will die soon and agrees to act as their gunman under the condition that his wife and son are well compensated financially. The killing occurs in a Paris subway station and Jonathan gets away clean. Minot is so impressed that he wants Jonathan to commit a second, more dangerous assassination, this time on a train, which will be a "revenge" hit to blame the first murder on a rival mob led by a nameless American pornographer (Fuller).

Much like the close professional relationship between Jeff and Wes in *The Lusty Men*, Jonathan and Ripley form an unlikely bond. Jonathan is attracted to the spirit of American travel and adventure that Ripley embodies as a whistling cowboy, and Ripley ingratiates himself to Jonathan by joking that he is trying to bring the Beatles back to Hamburg (Jonathan sings "Drive My Car" to himself at one point). Drawn to Jonathan's domestic stability and craftwork, Ripley admires and even envies him. Forced to keep secrets from his family, Jonathan engenders suspicion and hostility from his wife Marianne, who fears his new "American friend" may have lead him into danger, but she also appears jealous over their intimate friendship.[20] Elsaesser reads the friendship between Jonathan and Ripley as one of "two kinds of Americas" represented in the film that structure the narrative. The "violent America" reflects America's colonization and economic hold over Europe, "that of crime, of exploitation, shady deals, power struggles, pornography, labyrinthine international conspiracies, a cold and hostile, cruel and aggressive America" ("Spectators" 249). By contrast, Jonathan and Ripley's friendship is interwoven with that paranoid environment to reflect American egalitarianism, "the world of equality, of exchange rather than exploitation" and of "partnership rather than rivalry and competition" (250). When Jonathan agrees to Minot's second assignment, Ripley steps in to save Jonathan and perform it himself. Confessing to setting up Jonathan for the first murder, Ripley refuses to accept the money and insists that Jonathan inform Minot he acted alone. "I would like to be your friend," Ripley tells him, "but friendship isn't possible."

Ripley is certainly a queer figure in Highsmith's novels, and while there seems to have been an effort to turn him into a more normatively masculine character in *The American Friend*, his relationship with both Derwatt and Jonathan has a serious homoerotic undercurrent. As much as there seems to be a love triangle involving Ripley, Jonathan, and Marianne, there also seems to be one involving Ripley, Jonathan, and Derwatt. Questioning his loyalty to Derwatt and feeling guilty over his manipulation of Jonathan to commit the first murder, Ripley trades cryptic comments with the old painter in one peculiar scene.

This dialogue smacks of the "feint-and-parry" encounters between Ray's heroes and heroines that Geoff Andrew highlights in *The Films of Nicholas Ray* (26), the "blend of duet and duel" (26) that characterizes the "courtship dialogue" (92) between Bowie and Keechie in *They Live by Night*, Johnny and Vienna in *Johnny Guitar*, and Jim and Judy in *Rebel*:

> DERWATT: What's wrong with you?
>
> RIPLEY: I'm confused.
>
> DERWATT: Don't try to be a nice guy.
>
> RIPLEY: I want to go home.
>
> DERWATT: Let me love you for your money.
>
> RIPLEY: I'm confused!
>
> DERWATT: Close the doors, they'll come in through the windows.

Ripley departs in frustration as Derwatt says to himself, quoting a line from *Knock on Any Door*, "A little older, a little more confused." One could read this scene as a lover's quarrel between two gay men (both are presented in the film as confirmed bachelors), but also a session between analyst (Derwatt) and analysand (Ripley). If we put even more pressure on the latter reading, the scene plays like a session between teacher (Ray) and student (Hopper), in light of Ray's various teaching appointments, as Ray coaches Hopper in a strange exercise in improvisational acting. Ray's last line is a clear reference to the many films he directed about "confused" young people.

The film never entirely sorts out its attitude toward the Derwatt character, who disappears roughly halfway through the film, and the confounding, almost darkly funny climax leaves us unsure over the details of how and why the plot has taken us there. Ripley and Jonathan hide out at Ripley's mansion as they prepare for a counterattack from Fuller's character, who arrives in a stolen ambulance carrying one of his female porn stars and a man wrapped in plaster bandages (played by Wenders), with Minot in tow and badly wounded. Ripley kills the Fuller character with a blow to the head that sends him down a flight of stairs, Minot kills the bandaged man inside the ambulance, and the porn star vanishes into the night.

As Ripley and Jonathan prepare to dispose of the dead bodies in the ambulance, Marianne pulls up in her car with the news that Jonathan's recent medical results, which Ripley and Minot had orchestrated, were faked. The three of them head to the sea shore, Marianne driving Jonathan in her car and Ripley driving the ambulance with the corpses. While Ripley sets fire to the ambulance, Marianne and Jonathan speed away. Jonathan dies behind the wheel of Marianne's car—ironically, just as he learns he may have longer to live. Sitting by the dock on the beach, Ripley begins to sing Bob Dylan's "I Pity the Poor Immigrant," but we only hear the first line of the song. The first stanza, as Dylan fans will remember, describes Ripley's condition of physical and psychological homesickness: "I pity the poor immigrant / Who wishes he would've stayed home / Who uses his power to do evil / But in the end is always left so alone / That man whom with his fingers cheats / And who lies with every breath / Who passionately hates his life / And likewise, fears his death."

But what do we do with Derwatt? Wenders gives "the poet of nightfall" the final shot of the film. He is standing on a bridge over the West Side Elevated Highway at dusk, smoking a cigarette, before walking away from the camera as the title wipes across the screen and the credits roll (in red, which, we know is an important color for Ray).[21] The Oedipal father has not been slain or replaced, and he seems to have access to knowledge that neither the characters nor the viewers can possess. Further, the haunting specter of Ray's authorship imbues Derwatt with the role of criminal mastermind or puppeteer, designing events from his artist's loft—an Americanized Dr. Mabuse, if you will.

In the end, Ripley and Jonathan fall under the sway of the Law of the Father, who restores the order they threaten to disrupt in the same way that Wenders's critique of America's patriarchal dominance is negotiated by the Law of the Author. American mass culture was the fodder for both a tradition and the rebellion from that tradition in Wenders's cinema: the establishment and a hip alternative to the establishment. Wenders owes a debt to the country that gave birth to his masters of cinema—Ray, Fuller, Ford, and so on—even if it has colonized cultural memory of the artist/author. *The American Friend* is in many ways an allegory of ambivalence.

Jim Jarmusch: From New York to the New World

There is a scene in Jarmusch's first feature film, *Permanent Vacation* (1980), in which the pompadoured protagonist Allie (Chris Parker) wanders into a New York City movie theater showing *The Savage Innocents*. After staring at the poster, he asks the cashier whether she thinks he will like the film. "The 'Quinn, the Eskimo' film?" she asks,[22] replying that all she can remember is the scene in which the Eskimo hunter Inuk and his wife Asiak offer a white missionary a bowl of meat covered in maggots. She also recalls the scene in which Asiak's mother instructs her to suffocate their newborn with snow, if it is a girl, or to lick it clean and rub it with blubber, if it is a boy, since the latter will grow up to provide for their family.

Sitting down in front of the poster, his awkward efforts to flirt with the cashier aborted by her blunt assessment of the film, Allie strikes up a conversation with another patron. The man tells him a long, grim joke about a 1950s jazz saxophonist, whose "sound was different, way out, too advanced," and whose refusal to conform to traditional musical styles made him unemployable. How can one not think of Ray as the poster for the first film he directed outside of Hollywood hangs in the background? Allie is a disaffected teenager from the East Village who, in his search for philosophical truth, adopts Nick Romano's saying in *Knock on Any Door*, "You know, sometimes I think I should just live fast and die young . . . and go in a three-piece white suit like Charlie Parker. Not bad, huh?" Jarmusch dedicated the film to Ray, who might have created a character like Allie, a stranger in a strange land: his own.

The working title for all of Jarmusch's films could have been the same as Ray's—*I'm a Stranger Here Myself*. Although Jarmusch is an American filmmaker, born in Akron, Ohio, his films are better received in Europe and East Asia (they also rely on European and Japanese funding), and he thinks of himself as an estranged American (Suárez 2). This scene from *Permanent Vacation* is the only direct reference he makes to Ray in his films (although Nick Romano could have given Jarmusch the name for ex-con Jack Romano in *Down by Law* [1986]). Also, it illustrates where viewers are likely to find the markers of Ray's influence on Jarmusch. Ray comes into focus in the background, on the edges, and under the surface of his films.

Like Godard and Wenders, Jarmusch is a cinephile, and while he was never a film critic (Godard wrote for *Cahiers du cinéma* and Wenders wrote for *Filmkritik*, respectively), he grew up on repertoire programs. Jarmusch benefited from Cleveland's rock-and-roll scene and DJ Alan Freed's radio shows, but he also frequented the art house in Akron as a youth. During his senior year of college at Columbia University,[23] he traveled to Paris for a semester, which turned into a ten-month stay. Here, he was exposed to Langlois's unorthodox programming at the Cinémathèque Française that could span different genres and historical periods of film within a single evening.

After discovering the films of Classical Hollywood auteurs in Paris, Jarmusch had the opportunity to study under one of them, Nicholas Ray, in film school. Jarmusch was in his third and final year of New York University's MFA film program when Ray was dividing his time as a teacher between NYU and the Lee Strasberg Institute. "Before I even met [Ray]," Jarmusch later said, "he was like a hero to me, for his films; and then meeting him and finding that his films were just one aspect of the way he thought about things . . . I almost feel I learned more just talking to him about anything, books, music or baseball, anything besides the specifics of directing" (qtd. in Eisenschitz 476). This statement is telling in that it points to the influence of Ray's "character," what he represented for a future generation as a rebel filmmaker more than his actual philosophies or methods of film directing.

Jarmusch was on the verge of leaving school, and Ray, having grown weak from cancer (and tired of teaching in the rigid environment of an academic institution), was allowed to work from home. The chair of the NYU Tisch School of the Arts graduate program, László Benedek, was friends with Ray and described his teaching as "absolutely brilliant," encouraging Jarmusch to work as Ray's new assistant (qtd. in Eisenschitz 476). Students who wanted to take classes with Ray were required to come to his loft once a week, and after his class whittled down from a handful of students to one, Jarmusch was the only student left. Ray invited Jarmusch to join the crew of *Lightning over Water*, which he was in the process of making. They became friends, and although Jarmusch did finally drop out of NYU, he continued studying with Ray independently.[24]

Prior to writing and directing *Permanent Vacation*, which he shot on 16 mm just days after Ray's death, Jarmusch made a few short films (one was shown at the Museum of Modern Art and another at a Times Square art show in a former massage parlor). But *Permanent Vacation* established the minimalist style, deliberate pace, and quirky humor by which his subsequent feature films came to be known. In his monograph *Jim Jarmusch*, to date the only book-length scholarly work on the director published in

English, Juan A. Suárez identifies "classical American cinema, European art film, and downtown experimental culture" as the three principle influences on Jarmusch's early career that made up his experiences studying under Ray, working on *Lightning*, and making *Permanent Vacation* (9). The improvisational, communal, and noncommercial approach to *Lightning* (shot on location with a small crew, minimal equipment, and a low budget) played a formative role in Jarmusch's own working methods, as did the combination of fiction and documentary (11). Conceptually, the film gave Jarmusch a perspective on "death, the fragility of existence, and the difficulty to make sense out of experience," which Suárez sees as recurring themes (10). Suárez adds that Ray's Hollywood films inform Jarmusch's themes of exile and displacement; the marginal, dispossessed characters of both Ray and Jarmusch are social outcasts deprived of a secure home or family (2, 10).

Outside of cinema, Jarmusch's influences range from Beat literature to punk, new wave, and hip-hop music, but he was most immediately affected by experimental trends in the medium. The 1950s and 1960s auteurist filmmaking of Classical Hollywood and international art cinema were as vital as to him as the avant-garde of 1970s and early 1980s New York City. Inflected toward pop aesthetics, this latter artistic practice repurposed found images from advertisements, self-consciously imitating the iconography of Hollywood stars and genres, performing in rock clubs, and incorporating new media technologies.

Jarmusch was also a vocalist and the keyboardist in a band called the Del Byzanteens, which released its sole album in 1982, *Lies to Live By*.[25] As both a filmmaker and a musician who got to know reputed independent filmmakers such as Amos Poe and Bette Gordon and who convened at the legendary Manhattan club CBGB's, Jarmusch had a hand in this alternative culture. He worked on the sound for Eric Mitchell's No Wave film *Underground U.S.A.* and contributed his voice to *Vortex*, a film by the punk group the Bs. This network of artists kept Jarmusch in good company for years. For example: Mitchell has a part in *Permanent Vacation*; Bill Rice, who acted in films by the Bs, appears in Jarmusch's *Coffee and Cigarrettes* (2004); and Tom DiCillo, who was the cinematographer on *Underground U.S.A.*, shot three of Jarmusch's feature films (including his breakout sensation *Stranger Than Paradise*).

What Jarmusch learned from Ray most of all was his individualistic and "anti-authoritative" line as a Hollywood filmmaker, which Jarmusch praised in an extended interview on the Oscilloscope Laboratories DVD and Blu-ray of *We Can't Go Home Again*. Jarmusch lauded Ray's "elegance of storytelling," his deep empathy for his characters to whom he must have related, and his direction of "raw" performances that felt like "exposed nerves." Once again, Ray is invoked in the name of a modernist project, "breaking through something that was kind of staid." Paying special attention to *In a Lonely Place*, Jarmusch credited Ray for instilling in him the advice not to move to Hollywood, and Jarmusch added that he has remained an independent filmmaker ever since his apprenticeship at NYU.

Ray also counseled him to envision filmmaking as an always changing process, comparing it to stringing beautiful beads. In other words, each scene should function as a stand-alone film as much as a part of a larger film, and the mistakes of the experience will teach the filmmaker more than the successes. This "at the moment" method of directing—to "be there and be open"—is most evident in Jarmusch's episodic ensemble films, which slowly unfold more in a series of loosely connected vignettes than a linear, causal narrative (*Mystery Train* [1989], *Night on Earth* [1991], and *Coffee and Cigarettes*). "He always just looked so cool, too," Jarmusch reflected wistfully.

Although Ray had only begun to work independently in the 1960s after leaving Hollywood, his desire for autonomy in the studio era and his widely publicized and promoted independent ventures on returning to the United States in 1969 enshrined him as an American Independent, an image that Jarmusch has helped to construct for himself since the 1980s. Not only does Jarmusch's relationship with Ray enhance Jarmusch's mystique as a rebel against the contemporary Hollywood system, but it also retroactively places Ray among the independent avant-garde artists in New York who launched Jarmusch in this direction. Jarmusch's cinema is in some ways the link between the so-called "Film School Generation" of New American Cinema (a period in Hollywood generally demarcated from 1967 to 1976) and the American Independent Cinema of the 1980s and 1990s.

Auteurs such as Francis Ford Coppola, Martin Scorsese, and Terrence Malick each graduated from film schools (UCLA, NYU, and the American Film Institute, respectively), introduced European art cinema techniques to the practice of Hollywood filmmaking, and revised the formulas of popular genres. As Joe McElhaney observes in his book *The Death of Classical Cinema*:

> Ironically, during this period of "the death of the author," film directors increasingly became celebrity figures in their own

> right, particularly in U.S. cinema when the so-called Film School Generation [. . .] began to emerge in the aftermath of the decline of the traditional studio system. Many of these young directors were formed by the cinephilia and auteurism of the previous two decades, their work (like that of the French New Wave earlier) filled with citations from the work of favored films and filmmakers of the past. (16)

Jarmusch has done self-conscious takes on the road movie (*Stranger Than Paradise*), the prison movie (*Down by Law*), the crime movie (*Ghost Dog: The Way of the Samurai* [1999], *The Limits of Control* [2009]), the Western (*Dead Man* [1995]), the family melodrama (*Broken Flowers* [2005]), and, more recently, the horror movie (*Only Lovers Left Alive* [2014]), preferring character actors over star types and undercutting generic conventions and expectations. Educated and familiar with old movies themselves, his presumed audiences are hip to his sense of irony and intertextuality.

In twenty-first-century media culture, the term *independent* does not have the industrial meaning it had for Jarmusch when he started his career. Suárez contends that "the 1980s independent cinema is a recent—perhaps terminal—chapter in the history of alternative filmmaking in the United States" (40). At the time Jarmusch came of age with contemporaries such as David Lynch, Spike Lee, John Waters, John Sayles, and Steven Soderbergh, the term suggested a mode of auteurist production outside of Hollywood that gave voice to minority artists and supported the kinds of experimentation prohibited by commercial filmmaking aimed at a mainstream audience. Suárez explains that independent cinema "quickly became assimilated, first by a new brand of unaligned operators and later by the major studios, and eventually became a cross-over phenomenon that attracted an art-house audience but also made significant runs into the mainstream." While it may continue to provide an alternative to the aesthetics of blockbuster filmmaking, many independent films today are still financed and distributed by major studios or their subsidiaries, and are branded as a genre or style unto themselves (40).

Stranger Than Paradise was Jarmusch's first film as a writer-director after *Permanent Vacation*. Jarmusch shot the first thirty minutes on the leftover film stock from Wenders's *The State of Things*, which he acquired from Gray City Films (Wenders's production company), and released it as a short. Gray City Films agreed to cover the lab costs in exchange for the negative and the rights. The film screened at the 1983 International Film Festival Rotterdam, where it won the first award from the Dutch Circle of Film Critics. After he was able to purchase the rights back from

Gray City, Jarmusch secured funding to complete the film as a feature and shot it in black-and-white for $100,000 (Prince 275).[26]

Told in a three-act structure (with segments titled "The New World," "One Year Later," and "Paradise"), the film is essentially sixty-seven long takes shot with a static camera, each separated by black leader. The deadpan performances and laconic dialogue, spare compositions, leisurely progression of the narrative, and atmosphere of the mundane achieve a stark and muted tone. Jazz musician John Lurie, the cofounder of the Lounge Lizzards, wrote the somber string quartet score.[27] Grossing $2.5 million at the box office (Prince 275), *Stranger Than Paradise* generated instant critical acclaim and became a massive hit for 1980s American Independent Cinema, sweeping the Special Jury Prize at the Sundance Film Festival, the Camera d'Or Award for best first feature at the Cannes Film Festival, and the Best Picture Award from the National Society of Film Critics. The film may be a testament to Jarmusch's influences (Ray and, more plainly, Wenders), but it also influenced a new class of American independent filmmakers.

Lurie also plays the aimless main character, Willie, a young Hungarian immigrant living in the Lower East Side, caught between his obligations to his family heritage and his desire to assimilate to urban America. Former Sonic Youth drummer Richard Edson, another player in the punk/new wave subculture of the New York Underground, who then was drumming for the band KONK, costars as Willie's good-natured friend Eddie. They both sport retro Trilby hats, which, like Michel's fedora, Ripley's Stetson, and, for that matter, James Dean's red jacket, are part of their uniform of the coolly self-styled American outsider. Traversing the vast, empty spaces behind the facade of the American Dream, Willie and Eddie drive from the gritty streets and shabby apartments of New York City, to the austere, postindustrial landscapes of Cleveland in winter, to the bleak white beaches of Florida (all along the nocturnal highways that Ray and Wenders have made familiar to us) (see fig. 4.5). Neither Willie nor Eddie holds a job to speak of, coasting on their winnings from fixed card games.

The third character in the film is Willie's cousin Eva, played by Eszter Balint, whom we meet in the process of moving from Budapest to Cleveland, where she will live with their Aunt Lotte. Presently a singer-songwriter and violinist, Balint was a member of the radical avant-garde troupe Squat Theater, which settled in New York City during the late 1970s after their performances got them expelled from Hungary. Living

Figure 4.5. *Stranger Than Paradise* (1984): Traversing the vast, empty spaces behind the facade of the American Dream, Willie (John Lurie) and Eddie (Richard Edson) drive from the gritty streets and shabby apartments of New York City, to the austere, postindustrial landscapes of Cleveland in winter, to the bleak white beaches of Florida (all along the nocturnal highways that Ray and Wenders have made familiar to us). (The Criterion Collection, 2007; digital frame enlargement)

and operating out of a storefront theater on West Twenty-Third Street, they staged performances both inside and outside of the theater walls, and engaged in impromptu theatrical events with passersby.

While the troupe toured Europe in the summer of 1979, they turned their theater into a music club, where Lurie's Lounge Lizzards and Jarmusch's Del Byzanteens performed along with other acts, and they later invited filmmakers (including Jarmusch) to curate film series. The theater finally served as a venue for independent films in the downtown circuit, exhibiting *Permanent Vacation* among others, and opened an upstairs café that screened retrospectives and music and video programs (Suárez 37–38). *Stranger Than Paradise* allowed Jarmusch to elaborate on what he began with *Permanent Vacation*, synthesizing his subcultural training in the New York avant-garde with both the Classical Hollywood mainstream and art cinema canon on which he was brought up as a cinephile and film student. Jarmusch channeled this aesthetic for a more midrange audience of popular moviegoers.

Eva stays with Willie at his apartment until Aunt Lotte is released from the hospital, and Willie, insisting she speak in English, introduces her to the pop culture of "The New World": Chesterfield cigarettes, American football, late night science fiction movies on television, and TV dinners of meat and potatoes ("Where does the meat come from?" she asks). Carrying around a cassette player, she constantly listens to the 1956 recording of "I Put a Spell on You" by Screamin' Jay Hawkins—one of the few products of American pop culture Willie does not appreciate—and quickly tires of Willie's drifter lifestyle and antisocial personality. However, Willie develops sincere affection for Eva, and misses her after she leaves for Cleveland.

A year later, Willie and Eddie decide to borrow a car and visit her at Aunt Lotte's home. Eva now works at a hot-dog joint and has become more Americanized (she takes in a Kung Fu movie with her New York compatriots at the local theater), but she also feels stifled under the roof of her old world aunt and is bored by her dead-end job. On a whim, Eddie and Willie take Eva on a road trip to Florida where they check into a cheap roadside motel. Although their destination is hardly the paradise they expected, Eva has warmed to Willie.

The first morning of their vacation, Willie and Eddie leave Eva at the motel and head to the dog track, but they return after losing most of their money. Willie snaps at Eva for her incredulity over the situation, and tries to recoup their losses with Eddie at the horse track. Meanwhile, Eva comes into some good fortune when she is mistaken for another woman and given a handful of cash by a stranger on the beach. Leaving a portion for Willie and Eddie with a note, she takes the money and buys a plane ticket to Budapest. When the guys come back to the motel and discover that Eva is gone, they race to the airport to talk her into staying. Jarmusch subverts the romantic comedy cliché as Willie buys a ticket to find Eva on the plane and then Eddie, waiting by the car, sees the plane take off. We assume, as Eddie does, that Willie is en route to Budapest with Eva. The last shot reveals Eva entering the motel, suggesting that Willie has flown to Hungary to accept his homeland, while she remains in the United States.

I would not dispute that Jarmusch's signature style is all his own, but his characters are kindred spirits to those we have seen in Ray's films, people who forge alternative (i.e., rebellious) communities in their quest for acceptance, either because they have rejected their home or, like Jeff McCloud in *The Lusty Men*, no longer have a home which to return. Jim Stark in *Rebel* creates a surrogate family with Judy and Plato as a substitute for his parents with whom he cannot communicate. Ed in *Bigger*

Than Life, a self-professed "male school marm" who moonlights as a taxi dispatcher and speaks with a mid-Atlantic accent, longs to be the all-American breadwinner for his suburban family *and* to be an extraordinary individual in a conformist society (desires exacerbated by his addiction to cortisone). The gypsy Stephano in *Hot Blood* wants nothing more than to pursue professional dancing as he tries to begin his life as an American, but his dying older brother hopes he will succeed him as the gypsy king of Los Angeles and marry the eligible daughter of another gypsy family.

Ray's outlaws, both the juvenile delinquents and the adults who transgress the conventions of a society (e.g., Vienna and Johnny in *Johnny Guitar*), often find themselves robbed of a home. Characters in Ray's films are lost in time, either one generation too early (e.g., Jim, who looks forward to the counterculture of the 1960s) or too late (e.g., Jeff, whose nineteenth-century frontier ideal has faded). Home is a contested space of personal and cultural negotiation in the films of Nicholas Ray, as they investigate what responsibilities one has to a home under these conditions of impermanence.

The themes I have just outlined are not necessarily exclusive to Ray. For example, the Beat writings of Jack Kerouac, most famously the novel *On the Road* (1957), could be interpreted as the last gasp of the populist modernism of New Deal era America. Characters journey across the back roads of the country in search of a more authentic experience of their native land, freed from the consumerist and corporatist standards of living among the bourgeois class of 1950s suburbia. Photographer Robert Frank undertook a series of road trips in which he documented America's rural, working-class, and ethnic subjects for his 1958 collection *The Americans* (some of his films were later shown at the Squat Theater, such as the 1959 Beat short *Pull My Daisy*). Frank picked up where photographer Walker Evans left off in the 1930s. Using low lighting and shadows, unbalanced and unfocused compositions, and haphazard cropping, these photographs portray the estrangement of an America that lies outside the purview of dominant culture.

Ray's cinema is not exactly the ur-text for Jarmusch's cinema. In Suárez's estimation, "One could argue that *Stranger than Paradise* updates the mixture of modernism and marginality that characterizes Frank's and Evans's aesthetic and filters it through minimalist and post-conceptual art" (37). Yet, Jarmusch reanimates Ray as an alternative artist through these other influences and aesthetic forefathers, casting him not only as an American auteur, but as an international art filmmaker, a jazz musician, a Beat writer, a postwar art photographer, and an honorary member of the New York Underground. "It can be said that Jarmusch revived the aesthetics of the 1950s to portray the 1980s," Suárez reasons, "except that the 1950s he revived were not those of consumer paradise, small-town homogeneity, and suburban bliss [. . .] but the 1950s of Beat writers and artists" (36). While not actually an independent filmmaker in Hollywood, Ray can share that same reputation with postwar directors such as Fuller (another one of Jarmusch's idols), whose independence is defined through historical-material conditions of the American film industry (i.e., working for independent companies and producers, and making "B-films" exhibitors craved to play on the bottom half of double bills).

As differently as Ray's legacy registers across the films of Godard, Wenders, and Jarmusch, Ray is consistently evoked as a director whose rebellion resonates with the modernist iterations of cool in midcentury American culture, from racial discourses about the "philosophical psychopath" and the invisible Other to the experimental work of fashionably outsider figures in jazz, literature, and the visual arts. This exclusive club of rebels was defined against certain artistic norms, but was still formed within normative cultural parameters of who is allowed to be cool (i.e., white men). An auteur who demonstrated a modernist potential in mass culture, Ray left Godard with the means to explore the relationship between modern and classical cinema, and his own place within that continuum. A symbolic father figure, Ray passed on to Wenders an American lexicon with which to rewrite a cultural history and critique that history. And as a New York "independent" and teacher of film, Ray modeled an anti-authoritative ideology of filmmaking that Jarmusch took with him through the downtown avant-garde and the industrial practice of independent cinema.

What all three examples demonstrate is the building of a reputation by association. As Ray influences perceptions of the modernism of these art cinema auteurs, they, in turn, instill Ray's films with ideas about modernism related to the French New Wave, New German Cinema, and American Independent Cinema. Ray's intertextual position at the nexus of these three directors facilitates a reading strategy by which their reputations as rebels themselves begin to take shape. Those individual reputations in the contexts of their respective film cultures have yet to be fully historicized and theorized beyond what I have begun here.

Conclusion

Rediscovering Nicholas Ray

> In the years close to his death, he burnt a lot of burnt bridges. I think enough time has passed, the damage has been forgotten, and people can appreciate more the prophetic strengths of the body of work.
>
> —Susan Ray on Nicholas Ray
> Quoted in Patricia Cohen,
> "Reclaiming Causes of a Filmmaking Rebel"

How I Came to Ray from the Back Roads

MY PERSONAL LOVE FOR THE FILMS of Nicholas Ray began not through the repertory theaters that introduced him to a previous generation of cinephiles, but through cable television long after his reputation was established. American Movie Classics first exposed me to *Rebel without a Cause* in high school. I saw *In a Lonely Place* on Turner Classic Movies during my first year of college when I declared a cinema major. Of course, these were appropriate times for a film about teenagers and a film about filmmaking to make an impression, but as *On Dangerous Ground*, *Johnny Guitar*, and *They Live by Night* followed in the onset of my graduate studies, I realized that Ray was a director whose films I was continuing to discover in breathless revelations. Indeed, his films were among those to which I would continue to return.

Figure C.1. *They Live by Night* (1947): My personal love for the films of Nicholas Ray began not through the repertory theaters that introduced him to a previous generation of cinephiles, but through cable television long after his reputation was built. (Warner Home Video, 2007; digital frame enlargement)

What kept attracting me to Ray was a cinephilia not far afield from the *Cahiers du cinéma* critics and their ideas about modernist film authorship. Ray has been one of the few commercial American directors I have encountered whose films envision a sense of being in the modern world that can only be made manifest by the inherent properties of the medium itself. We need look no further than his debut film, the achingly romantic *They Live by Night*, for one example. Night falls on our outlaw couple Bowie (Farley Granger) and Keechie (Cathy O'Donnell), who check into a roadside motel with the police in pursuit. Believing the only way to protect Keechie and their unborn child is for him to flee and send for them later, Bowie walks into a fatal trap—the motel proprietor, sister-in-law of one of his old gang members, has informed on him in exchange for her husband's release from prison. Keechie awakens in horror to the sound of gunfire and finds Bowie dead in front of their motel room with the police standing over his body.

A high-angled medium shot reveals O'Donnell prostrate beside Granger with her back to the camera as she picks up a crumpled piece of paper (Bowie's good-bye letter) and then turns to face the police (and the viewer). The découpage is striking in the way the angle and scale change with the next shot. Now in a straight-on close-up, O'Donnell kneels at eye level before the viewer, looking up at the police with doe-eyed fear and confusion as she begins to rise. Although the shot lasts a mere four seconds, its intimacy anchors our emotional identification with Keechie, who pleads with us in a private moment of interruption. Cut back to a high-angled medium shot as she stands and the camera tilts up. With her head pointed down and her eyes cast upward beneath her eyebrows, O'Donnell accomplishes a subtle transformation to reflect Keechie's contempt for the officialdom the police represent. We have learned that Bowie and Keechie may be "thieves" according to governmental definitions of the law, but that law-abiding society has failed to uphold the principles by which it ostensibly functions (wrongfully accused of a killing, Bowie's only intention of stealing was to use the money to hire a lawyer and clear his name).

Turning away from the police, her back to the camera once again, she attends to Bowie's letter and slowly walks toward the hotel. The Scottish folk ballad "I Know Where I'm Going," which has been a melody in Leigh Harline's score and the couple's leitmotif in the film, starts to make its final appearance on the soundtrack.[1] Almost in a whisper, she reads aloud to herself: "Little old girl, I'm gonna miss you, but I gotta do it this way. I'll send for both of you when I can, no matter how long it takes. I've gotta see that kid. He's lucky, he'll have you to keep him squared around." There is a bittersweet irony in the fragile optimism of Bowie's words that O'Donnell speaks over this music. The camera tracks in to follow her until she pauses at the door to her room. After reading his last lines, she turns and faces the police only to look off-screen at Bowie lying in the dirt. "I love you," she says quoting the letter and then reads Bowie's signature aloud. O'Donnell is lit by police floodlights in a luminous close-up against the blackness of the hotel room behind her. Eyes welling, head cocked, and continuing to gaze off-screen, she repeats his name under her breath and pouts mournfully. The lights gradually dim until she is left only in silhouette with a halo glowing around the edges of her hair before the film fades out.

They Live by Night moves me with its purity, its utopic imagining of love that the characters desperately, even obsessively seek. Bowie and Keechie know the possibilities are only fleeting, but the potential is real for them, lovers so earnest and uncompromised in their passion that they must live outside conventional bounds of society, home, the law, and time altogether. Why their love remains as real for me is because the elemental qualities of cinema—mise-en-scène, cintematography, editing, and sound—match such an elemental ideal in Ray's marriage of form and content. Form dictates content in his films, but it also *is* the content. I linger on my affective response to this haunting sequence of three shots to explain, auto-ethnographically, my investment in Ray and the pleasures I take from his films. The poetry of light and shadows, O'Donnell's expressive performance (especially in close-up), her system of looks to and from the camera, and the camera's deliberate movement with her are all part of the Classical Hollywood style from which Ray draws.

Ray has inspired some of the formative writing in contemporary film scholarship, and reading through his critical history one finds descriptions of similar relationships with his films. Jacques Rivette gets at some of my feelings about *They Live by Night* with his comments on Ray's "return to lyricism, powerful feelings, melodrama," comparing him to Griffith. I remember those closing images in the film as Rivette describes "the childlike clarity of his look, the provocative humility of his narratives," and by turns I also remember Rivette whenever I see them again on-screen. Rivette has therefore become a part of the way in which I experience Ray. Through my admiration for Ray as a director, the impetus for this book was to gain an understanding of how his films structured a larger social experience of Hollywood cinema within historical communities of modernist practices. Reading about Ray in many ways tells us the story of how the discipline of cinema studies developed as an institution, and how artistic labels such as "rebel" were defined and deployed across certain social-historical constellations. Biographical and auteurist studies by Bernard Eisenschitz, Geoff Andrew, and others have already contributed to our understanding of Ray's work in his own vision. In this book, which has been more about Ray's aesthetics in culture, my goal was to reach for a metacritical grasp on the ideologies of film authorship that his reputation exemplifies.

Rather than taking Ray's auteurism as a given, I wanted to travel backward from critics and other user groups to know *how* Ray became Hollywood's quintessential rebel auteur, how his marginalization in Hollywood actually made him a critical and scholarly subject. As Rick Altman proposes in his groundbreaking book *Film/Genre*, "genres do not exist until they become necessary to a lateral communication process, that is until they serve a constellated community" (161), which coheres in film reception through a shared taste and "a common orientation towards the genre" (162). Unlike genre studies, the area of director studies has only begun to investigate fully what a lateral approach authorship could yield.

Whereas a traditional, production-based paradigm of film authorship conceives of a "frontal communication" between director and spectator, I hope to have shown what a "lateral communication" among a director's constellated communities bears on the readings and meanings of films.

I have suggested that the interpretive and evaluative systems by which Ray earned a reputation operate through four fields of discourse, each representing a context of modernism that determined the aesthetic significations of his films. A project of auteurist film criticism among radical French cinephiles after World War II saw Ray as a populist producer of American culture, crediting his films with an autonomous, medium-specific style that challenged fascist, bourgeois taste politics. Ray's work with "the Method" and the innovative performances he elicited from his actors linked him to 1950s male stars such as James Dean, Robert Mitchum, and Humphrey Bogart, personifications of the rebel figure whom Ray himself would later be cast. The experimentations in the political avant-garde in which Ray participated as a teacher in the 1970s not only allowed him to efface his individual authorship through collaboration, but also paradoxically to promote his auteurist celebrity in the waning years of the counterculture. Finally, Ray was the source of nostalgia and American coolness in his influence on generations of hip, art cinema auteurs such as Jean-Luc Godard, Wim Wenders, and Jim Jarmusch, whose associations with Ray gave his films a rebellious afterlife. Each of these modernisms provided Ray with different public roles as the rebel artist/author, bringing him into focus as the central point of overlap among four distinct fields of possible meaning.

Preserving an Image

Since I began writing on Ray, the area of reputation studies has produced work on contemporary American film directors that demonstrate the ongoing vitality of the auteur as a subject in cinema studies. Antony Todd's book *Authorship and the Films of David Lynch: Aesthetic Receptions in Contemporary Hollywood* looks at the ways in which public opinions about aesthetics shaped the rise, fall, and reassembling of Lynch's reputation. In his book *Hollywood's New Yorker: The Making of Martin Scorsese*, Marc Raymond focuses on Scorsese's relationship with the social institutions that formed his reputation, such as his alma mater NYU (where he was also an instructor), the Hollywood studios in the 1970s, and the Museum of Modern Art, as well as his investment in film preservation. Rethinking authorship in collaborative terms, Mark Gallagher in his book *Another Steven Soderbergh Experience: Authorship and Contemporary Hollywood* situates Soderbergh in the multimedia production and distribution practices, textual and intertextual communication modes, and cultural and industrial developments of Hollywood and American cinema that constructed his reputation as the poster child for independent filmmaking since the late 1980s.[2]

By way of conclusion, in these remaining pages I sketch an avenue for further research—the *preservation* of a director's reputation—that looks at how an image is sustained through sponsors of a director's posthumous legacy. Once a director becomes canonized, how is his or her place in the film canon justified, secured, or perhaps even reconsidered for a new audience? To be sure, familiar words about Ray keep the romantic myth alive, such as David Thomson's statement in the *New Republic*: "There's no doubt that Ray embodied the idea that, in the mid and late twentieth century, the place to look for America's tragic heroes was among its filmmakers" ("Lonely"). Moreover, he attributed Ray's downfall to his "helpless, persistent compromise coupled with a sense of artistic ambition and integrity that was more than Ray could sustain for a day or two" ("Lonely"). Looking at recent career overviews and retrospectives, documentaries such as *I'm a Stranger Here Myself* and *Don't Expect Too Much*, and the efforts of Ray's widow Susan, who spearheaded the Nicholas Ray Centenary Project, another role for Ray has been established.

The romanticization of Ray's authorship has moved from the realm of modernism to academic citizenship, and what constitutes Ray's reputation in the new millennium is a progressive social consciousness and pedagogical engagement with cinema studies. Ray as rebel now teaches a kind of humanist or "responsible" rebellion, while the tragic, studio-era Ray, who fought with producers and executives, who indulged in drugs and alcohol, and who was celebrated for his high formalism in excess of classical realism, belongs more to the postclassical period of the 1970s.

Over the course of my preliminary research for this book, I realized that I was rediscovering Ray at the same moment that a wider rediscovery was taking place. In the summer of 2009, the New York Film Forum ran a Ray retrospective. Coinciding with the event, a group of critics (Evan Davis, Kevin Lee, David Cairns, Zach Campbell, and Daniel Kasman) published a Ray dossier titled "Homes for Strangers" on the popular website *MUBI*, which included articles on nearly all of Ray's films, along with a video essay on *The Lusty Men*. The following summer, the Harvard Film Archive curated a Ray series.[3]

Contemporary programs dedicated to Ray or screenings of his classic films were not an anomaly (for example, a notable retrospective played at the Museum of Modern Art in the spring of 2003[4]). What made this attention unique was that it signaled a centennial celebration culminating in the premiere of the reconstructed and digitally restored version of *We*

Can't Go Home Again at the Sixty-eighth annual Venice International Film Festival in 2011, which was promoted as the complete cut of the film to be shown with the "making of" documentary *Don't Expect Too Much*. At long last, the much-maligned film could be viewed with fresh eyes.

If Ray was regarded as a has-been in the 1970s, wasting his last years on a failed production, he is now recognized as an avant-garde prophet who was, once again, ahead of his time. Marco Müller, the director of the 2011 Venice festival, declared, "the sophistication and emotional power of Ray's multiple images have not yet been matched, even now that digital technology makes this technique immediately accessible" (Cohen). Having worked on the film from the beginning, Ray's widow Susan prepared it for the highly anticipated exhibition with the Academy Film Archive and the EYE Film Institute. Meanwhile, she sold Ray's collected papers to the Harry Ransom Center at the University of Texas–Austin: annotated original scripts, treatments, and drafts; storyboards; production photos and film stills; journals and notes; correspondences; artworks; photographs; interview transcriptions; video recordings; material for unfinished projects; address books; and personal effects.

Journalists responded to this rediscovery of Ray with overwhelming enthusiasm. Patricia Cohen in the *New York Times* trumpeted the *We Can't Go Home Again* premier, quoting Susan's prediction that the event will facilitate reappraisals of Ray's later work. Referring to his experimental techniques in the film, Cohen connects Ray to reality television and digital technologies of the present. With Susan's plans to sell his papers, Cohen highlights the "substantial collection of artifacts that had never, or rarely, been seen." Among the documents she surveys are fifty-three storyboards for *Rebel without a Cause* (each 8½-by-11 inches, complete with Ray's notes about dialogue changes and camera positions), which reveal an alternate ending in which Plato falls to his death from the roof of the Observatory after getting shot down by a police sharpshooter. Cohen also points to Ray's charcoal storyboards from *55 Days at Peking*, his annotated script for Kazan's *A Tree Grows in Brooklyn*, the costume designs and script he wrote with Norman Mailer for the aborted Rip Torn/Marilyn Chambers film *City Blues*, and material for his unrealized film about the Chicago Conspiracy Trial.

Writing for the *Boston Phoenix*, Chris Fujiwara reported on the Harvard Film Archive retrospective by musing how Ray's place in the canon (once the subject of derision) is no longer in question, thus rendering the defense of Ray a moot position. Fujiwara claimed, "the battle for Ray as a major artist has been won," adding that at this point Ray's films "speak for themselves; they need no mythologizing" ("Bigger"). The legend of Ray—"America's poet of outlaws, outsiders, and adolescents, a self-destructive artist ruined by alcohol, drugs, and being too good for Hollywood"—may convey a certain truth, but for Fujiwara, we still have a great deal to learn about Ray from the films themselves ("Bigger").

The *Chronicle of Higher Education* deemed the new archival holding at the Ransom Center so significant for cinema studies research and pedagogy that it featured a front-page article by senior editor Jean Tamarin on the acquisition, covering some of the same ground as this book. Ray was pictured with Dennis Hopper in 1971, while teaching in Binghamton, and with James Dean and Jane Russell, on the sets of *Rebel without a Cause* and *Hot Blood*, respectively. Under a headline that boldly read "Nicholas Ray, Auteur," the piece underscored his influence on Jarmusch, Wenders, and the *nouvelle vague*, as well as his post-Hollywood activities living in Europe and teaching in New York. In addition to linking to the inventory of the archive, the article closed with a series of Ray's quotes on acting.

From 2010 to 2015, ten feature films directed by Ray became available for the first time in the United States for home viewing on digital formats, and during the month of October in 2011, Turner Classic Movies aired all of Ray's films, including *We Can't Go Home Again*. Neglected titles were newly remastered and released through made-to-order services, such as *A Woman's Secret*, *Born to Be Bad*, *The Lusty Men*, and *Wind Across the Everglades* from the Warner Archive Collection, and *Hot Blood* and *Knock on Any Door* from Sony Pictures Home Entertainment. Despite the sudden accessibility of his films, independent distributors and boutique labels have branded Ray as an alternative director for niche audiences of film collectors (i.e., cinephiles and auteurists), and thus still something of a "stranger" to the mainstream cinema culture. The canonical *Bigger Than Life* was restored and issued on DVD and Blu-ray by the Criterion Collection, which is known for its "important classic and contemporary films" and director approved editions with superior technical quality and extensive supplements. Olive Films, which specializes in independent, foreign, documentary, and classic films, released two of Ray's Westerns on DVD and Blu-ray: the old favorite *Johnny Guitar* and the lesser-known *Run for Cover*. Oscilloscope Pictures, which distributes "unique, independently produced films," brought *We Can't Go Home Again* on a two-disc DVD and Blu-ray set with *Don't Expect Too Much*, Ray's short "The Janitor," and the rushes from his film *Marco* shot at the Lee Strasberg Institute. Previously available on DVD from Sony Pictures Home Entertainment, *In a Lonely Place* received an upgrade when the Criterion Collection released the 2K restoration on DVD and Blu-ray with several attractive supplements, including a slightly condensed version of *I'm a Stranger Here Myself*.

Ray's films also received renewed interest through the 2011 publications of the biographies *Nicholas Ray: The Glorious Failure of an American Director* by Patrick McGilligan and *Nicholas Ray: An American Journey* by Bernard Eisenschitz, a reprint of his authoritative book first published in English in 1993. My own anthology of new essays on Ray, *Lonely Places, Dangerous Ground*, which I co-edited with Steven Rybin, was published in 2014 by SUNY Press. Critics online have been the most active group of supporters since 2008, publishing appreciations that range from video essays, reevaluations of single films, and careerwide assessments.[5]

Whether drawn to Ray's films, his life, or (in most cases) both, revisiting Ray over the past six years also revisits the pedagogical discourses that gave him such a prominent standing in the 1970s (critical-academic writing on Ray coupled with his public persona as a teacher). The difference is that in the 1970s, Ray was taken up by scholars as a subject for academic film study and criticism when the field had just begun to establish its theoretical and methodological objectives within the institutional setting of higher education. In a response of sorts, he used his teaching career as a platform to promote his new image, an embodiment of the counterculture who spoke to the emerging practices of political modernism. As I hope to have illustrated in this book, Ray's canonicity was predicated on these varying moments of modernism and the sources of rebellion. However, as Fujiwara affirmed, "the battle for Ray as a major artist has been won," and therefore the mechanisms currently at work in Ray's reputation (the archive, retrospectives and restorations, new or reprinted writing, etc.) sustain rather than erect those ties to a cinema studies education. Instead of the antagonistic figure of Ray, burning his bridges with institutional authority in the film industry and the university system, we now have the figure of Ray as a model for what might be called "responsible" rebellion for students and filmmakers.

Teaching Rebellion

The precedent for this current strain in Ray's reputation came in 1975 with the rarely seen film *I'm a Stranger Here Myself*, directed by David Helpern and produced by James C. Gutman, an hour-long independent documentary made by Films Incorporated and distributed by October Films. Helpern and Gutman chronicle the rough-hewn production of *We Can't Go Home Again* at Harpur College. *Take One* contributor Jay Cocks, who went on to become a Hollywood screenwriter, called it an exercise in "ass kissing," a "grave, highly superficial homage" to Ray that characterizes him "as the still embattled, still vigorous rebel." "Watching him in the documentary," he opined, "it is clear that Ray is wasted now, has wasted himself, but the people who made this film [. . .], like the Harpur students, are getting off on Ray's own shabby glory." Although Ray's films met a fairer assessment from English-language critics in the 1970s, critics such as Cocks were less sympathetic to Ray himself. Cocks accused Ray of allowing the film industry to victimize him in the studio era, while exploiting sentimentality and nostalgia for Hollywood history (not to mention his personal flamboyance) in the interest of a contemporary appeal (17).

I'm a Stranger Here Myself premiered in January at the First Avenue Screening Room in New York City, where *We Can't Go Home Again* was shown in the fall of the previous year. Ray introduced the film, with his Harpur students in attendance, and was greeted with starry-eyed admiration from a young audience of devotees (Eisenschitz 453–54). Admittedly, the film's reverent tone inhibits opportunities for genuine critical insight, and the information presented about his career is not terribly new in the wake of the numerous articles on Ray published by 1975. The film succeeds most, as Cocks acknowledged, when it simply shows Ray and his students at work on their unorthodox film school project (and it is in those scenes where we see the image of Ray that has circulated since his centenary). Howard Da Silva, who costarred in *They Live by Night*, narrates the film with avuncular authority—his deep, nasal gruffness instantly brings his criminal character Chickamaw to mind—and the interview subjects include John Houseman, Tom Farrell, François Truffaut, and Natalie Wood. Interspersed throughout are clips from *They Live by Night*, *Rebel without a Cause*, *Johnny Guitar*, *In a Lonely Place*, and *55 Days at Peking*.

Following Da Silva's brief biographical outline, which covers Ray's apprenticeship under Frank Lloyd Wright, his service for the Federal Theatre Project, and his involvement in the Theatre of Action, the film proceeds through a series of "talking heads," confirming rather than questioning his reputation through repetition. Truffaut orients the documentary in the French auteurism dealt with in chapter 1, championing Ray's directorial "sensitivity" (evinced by the psychological and emotional "fragility" of his male characters). According to Truffaut, Ray's films brought a "European sensibility" and an uncommon degree of realism to sentimental Classical Hollywood fare, imbuing it with the feeling of a "true story" at a time when American cinema was rarely personal or autobiographical. Houseman reinforces Ray's biographical legend to which chapter 2 alluded, declaring that Ray's films are "about people whom society was opposing and whom society was crushing, and who were almost doomed to be defeated by society." "Nick himself is not altogether outside that category," Houseman continues, noting how Ray was so "vulnerable" he was "partly destroyed" by interference from Hollywood—and came to expect it. Farrell talks about his experiences making *We Can't Go Home Again* with Ray, indicating Ray's relevance for the counterculture, which chapter 3 detailed: "He's always wanted to be cherished by young people, and he scorns his own generation, which has rejected him, apparently."

The film also spends a good deal of time with Ray, who, employing the documentary mode as a self-promotional tool in the 1970s, touches on his commitment to Method acting and improvisation, his relationship with James Dean, his recent efforts to make a film about the Chicago Conspiracy Trial, and his incredulity over his auteurist status with critics (insisting that a director shouldn't "moralize" or "consciously put their neurosis onscreen"). Ray expounds on the medium, an apparent overture to the cult of cinephiles for whom the film was intended, asserting that cinema is the "most communicative art in the world" and one of "only two great ambassadors we've ever had from the United States" (the other, he said, was jazz). We hear about Ray's disappointments and compromises as a director who was forced to relinquish control of his Hollywood films in the editing stage, and who abandoned film after film in the 1960s as a result of "personal problems" and "failing health." Nevertheless, *I'm a Stranger Here Myself* sees Ray as a hero, whose intransigence and optimism were validated by his mentorship to his students in spite of his uncertain future.

Ray may not have been welcomed back by Hollywood, and he never lived to see *We Can't Go Home Again* as he intended it, but his centenary retrospectives have illuminated this "failure" as a glorious one (to quote the subtitle of McGilligan's biography). Instead of viewing Ray as a victim of the industry, the apparatus of fan-critical rhetoric has rewritten Ray's final years as a testament to his honor and courage. The resurrection of *We Can't Go Home Again* puts it this way: Ray survived the dark days of Hollywood to continue making movies as an auteur, and did so by teaching students how to make films outside the confines of the industry, free from the creative restrictions of commercial filmmaking.

Preserving Ray's reputation, in addition to his films and archival material, has been the primary goal of the nonprofit organization The Nicholas Ray Foundation. The website for the foundation, which is currently in development at http://nicholasrayfoundation.org, proclaims its mission clearly: "Dedicated to honoring the pioneering spirit of Nicholas Ray by preserving and restoring his films and archives, and by facilitating innovation and experimentation in contemporary movie making." On the Board of Directors sits President Susan Ray, Vice President Timothy Ray (Nicholas Ray's son from his marriage to Gloria Grahame), and Secretary

Myron Meisel (the associate producer of *I'm a Stranger Here Myself*). The Board of Advisors includes Geoff Andrew, Bernard Eisenschitz, Jonathan Rosenbaum, and Jim Jarmusch. Susan, who is also the foundation's creative director, envisioned *We Can't Go Home Again* as the first of three films in its Nicholas Ray Centenary Project.

The second film was the full-length documentary *Don't Expect Too Much*, which Susan wrote, directed, produced, and narrates. A heartfelt love letter to Ray, the film imagines him as a representative of freedom, rebellion, and possibility during the early 1970s, marking the end of the era of "heroic bohemianism." Ray was in this way a transitional figure between the leftist political activism of the 1960s, and the politically conservative "me generation" of the 1980s. "Nick rejected authority of every kind," Susan comments sagaciously in the voice-over, "whether as a person, protocol, belief, or boundary. Authority meant limitation, which to Nick was a kind of death. He truly believed we each and all have the infinite within us, and he was determined to touch it." The film emphasizes how Ray worked by instinct and intuition, not hard-lined theories or methods, but it does reflect his driving philosophy that the camera should be deployed as an instrument for the actor, allowing the director to record the range of human emotion. Conflating Ray's role of director with his role of teacher, the film implies that his appointment at Harpur College lifts the veil off his career-long ambition to access the infinite that we "each and all" possess.

The three main actors in *We Can't Go Home Again*—Tom Farrell, Richard Bock, and Leslie Levinson—each share their thoughts, as do a parade of Ray's student crewmembers: Phil Weisman, Steve Anker, Peer Bode, Ken Ross, Helene Kaplan White, Pam Maurer Araujo, Doug Cohen, Charles Bornstein, David Mare, Jane Heymann, and Danny Fisher. Ray's most famous former student, Jim Jarmusch, talks about his training under Ray at NYU. Other interview subjects include Bernard Eisenschitz, actor Gerry Bamman (Ray's teaching associate at the Lee Strasberg Institute), editor and sound designer Walter Murch (who worked at Zoetrope Studios, where Ray temporarily edited *Home*), and Spanish director Victor Erice (who, with Jos Oliver, cowrote the book *Nicholas Ray y su tiempo*). *Don't Expect Too Much* does not shy away from Ray's addictions and temperament that plagued him in the 1970s, or the funding problems of *We Can't Go Home Again* and its baffled reception at the Cannes International Film Festival in 1973. Still, it obviously respects Ray's passion and dedication for the project, both when it was going well and when it was not. Borrowing Ray's advice to Farrell in *Home* ("don't expect too much from a teacher"), in the end the film speculates whether

Ray's audience in the 1970s may have expected too much from him, and that the film is ultimately misunderstood.

At the beginning of *Don't Expect Too Much*, Ray quotes Abbie Hoffman's instruction to a group of art students: "What is art? Fuck art! Art is what you're doing. What is politics? Politics is living." This sentiment is indirectly absorbed in the forthcoming third film of the Nicholas Ray Centenary Project, *ACTION! Master Class with Nicholas Ray*, which, according to the Nicholas Ray Foundation website, is a full-length documentary that will serve as a "teaching tool in both undergraduate and graduate film classes around the world." Susan, who is directing the film, financed the project through a Kickstarter campaign. The foundation explains that the documentary material will follow the course of Ray's life, "which touched on every major cultural and political development in the United States in his lifetime," and will thus not only render "a portrait of this country at one of its most culturally fertile times," but "a portrait of the artist as committed humanist."

Cut from over 90,000 feet of film and video from the Ray archive at the Harry Ransom Center, 300 hours of audio recordings, and clips from Ray's films, the documentary will be available for students to stream online. Accompanied by American folk and jazz music, the material will include: behind-the-scenes information about the making of Ray's films; audio of Ray's public talks and his classes at NYU and the Lee Strasberg Institute; private journal entries and oral autobiography; and interviews with members of Theatre of Action and ethnomusicologist Alan Lomax. The thesis of the film comes out of Ray's rebellious personal credo that he adopted as the basis for his pedagogy: "An action in life is not so different from an action onstage or on a film set. Acting is living and living is acting."

In contemporary Hollywood, the image of the American rebel is, paradoxically, hardly unconventional among directors who have achieved a reputation in the public. Quentin Tarantino trades on a roguish celebrity in his films' liberal uses of violence and profanity, and his penchant for trash aesthetics of "low culture" and "bad taste" (one need only think of the way he choreographed an ear-severing to the Stealers Wheel song "Stuck in the Middle with You" in his 1992 indie hit *Reservoir Dogs*). Both for his films' mysterious promotional strategies, and for their unusual storytelling forms, Christopher Nolan has earned a name as a quasi-nonconformist (playing with reverse chronology *Memento* [2000], fragmented, nonlinear narrative in the *The Prestige* [2006], and illusionist dreamworlds in *Inception* [2010]). Admired for tackling a patriarchal industry, often by subverting masculine genres and archetypes, Kathryn

Bigelow has been praised as a feminist maverick unafraid of controversial subjects (as in the hunt for Osama bin Laden after September 11 in *Zero Dark Thirty* [2012]). Even cross-over international auteurs such as Lars von Trier and Nicolas Winding Refn have attained notoriety for their personas as politically incorrect provocateurs, whose films seek to shock and offend while at the same time make claims to artistic integrity.

All of these examples are measured by different standards of rebellion that are contingent on different historical forces, but the image of the rebel is more or less fundamental to today's public image of the narrative film auteur as a commercial figure. As one particular case of directorial rebellion, Ray shows us how we can map the routes by which those reputations culturally circulate. The "real" or "complete" author may be unknowable as a coherent subject. Moving through the discursive pathways of modernism, however, Ray's films became symptomatic of the ideological meanings that his evolving reputation as a rebel opened to his directorial aesthetics. Film directors may be taken for granted or dismissed as too elusive a presence for which to fully account, but, as we have seen with Ray from the 1950s to the 1980s and beyond, they often give a dynamic life to their films well past the momentary instance of creation behind the camera.

Notes

Introduction

1. As Ray's films receive copious citation throughout, I have made the choice not to cite release years inside the chapters, but instead to provide a full chronological filmography at the end of the book.

2. One of my referees informed me that part of the film was also shot on location in the Arctic, but most of this footage was lost in a plane crash.

3. In the introductions to their anthology, *Authorship and Film*, David A. Gerstner and Janet Staiger make a similar case for the analysis of film authorship. For Gerstner, the emergence of cultural studies in academia gave the position of the film author a new force as "the interface of race, class, and gender with the production of art took on a particular urgency" (6). Cautioning cinema studies not to silence the voices of feminists, gay and lesbian activists, and antiracists, Staiger insists, "Authorship discourse may have positive political effectivity," and "forgetting authorship and individuals takes away a historical necessary for social activism and utopic imaginings" (28).

4. See also Bennett, "Texts."

5. See Corrigan, "Commerce."

6. Ray borrowed the phrase from Ogden Nash's 1938 book of verses and later gave it to Sterling Hayden in *Johnny Guitar*. Nash was the lyricist for the 1943 Broadway musical *One Touch of Venus*, composed by Kurt Weill with a libretto by S. J. Perelman, which featured a number titled "I'm a Stranger Here Myself." Ray has said that "I'm a stranger here myself" was "the working title of nearly every poem, play, short story, any screenplay I've ever written" (McGilligan 472). The falsity of Ray's statement is beside the point; it is part of the persona he created for himself.

Chapter 1

1. Albert Camus's *The Rebel*, which was published in English for the first time in 1954, also made Ray amenable to taking Robert M. Lindner's book title

for his film of the same name, *Rebel without a Cause*, per the studio's demands (Eisenschitz 233).

2. See also Hansen.

3. See Rivette, "On Imagination."

4. Ray worked as Losey's stage manager again for a Franklin Delano Roosevelt memorial at the Hollywood Bowl and for the 1946 Academy Awards.

5. For more on Ray's federal service, see Deutsch and Shaw, and Wollen "Never."

6. Ray's first film, *They Live by Night*, was completed for RKO in 1947, but it was shelved when Howard Hughes took over the studio in 1948. After quarrels between Schary and Hughes, Schary left and the film was released in Britain later that year. However, it did not receive its American theatrical premiere until Hughes released it with other backlogged productions in 1949, *after* Columbia Pictures distributed *Knock on Any Door*, which Ray had directed for Humphrey Bogart's independent company Santana Productions (see Gomery). *They Live by Night* was originally titled *I'm a Stranger Here Myself* in a version of Ray's treatment and then became *Your Red Wagon* (the title of the song performed by Marie Bryant in the nightclub and a New Orleans expression meaning "it's your business"). Schary retitled it *The Twisted Road* before an audience research poll finally settled on *They Live by Night* (Eisenschitz 91, 95, 103).

7. See also Cagle for a discussion of the relationship between realist form and popularized social science in *Knock on Any Door*.

8. Budd Schulberg wrote *Everglades* and also produced the film with his brother Stuart. Upon dismissing Ray two weeks before shooting ended, he eventually took over as director. For more on the film's disastrous production conditions, see Eisenschitz 316–38 and McGilligan 365–73.

9. The Paramount Case of 1948 ruled Hollywood's system of vertical integration a monopoly, requiring the studios to sell off their theater chains and operations and sever their financial connections. In addition to the loss of their distribution and exhibition arms, the studios met competition with television and the development of privatized leisure entertainments, while facing a rise in production and operation costs throughout the postwar era.

10. See Borde and Chaumeton, in addition to Chabrol, for elaborations on this definition of American film noir by French critics in the 1950s.

11. For more on Ray's use of widescreen, see Cossar.

12. In this way, the modernist film criticism of *Cahiers du cinéma* is similar to Walter Benjamin's Marxist critiques of media written in Weimar Germany. Benjamin viewed all mechanically reproduced art since 1900 is a potential tool of revolution. According to his most well-known essay, the mass production of art vanquishes the "aura" of the authentic original and signals the rise of a political body, as opposed to an elite few, who ascribe to the authority of an artistic genius. See Benjamin.

13. Donoghue, who coached Brando during the shooting of *On the Waterfront*, had expressed interest in casting James Dean for a boxing film he cowrote with Budd Schulberg. Intrigued by the project, Ray recruited Donoghue as his assistant and consultant on *Rebel*, which gave Donoghue an opportunity to work with Dean (Eisenschitz 257).

14. Captivated by Elvis Presley, who had just made his acting debut in the Fox Western *Love Me Tender* (1956), Ray wanted the twenty-two-year-old rock-and-roll star to play Jesse, seeing him as another James Dean. However, Presley was under contract with independent producer Hal B. Wallis, and Paramount distributed Wallis's Elvis movies (Eisenschitz 283–84). Although Presley's next film was to be *Loving You* (1957), he modeled himself after James Dean, his favorite actor, and had memorized Dean's lines from *Rebel without a Cause*. On meeting him, Ray recounted, Presley dropped to his knees and recited whole pages of script (Guralnick 119). See also Johnson for more on the relationship between 1950s rock-and-roll and male performances in Ray's films.

15. Christopher Anderson argues that the film is "not primarily concerned with the material events in the life of Jesse James," but more about "the process of telling James stories and about the transformation of James into a cultural figure" (43). Crediting Nunnally Johnson's screenplay for the original 1939 film as its basis, and not the actual historical material, ironizes its claims to the "true story" of Jesse James.

16. Ever devoted to the Method, Ray's first choices for the part of Leith were Montgomery Clift and Paul Newman, and he wanted Burton instead to play Brand (Eisenschitz 294–95).

17. See Pomerance, "1957" for an analysis of the ways in which the film's moral-ethical conflict is played out in distinctly CinemaScope proportions (191–95).

18. Trucolor was a three-strip process owned and developed by Consolidated Film Industries (a division of Republic), but was rendered obsolete by the cheaper and less cumbersome Eastman Kodak "monopcak" process at the end of the 1950s (the same time at which the studio happened to go under). After working with Technicolor on *Flying Leathernecks*, *Run for Cover*, and *Hot Blood*, Ray shot most of his films from the mid- to late 1950s in Eastmancolor, which was credited as one of the studio's Eastmancolor brand names: Warnercolor (*Rebel without a Cause* at Warner Bros.), Deluxe color (*Bigger Than Life* and *The True Story of Jesse James* at Fox), and Metrocolor (*Party Girl* at MGM). For more on Ray's use of color, see Williams.

19. Among the other left-wing stars who worked with Ray were Humphrey Bogart, Robert Ryan, James Cagney, and Lee J. Cobb.

20. See Scheibel.

21. Faulkner also hailed the film as a masterpiece, supposedly declaring, "*Rebel Without a Cause* will remain a masterpiece, because it is the American cinema's only Greek tragedy" (qtd. in Rathgeb 7).

22. Peter Wollen submits that Wright's influence on Ray is less evident in his mise-en-scène than in his internalization of Wright's "patriarchal image [. . .] as tempestuous sage" (*Paris* 209). The home functions less in terms of its architecture, Wollen argues, than its symbolic meaning as a common theme in Ray's films (*Paris* 209–10).

23. Sarris was actually less instrumental in introducing Ray to an English-speaking audience than the critics at both of these publications. Writing for *Film Culture* in 1963, he opined, "Nicholas Ray is not the greatest director who ever lived, nor is he a Hollywood hack. The Truth lies somewhere in between. [. . .] Ray does not represent the triumph of form over

content. His form is not that impeccable, and his content has generally involved considerable social issues" ("Ray" 15–16). Later in *The American Cinema*, Sarris categorized Ray below his crop of "Pantheon Directors" in "The Far Side of Paradise."

24. *Rebel* also received positive notices from critics Eugene Archer and Ray's soon-to-be collaborator Gavin Lambert, both of whom published on the film in the highbrow periodicals *Film Culture* and *Twentieth Century* in 1956, respectively. Archer credited its success to James Dean, not Ray (18). Lambert, who had already been a proponent of *They Live by Night* in journal *Sequence*, was more glowing, and appreciated the film's approach to the "question of human beings and their relation to society" ("Rebels" 275).

25. Director Lindsay Anderson overtly took Ray and his contemporaries to task in *Sight and Sound*, chiding them for preferring "lavishness and hack-show biz formulae" to "sincere expression or the stimulus of controversy" ("Ten" 35).

26. See Perkins, "Must," for more on "questions of artistic method, structure and effect" (2) posed in *Movie*, which he distinguishes from both traditional auteurism and David Bordwell's cognitivist and neoformalist analysis.

27. Godard has also stated this idea in a less cheeky manner: "To me, style is just the outside of content, and content the inside of style, like the outside and inside of the human body—both go together, they can't be separated" (qtd. in Roud, *Godard* 13).

28. For example, Richard L. Coe of the *Washington Post* harshly criticized the film for sensationalizing the subject of juvenile delinquency ("Delinquency?" 21), while Philip K. Scheuer of the *Los Angeles Times* admired the sensitivity with which it addressed themes of innocence and belonging ("James" B12). Mae Tinee, the pseudonymous reviewer of the *Chicago Tribune*, described moments of the film as "overdone," but also admitted that it has a cumulative dramatic impact ("James" B5).

29. See, for example: Crowther, "Sheriff"; Crowther, "*Guitar*"; Crowther, "Tax"; Crowther, "*Everglades*"; Crowther, "*Ground*"; and Crowther, "*King*."

30. See Taylor for a complete history of Farber and Tyler's film criticism.

31. See Biskind, "Rebel" and Biskind, "*They*" for exceptions to this critical consensus in the 1970s. In both articles, Biskind make a case for a conservative ideology in Ray's films.

32. Ray was also covered in key books on film published during the 1970s and early 1980s, such as Colin McArthur's *Underworld U.S.A.* (1972), Thomson's *Biographical Dictionary of Cinema* (1975, eventually updated, expanded, and retitled *The New Biographical Dictionary of Film*), and Thomas Schatz's *Hollywood Genres* (1981).

33. More recently, academic film scholars have also expanded this interpretation with exegeses on its "dialogue between containment and excess" (Charney 25), its "representations of gender" (Peterson 4), and its mode of "feminist camp" (Robertson 33). The documentary *The Celluloid Closet* also implies a coded lesbian subtext in Vienna and Emma's relationship.

Chapter 2

1. When asked whether Mitchum hated the Method, Ray said, "he doesn't know what he's hating." "But without knowing it," Ray continued, "just by using different terms than 'improvisation,' terms like 'we'll ad-lib this one, or 'we'll play around with it and see what comes,' or whatever, you're using the same technique, without using the language" (Krohn, "Class" 260).

2. "No one ever gives a bad performance in a Ray film," declared Robin Wood (qtd. in Rosenbaum, "Guilty" 50), and even Ray's actors who were not in fact stars deserve a separate study unto themselves. Apropos of the actors who did not enjoy the same celebrity as Dean or Bogart, Jonathan Rosenbaum insisted, "Ray's most remarkable work with relatively unskilled or inexpressive players is among the steadiest pleasures to be found in his canon" (50). Experimental filmmaker Larry Gottheim, Ray's colleague at Harper College, reflected that "Nick's genius was his ability to drive potentially gifted actors into performances that pushed them into states that transcended their previous limits." Gottheim added, "This involved a relationship with the actors outside the actual filming, driving them to extremes that would lead to great performances" (94).

3. See, for example, *Life* magazine's 1949 profile of Jackson Pollock, which asks, "Is he the greatest living painter in the United States?" (42).

4. Sloan Wilson's novel *The Man in the Gray Flannel Suit* (1955) and William H. Whyte's nonfiction book *The Organization Man* (1956) named these male social symbols in the 1950s.

5. J. David Slocum's collection of essays for the film's fiftieth anniversary contains some of the finest scholarship to date on *Rebel*, to which my own reading is indebted. In particular, see: Broderick; Pomerance, "Stark"; Lewis; Mitchell; White; and Wilson.

6. For more on Dean in *Rebel*, see: Pomerance, "James"; Medovoi; and McCann.

7. Ray's original treatment made this theme explicit in the opening sequence, which was never shot, as the all-American suburb regresses to a primordial state of chaos and savagery. Three vignettes involving teenage delinquents set a nightmarish tone for what was intended to be a straightforward social problem melodrama from Warner Bros.: a man lit on fire runs toward the camera, a gang whips a teenage girl stripped to the waist, and two hot rods drive into a head-on collision (Frascella and Weisel 11, Rathgeb 16). This opening would have been more of a piece with Luis Buñuel than Hollywood melodramas of the 1950s, and Ray greatly admired both the surrealist filmmaker and his *Los Olvidados* (1950), which focused on a young Mexico City street gang. The success of *Rebel* with youth audiences, especially on the heels of popular juvenile delinquency films such as *The Wild One* (1953) and *Blackboard Jungle* (1955), led to studios producing and marketing films for a new teenage demographic, signaling the juvenile delinquency exploitation cycle of the 1950s, wherein this sort of violent, sexualized imagery was commonplace.

8. The film's stereotypical portrayal of Jim's mother and grandmother as castrating women of the 1950s echoed what sociologist Philip Wylie called "momism" in his misogynistic critique of the cult of American motherhood, *Generation of Vipers*, first published in 1942 and reprinted in 1955.

9. In *Hollywood Babylon II*, the sequel to his fabular *exposé* of star scandals, underground experimental filmmaker Kenneth Anger told the story that Ray "dragged Dean off to a Burbank drugstore" to treat a case of crabs (135). Anger's imagery here could have come directly from one of his own homoerotic films, portraying Dean's penchant for drugs, leather bars, anonymous sex, and S&M (Dean allegedly begged his masters to extinguish cigarette butts on his bare chest when he was stoned) (135).

10. The matter of intentionality on this subject is open to debate. Stern denied Plato's latent homosexuality and thought Plato's feelings for Jim should be less clearly defined (Frascella and Weisel 173). Despite Stern's stated intentions and no mention of a homosexual relationship in his script, studio censor Geoffrey Shurlock wrote a memo to Warner Bros. cautioning, "It is of course vital that there be no inference of a questionable or homosexual relationship between Plato and Jim" (qtd. in Frascella and Weisel 172), as the Production Code prohibited the subject of homosexuality in Hollywood movies during the 1950s.

11. Gavin Lambert discloses his relationship with Ray in his 2000 book *Mainly about Lindsay Anderson*. The two men met in England when Ray was promoting Rebel and Lambert was working as a critic. In his biography of Wood, he also mentions living with Ray in his Chateau Marmont bungalow, while working as his assistant and script collaborator, when he first met Wood in the fall of 1956: "'I was wondering exactly what was going on with you and Nick Ray,' Natalie said. 'What was going on,' I said, 'was exactly what you wondered'" (221). See also Doty for a discussion of the ways in which Ray queered the Classical Hollywood style in *A Woman's Secret* and *Born to Be Bad*.

12. The biography authorized by the James Dean Estate, written by George Perry, attempted to "straighten" his image by asserting, "The belief that he was a homosexual is a persistent myth. The truth is that he was a great experimenter, and that he avidly and almost greedily soaked up all the experiences that life could offer" (216). Dean's longtime biker friend John Gilmore, best known for his true crime and hard-boiled literature, detailed in his memoirs their "experimentations" with gay sex. Television writer and Dean's former roommate William Bast described their own sexual relationship, in addition to Dean's involvement with other men in show business, such as radio producer and television director Rogers Brackett, who helped his career. Biographer Donald Spoto commented, "Dean's conduct throughout his short life indicates that he was not entirely heterosexual, as even his girlfriends confirmed" (81). Elaborating on Dean's transgressive sexual practices, he went on to write, "Jimmy became known as something of a dabbler in the varieties of sexual experience; even in the repressed 1950s, it seemed, sex could have a political subtext" (134).

13. See DeAngelis and Hankin for examinations of Dean's homosexual star text from the perspective of gay and lesbian fandom, respectively. Dean's

performance in *Rebel* has also inspired queer readings from canonical works of LGBT studies, such as Parker Tyler's 1972 book *Screening the Sexes* and the 1995 documentary *The Celluloid Closet*.

14. How far Ray wanted to take these implications is unclear. In a four-page memo, studio executive Steve Trilling curiously wrote, "Jim kisses Plato?" Trilling advised that Jim instead stroke Plato's head when he takes him home after Buzz's death (qtd. in Frascella and Weisel 171–75). Considering how Stern's script does not refer to this kiss, it is possible that Ray was the one who made this suggestion about their mutual attraction.

15. As Richard Barrios makes clear in his book *Screened Out*, Plato was not the first implicitly homosexual character in a Ray film. Barrios cites the gay portrait artist Gobby Broome in *Born to Be Bad* (205), the lesbian masseuse Martha in *In a Lonely Place*, the "sinewy rodeo rider" Rosemary Maddox in *The Lusty Men*, and the "butch vs. butch sight" of the antagonistic female characters in *Johnny Guitar* (223).

16. *Look* magazine opined, "The teen-ager who appears to conform, yet rebels successfully against conformity and gets away with it—that fellow is a hero. James Dean not only got away with it, he got so rich in the process that he was his own boss" (Scullion 122). The *Saturday Review* attributed Dean's popularity to the maternal feelings and sympathy he aroused from hundreds of thousands of teenagers. "Perhaps they saw mirrored in him their own problems," the author speculated, "and perhaps, also, Dean provided a symbolic channel for their own pressures of conformity, lacks of love and feeling" (Alpert 29). A rather conservative article in the *Reporter* mourned less over Dean's loss than the loss of more adult, traditionally masculine film heroes. The author insisted that Dean's acting abilities were "concerned only with an image of constructed surface mannerisms," and that the rebellion of his characters stemmed from "father failure" (Weales 41). "The image is not that of an adult hero to be emulated," he continued, "but an extension of all the confusion of adolescence, the concretizing of immaturity until it becomes a swagger, a boast, a sudden explosion" (Weales 41).

17. Pomerance extends some of these ideas elsewhere with a close reading of the scene in which Jim and Judy meet on their way to school. With Judy's rhetorical question, "Who lives?," Ray collapses the boundaries between Wood's performance and the composition of the shot to maximize the viewer's affective relationship with Judy in this moment (see "Who").

18. According to Wood, "Very often, he would kind of take over and almost say fuck off to Nick Ray," while Backus called him "practically a co-director" (qtd. in McGilligan 302). Hopper went as far as to say that "James Dean directed *Rebel without a Cause*, from blocking all the scenes, setting the camera, starting the scene and saying 'cut.' Nicholas Ray intelligently allowed him to do this" (qtd. in McGilligan 302).

19. The film's title changed to *Rough Company* and *This Man Is Mine* (McGilligan 217–18) before studio head Howard Hughes named it *The Lusty Men* prior to the film's release (227).

20. McCoy had garnered a reputation for his hard-boiled novels *They Shoot Horses, Don't They?* (1935) and *Kiss Tomorrow Goodbye* (1948). During the

shooting, the script underwent additional rewrites by Andrew Solt, Alfred Hayes, and Norman Krasna, although none of them were credited (McGilligan 222).

21. RKO assigned Ray to direct additional scenes for John Cromwell's *The Racket* (1951) and Josef von Sternberg's *Macao* (1952). Mitchum, who starred in both films, attested that Ray allowed him to write some of his own scenes in *Macao* ("TCM *Private Screenings*"), and Ray claimed to have shot 50 percent of the film (Goodwin and Wise 12).

22. See also McElhaney, "Nicholas" for more on Ray and gesture, as well as Rybin, "Nicholas" for more on *The Lusty Men* and cinephilia.

23. See also Campbell for more on *The Lusty Men* and the Western.

24. See Telotte for a comparative analysis of Ray's film and Hughes's novel.

25. See J. Palmer for an interpretation of the film as a metacommentary on Hollywood of the HUAC era.

26. The former Group Theatre actor Art Smith, who plays Mel, became a victim of the blacklist. Other character actors who had worked with Ray by this point would suffer the same fate, such as Howard Da Silva and Will Lee, the latter of whom cofounded the Theatre of Action and was a member of the Federal Theatre Project (both men appeared in *They Live by Night*).

27. Peppering this scene are at least three insider's references. First, the line, "You have put the son-in-law-business back fifty years," which Charlie directs at Junior, was originally said to producer Milton Sperling, Harry Warner's son-in-law. Second, there are similarities between Dix and Herman J. Mankiewicz, who wrote the screenplay for *A Woman's Secret*, but who is best remembered for *Citizen Kane* (1941) (Perkins, "*Lonely*" 224). Third, Charlie was loosely based on actor John Barrymore (Silver and Ursini 116).

28. Close viewers will notice three paintings on the main wall of Laurel's living room: *La Mousmé* (1888) by Vincent van Gogh, *La Loge* (1874) by Pierre-Auguste Renoir, *The Flower Carrier* (1935) by the Communist Mexican painter Diego Rivera. Frank Krutnik calls the painting a depiction of "a scenario of exploited labor that is readily amenable to interpretation as a political statement" (53), which, in turn, becomes "a blatant signifier of left-wing affiliation" in the mise-en-scène (51). "A semiotic calling card for political voices that have been silenced during an era of repression and compromise," he concludes, "the painting's very muteness testifies to the legacy of such repression" (78). The same painting appears in Joseph Losey's *The Prowler* in 1951 and Robert Stevenson's *The Woman on Pier 13* (aka., *I Married a Communist*) in 1949. According to Losey, before Stevenson took over the latter film, Ray was offered the job to direct and worked on the script, prepared actors, and built sets (Krutnik 61).

Chapter 3

1. The working title was *The Gun under My Pillow*, a reference to Plato in *Rebel without a Cause* (Eisenschitz 431).

2. An earlier example is Charles and Ray Eames's *Think*, the main attraction of IBM's Pavilion at the 1964 New York World's Fair, which was a slide show

that simultaneously projected animated, still, and live-action images on fourteen large and eight small screens of varying sizes. Multiple screens were also used in narrative films such as *Grand Prix* (1966), *The Boston Strangler* (1968), and *The Thomas Crown Affair* (1968), and performance films such as *Dionysus '69* (1970) and *Woodstock* (1970). See Krohn, *We*.

3. A second cut of the film was made available in 1976, which no longer exists, but the 1973 version was the most widely circulated, courtesy of Spanish film distributor Jos Oliver, who held the sole 35 mm distribution print (G. Klinger 18).

4. She has reported that no 35 mm prints will be made of the film. The 2011 and 1973 negatives are almost identical; only the soundtrack contains noticeable changes, such as the substitution of Ray's voice and more detailed narration in the opening voice-over, which was lifted from the 1976 version (G. Klinger 20). For essays on the film published since the 2011 release, see: Allan, "Old"; Martin, "Nicholas"; and Rybin, "Pedagogical."

5. Ray supposedly picked up a couple of radicals when he was driving a car in the Latin Quarter of Paris during the uprisings. As the story goes, he reached into his glove compartment, pulled out a gun, and said, "James Dean gave this to me, and I'm passing it on to you because you'll know what to do with it" (Rosenbaum, "Looking" 72).

6. Marcel Ophuls's TV documentary *Auf der Suche nach meinem Amerika* (1970) covers Ray's unfinished work in Chicago.

7. Coincidentally, Tom Farrell is also the name of Robert Taylor's character in *Party Girl*.

8. See Harvey for the first use of the term *political modernism*.

9. See Wollen, "Counter" for the first used the term *countercinema*.

10. See, for example, Kleinhans.

11. See, for example, Doane, "'Woman's'" and Cook. Studies of the Hollywood melodrama, in particular, continued in the tradition of progressive genre criticism even after the heyday of political modernism (see de Cordova, Walker, Studlar, and Fischer).

12. See Nowell-Smith, Mulvey, and Modleski for other articles on melodrama auteurs.

13. In her book on directorial self-inscription, *Performing Authorship*, Cecilia Sayad shows how "the filmmaker's physical presence challenges the understanding that the charges of lack of control, unoriginality and ephemerality point to the author's absence. The director's corporeality, on the contrary, gives substance to the author, situating this author in the space of the work and, consequently, in the world that surrounds it" (xxvi).

14. In addition to Gottheim and Jacobs, between 1967 and 1977 the Cinema Department faculty included Hollis Frampton, Ernie Gehr, and other moving-image artists. Scott M. MacDonald's book *Binghamton Babylon* recounts this formative moment in the academic development of cinema studies and the history of the film avant-garde, and contains interviews with participants in the department who discuss the making of *Home* (97–116). Like films by Gottheim,

Jacobs, Gehr, and Frampton, Ray's film represents what MacDonald calls the "pedagogical" dimension of film practice at the department. Creative work by faculty and students aimed to make contributions to film history and the teaching of film by theoretically analyzing the ontology, function, and possibilities of the medium (221–24). *Home*, which he describes as the department's "most notorious and controversial film" (221), was distinctive in that Ray's politics were based in the material context of the 1970s, and his approach to filmmaking was thoroughly collaborative.

15. Ray and his crew shot the footage of Hampton's blood-stained bedroom that we also see in the film (Eisenschitz 414).

16. See Smirnova and Fujiwara for more on *The Doctor and the Devils*. Ray envisioned the film as a multiple-image project not unlike *Home* (Eisenschitz 396), but he began experimenting with the process as early as his work on *Rebel*, in which he conceived of split-screen sequences that were later scrapped (Eisenschitz 239). *King of Kings* allowed him to return to some of these ideas for the purposes of condensing narrative action and simultaneously shooting the foreground and background. While making *55 Days at Peking*, he wanted to achieve a level of subjectivity onscreen with the use of multiple images, although the plan never came through (Eisenschitz 380–81).

17. Other unfinished projects in the 1960s included an adaptation of Henrik Ibsen's *The Lady from the Sea* (1888), a Western scripted by novelist James Jones, and a science fiction film starring the Rolling Stones titled *Only Lovers Left Alive* (Andrew 152). Ray was also preparing a thriller with French art house producer Stéphane Tchalgadjieff titled *In Between Time*, starring Terrence Stamp, which never materialized (Rosenbaum, "Looking" 74). Jim Jarmusch later used the title of the would-be Stones project for his 2014 vampire film.

18. Grove specialized in the literary avant-garde, including: the U.S. editions of Harold Pinter and the Marquis de Sade; Samuel Beckett's *Waiting for Godot* (1954); writing by the American Beats (Jack Kerouac, Allen Ginsberg, and Burroughs), the New York School (Frank O'Hara), and the French avant-garde (Alain Robbe-Grillet, Jean Genet, Eugène Ionesco); and the magazine *Evergreen Review*, which included the work of Albert Camus, Lawrence Ferlinghetti, Bertolt Brecht, LeRoi Jones, and Edward Albee.

19. In a later interview with Ray, he said that he offered Judge Julius Hoffman $100,000 to play himself, and even asked James Cagney, the star of his Western *Run for Cover*, to come out of retirement for the role. Ray's other choice was Groucho Marx (Goodwin and Wise 12).

20. See also Higashi on DeMille and Gunning on Griffith.

21. See Ray, "Rebel" and Ray, "Always."

22. Audiences well-read in interviews with Ray will recognize this interaction as a reference to one of Ray's first meetings with James Dean. Ray described Dean doing a backward somersault into his home one night, sitting on the floor, and asking, "Hey are you middle-aged?" When Ray responded, "Yeah, I think so," Dean asked, "Are you the guy who was trapped by a fire and ran back to pick up a box of puppies Bogart had given him, and went running bareass across

Sunset Boulevard with it?" When Ray responded, "Yup," Dean turned to one of his friends and remarked, "See? Same guy," and then got up to leave (Goodwin and Wise 13). A slightly different version of this anecdote appears in a 1956 story Ray wrote for the *Daily Variety*, reprinted in his memoir, *I Was Interrupted*, in which Ray identifies Dean's two friends as unemployed actor Jack Simmons and television horror host Maila Nurmi (aka, Vampira). According to Ray, Nurmi first told the puppy story to Dean, who came to Ray's house to see if it was true (109).

23. I have not been able to determine whether Joseph Lederer and the journalist Joe Lederer who appears in the film are the same person (there is no screen credit), or whether Ray was consciously referencing 1970s film criticism by including a character with this name.

24. Thanks to Bill Krohn, the Los Angeles correspondent at *Cahiers du cinéma*, I was informed that Jean-Luc Godard made the first contribution to financing the completion of *Home*, slipping Susan Ray $30 at the Pacific Film Archive.

25. Ray has also told the story that he spent a month riding in a patrol car with three police officers from the Boston Violence Squad to prepare for *On Dangerous Ground*. When Ray returned to Hollywood shortly after the Great Brink's Robbery of 1950, he claimed that the three officers suspected that the robbers planted him in their squad to obtain inside information (Krohn 257).

26. See Krohn, "Class" for one of the final interviews with Ray, conducted at the Lee Strasberg Institute during the shooting of this film and published in French in *Cahiers du cinéma* in 1977. The interview was published in its entirety in English for the first time in 2014. Ray talked about *Home*, his "Chicago Seven" film project, and his longtime work in the Method.

27. See Allan, "Nick."

28. While he was teaching in Binghamton, Ray actually stole a new 16 mm print of *Bigger Than Life* rented to the Harpur film program, but he denied possession to authorities (the cost of the print was still taken out of his salary). Ray and Wenders considered making *Lightning* a caper in which Ray steals the negative of *Home* out of the Harpur film lab, which was confiscated as a result of his unpaid bills (Farrell, "Ray's" 61).

29. Ray's real son Timothy (from his marriage to Gloria Grahame) was actually one of the crewmembers. See Corrigan, "Cinematic" for an interpretation of the film as a kind of "anti-Oedipus" story that works to "confront, refuse, and overturn" the Oedipal structure of classical narrative (12).

30. See also Pomerance, "Teacup," and Pomerance, "Hero" for more on Ray's staging of action in his Hollywood films.

31. See also Geist, *Cinema*.

Chapter 4

1. In a recent counter-example of Ray's popularity among cinephile-filmmakers, writer-director, actor, and self-identified "movie geek" Lena Dunham criticized what she deemed a nonnaturalistic acting style in his films. Regarding *Bigger Than Life*, she told the *Village Voice*, "I can't get into movies like Nicholas

Ray's. I'll go with my friends and they'll say, '*Bigger Than Life*—that was incredible.' And I was so distracted the entire time watching James Mason act in that fashion." Dunham added, "I was watching with a boy who [*sic*] I wanted very much to think I was cool, but the whole time I was like, ugh, yawn, bring a book, I can't deal with this . . ." (Kaufman).

2. See Kovács on "late modern cinema" and Orr on "neomodern cinema."

3. See Martin, "Disequilibrium" for more on Ray's style as it pertains to European modernist art cinemas.

4. See also Broyard. Mailer's definition of the "hipster" builds from Anatole Broyard's 1948 article, "A Portrait of the Hipster," published in the *Partisan Review*, which considered the jive-talking, marijuana-smoking delinquent, who listens to blues, jazz, and bebop. This delinquent expresses his aggressive resentment symbolically through a poetic philosophy, an attempt at self-definition and reconciliation with society that involves a disarticulation of self and redefinition of society according to his jive vocabulary.

5. The cast also included Shelley Winters, Jean Seberg, Ricardo Montalban, Ella Fitzgerald, and Ray's old friend Burl Ives, but the film is best remembered for the jazz album *Ella Fitzgerald Sings Songs from "Let No Man Write My Epitaph."* Working for the Federal Writers' Project, Motley, like Ray, cut his creative teeth in the Works Progress Administration.

6. West Coast modernism at midcentury was not exclusively the domain of American cool culture. A group of German *émigrés*—including critical theorists Theodor Adorno and Max Horkheimer, playwright and theater director Bertolt Brecht, writers Thomas Mann, Alfred Döblin, and Franz Werfel, and painter and composer Arnold Schoenberg—fled the Nazis and settled in L.A., participating in the high modernism of the era (see Bahr). The "cool modernism" of American artists and the high modernism of the German intellectuals eventually converged in the 1960s with the cultural practices of the New Left, yielding the transnational mix of "high" and "low" styles and avant-garde political agendas in cinema at work in the *nouvelle vague* and New German Cinema.

7. Godard's love for both films and their directors is well known. One might be tempted to include Joseph H. Lewis's *Gun Crazy* (1949) in Godard's outlaw couple canon, but critic and filmmaker Fergus Daly insists that, contrary to received wisdom, Godard's perspective on the film is mostly a matter of conjecture. *Gun Crazy* was made by an independent production company, not Monogram Pictures, and distributed by United Artists. Although the main characters watch the film in Jim McBride's 1983 American remake, no explicit reference exists in Godard's original. Finally, Godard never even covered the film or Lewis in any of his writing as a journalist during the 1950s.

8. Other cameos include critics Jean Domarchi and Jean Douchet, and actor Van Doude as himself.

9. The Hungarian-born cinematographer László Kovács is often thought to be Michel's namesake, but Godard would not know of his work until the late 1960s and early 1970s with films such as *Easy Rider* (1969) and *Five Easy Pieces* (1970).

10. The dialogue we hear is not from *Westbound*, but from twentieth-century French poets Louis Aragon and Guillaume Apollinaire. This dissolve between high art and mass culture happens frequently around Patricia in the film.

11. Another exception is when Michel picks up a copy of Maurice Sachs's novel *Abracadabra* (1952) while Patricia plays Mozart's *Concerto for Clarinet*, which Michel says he likes because it reminds him of his clarinetist father. On the cover of the novel, Michel reads a quote by Lenin that anticipates his fate: "We are dead men on leave."

12. In addition to fielding questions about Brahms and Chopin, both of whom he dismisses, Parvulesco comments on the twentieth-century Austrian poet Rainer Maria Rilke and agrees with his belief that "modern life comes between men and women." Parvulesco also opines, "Love is all one can believe in." Both of these statements seem to make up the philosophical yin and yang of *Breathless*.

13. Critics such as Sterritt and Dixon have made important claims about Godard's relationship to modernism more generally. Sterritt determines that Godard's aesthetics are based in two traits of modernist creativity in the arts: "(a) its self-aware investigation of the processes and motivations of art making in itself and (b) its insistence on the reality and importance of the raw materials used in fabricating artistic works" (32). Writing on *Breathless*, specifically, Dixon concludes, "Godard seized upon the *policier* genre to create a document which ruptures not only the grammar and syntax of the classical cinema, but also the unspoken societal contract between spectacle and spectator in the traditional narrative film" (23). Dixon calls *Breathless* a "marker of rupture" that signals "the end of classicism, and the birth of 'Bop' cinema on a commercial scale" (24).

14. The film suffered from a series of script versions and contention between Wenders and Coppola, leaving the question as to whether the completed work belongs to Wenders or Coppola. Wenders documented his disputes with Coppola in his short *Reverse Angle* (1982).

15. Ray's former student Tom Farrell has cameos in both films.

16. See Gemünden and Elsaesser, *New*, for more on the political, economic, and industrial conditions that determined West Germany's historical reception of American films.

17. More obscure filmmakers—Peter Lilienthal, Daniel Schmid, Jean Eustache, Sandy Whitelaw, and Lou Castel—also have cameos.

18. Wenders adapted the Derwatt subplot from Highsmith's previous Ripley novel, *Ripley under Ground* (1970).

19. The authors also elucidate how Wenders's realism is different from other realists, as well as other modernists in film. As one of the last directors of modernist art cinema, Wenders "begins questioning the power of representation." According to Kolker and Beicken, "He falls back on modified realist premises, believing that, with care, the cinematic image can permit 'people or objects to show themselves as they really are,' but cannot authenticate or even stimulate the authentic self" (90).

20. Marianne is an aspiring actress who dubs American movies, but the scenes devoted to her career were cut.

21. An alternate ending was shot in which Derwatt, humming a Woody Guthrie song, covers one of his works in black and then paints an open black eye in the middle of the canvas (Ray again as the author whose self-effacement reinscribes his imprint on the text). Wenders and Ray improvised the scene. Regarding the color red, Wenders notes in his DVD commentary on the deleted scenes that he used it to illustrate Ripley's menacing presence in Jonathan's life (such as his red bed sheets and curtains).

22. Bob Dylan supposedly took inspiration from *The Savage Innocents* starring Anthony Quinn when he wrote his hit song "Quinn the Eskimo (Mighty Quinn)," first recorded during his 1967 Basement Tapes sessions and made famous by Manfred Mann in 1968 (Goodwin and Wise 18).

23. He began college as a journalism major at Northwestern University, but transferred to Columbia to study English literature (where New York School poet Kenneth Koch was one of his teachers).

24. After receiving a grant from the Louis B. Mayor Foundation for his tuition, Jarmusch instead parlayed the funds into making *Permanent Vacation* and submitted the film as his graduate thesis. NYU rejected the film for its length, and it never received commercial distribution. Jarmusch did not return to school, but NYU awarded him an honorary degree years later (Suárez 21).

25. Wenders included two of the band's songs on the soundtrack for *The State of Things*.

26. Jarmusch's backers included the German channel ZDF and Munich businessman Otto Grokenberger. Fellow independent filmmaker Paul Bartel loaned him the money for the film's rights (Suárez 28–29).

27. Lurie is responsible for several of Jarmusch's soundtracks, including *Permanent Vacation*, *Down by Law*, and *Mystery Train*, and he plays a street saxophonist in *Permanent Vacation*.

Conclusion

1. See Martin, "Where" for more on Ray's use of this tune in the film.

2. Recent book series devoted to director studies, such as the Contemporary Film Directors series at the University of Illinois Press, the Director's Cuts series at Columbia University Press's Wallflower imprint, the Wiley-Blackwell Companions to Film Directors Series, and ReFocus at Edinburgh University Press, also show how auteurism is growing in different national and industrial contexts, historically underrepresented identities, and theoretical and transnational approaches.

3. In 2006, Philip Kaufman signed to direct a Ray bio-pic titled *Interrupted*, written by Oren Moverman and based on Ray's memoirs *I Was Interrupted* (Zeitchik), but there has been no news on the production of this film.

4. See Lane and Thomson, "Director."

5. See the following examples: Bramble, "Heart"; Bramble, "Mystic"; Danks; Gallagher; Kaplan; Kuersten; Morgan and Seitz; Rybin, *Party*; Sanjek; Slocum, *Rebel*; Weisman. In 2013, *La Furia Umana* published a multilingual dossier on Ray that included his last interview conducted in 1979 by filmmaker

Kathryn Bigelow, then a graduate student at Columbia University, and her friend Sarah Fatima Parsons, a journalist from West Germany (only part of this dossier was published in the online version of the journal). See Bigelow and Parsons.

Works Cited

Allan, Blaine. "Nick's Movies." *Senses of Cinema* 68 (Sep. 2013). Web 9 Nov. 2013. <http://sensesofcinema.com/2013/feature-articles/nicks-movies/>.

———. "Old Saint Nick: *We Can't Go Home Again* and *Don't Expect Too Much*." *Senses of Cinema* 63 (Jul. 2012). Web. 9 Nov. 2013. <http://sensesofcinema.com/2012/63/old-saint-nick-we-cant-go-home-again-and-dont-expect-too-much/>.

Alloway, Lawrence. *Violent America: The Movies, 1946–1964*. New York: Museum of Modern Art, 1971. Print.

Alpert, Hollis. "It's Dean, Dean, Dean." *Saturday Review* 39 (13 Oct. 1956): 28–29. Print.

Altman, Rick. *Film/Genre*. London: BFI Publishing, 1999. Print.

Anderson, Christopher. "Jesse James, the Bourgeois Bandit: The Transformation of a Popular Hero." *Cinema Journal* 26.1 (Autumn 1986): 43–64. Print.

Andersen, Thom. "Red Hollywood." *"Un-American" Hollywood: Politics and Film in the Blacklist Era*. Ed. Frank Krutnik, Steve Neale, Brian Neve, and Peter Stanfield. New Brunswick, NJ: Rutgers UP, 2007. 225–63. Print.

Andrew, Geoff. *The Films of Nicholas Ray: The Poet of Nightfall*. New ed. London: BFI Publishing, 2004. Print.

Anger, Kenneth. *Hollywood Babylon II*. New York: E. P. Dutton, 1984. Print.

Aprà, Adriano, et al. "Interview with Nicholas Ray." *Movie* 9 (May 1963): 14–25. Print.

Armstrong, Elizabeth. "The Square and the Cool: California Art, Design, and Culture at Midcentury." *Birth of the Cool: California Art, Design, and Culture at Midcentury*. Newport Beach, CA: Orange County Museum of Modern Art and Prestel Publishing, 2007. 23–61. Print.

Archer, Eugene. "Generation without a Cause." *Film Culture* 7 (1956): 18–21. Print.

Auty, Martyn. "Rebel without a Cause": Movies of the Fifties. Ed. Ann Lloyd. London: Orbis Publishing, 1982. 78–79. Print.

Bahr, Ehrhard. *Weimar on the Pacific: German Exile Culture in Los Angeles and the Crisis of Modernism*. Berkeley: U of California P, 2008. Print.

Baron, Cynthia, and Sharon Marie Carnicke. *Reframing Screen Performance*. Ann Arbor: U of Michigan P, 2008. Print.

Barrios, Richard. *Screened Out: Playing Gay in Hollywood from Edison to Stonewall*. New York: Routledge, 2003. Print.

Barthes, Roland. "The Death of the Author." *Image-Music-Text*. Trans. Stephen Heath. New York: Hill & Wang, 1977. 142–48. Print.

Bast, William. *Surviving James Dean*. Fort Lee, NJ: Barricade Books, 2006. Print.

Bazin, André. "The Death of Humphrey Bogart." Trans. Phillip Drummond. *Cahiers du cinéma, the 1950s: Neo-Realism, Hollywood, New Wave*. Ed. Jim Hillier. Cambridge, MA: Harvard UP, 1985. 98–101. Print.

Bennett, Tony. "Texts and Social Process: The Case of James Bond." *Screen Education* 41 (1982): 3–14. Print.

———. "Texts, Readers, Reading Formations." *The Bulletin of the Midwest Modern Language Association* 16.1 (1983): 3–17. Print.

Benjamin, Walter. "The Work of Art in the Age of Its Technological Reproducibility." 2nd version. Trans. Edmund Jephcott and Harry Zohn. *The Work of Art in the Age of Its Technological Reproducibility and Other Writings on Media*. Ed. Michael W. Jennings, Brigid Doherty, and Thomas Y. Levin. Cambridge, MA: The Belknap P of Harvard UP, 2008. 19–42. Print.

Bickerton, Emilie. *A Short History of Cahiers du cinéma*. London: Verso, 2009. Print.

Bigelow, Kathryn, and Sarah Fatima Parsons, et al. "Confidential Report: Nicholas Ray's *Rebel without a Cause*." *La Furia Umana* 4 (Autumn 2013). Print.

Biskind, Peter. "Rebel without a Cause: Nicholas Ray in the Fifties." *Film Quarterly* 28.1 (Autumn 1974): 32–38. Print.

———. "*They Live by Night by Daylight*." *Sight and Sound* 45.4 (Autumn 1976): 218–22. Print.

Bitsch, Charles. "Interview with Nicholas Ray." Trans. Liz Heron. *Cahiers du cinéma, the 1950s: Neo-Realism, Hollywood, New Wave*. Ed. Jim Hillier. Cambridge, MA: Harvard UP, 1985. 120–24. Print.

"Bogart Battles to Rescue Toys." *Los Angeles Times* 29 Sep. 1949: 2. Print.

"Bogart Gets Court Call as Panda Battle Sequel." *Los Angeles Times* 30 Sep. 1949: 2. Print.

Borde, Raymond, and Étienne Chaumeton. *A Panorama of American Film Noir, 1941–1953*. Trans. Paul Hammond. San Francisco: City Lights Publishers, 2002. Print.

Bramble, Serena. "Heart Is a *Lonely* Hunter, The: On Nicholas Ray's *In a Lonely Place*." *Senses of Cinema* 59 (Jun. 2011). Web. 9 Nov. 2013. <http://sensesofcinema.com/2011/cteq/the-heart-is-a-"lonely"-hunter-on-nicholas-ray's-in-a-lonely-place/>.

———. "The Mystic: An Appreciation of Nicholas Ray." *Vimeo* 3 Sep. 2011. Web. 9 Nov. 2013. <http://vimeo.com/28491452>.

Braudy, Leo. "'No Body's Perfect': Method Acting and 50s Culture." *Michigan Quarterly Review* 35.1 (Winter 1996): 191–215. Print.

Broderick, Mick. "'Armageddon without a Cause': Playing 'Chicken' in the Atomic Age." Rebel without a Cause: *Approaches to a Maverick Masterwork*. Ed. J. David Slocum. Albany: State U of New York P, 2005. 149–70. Print.

Broyard, Anatole. "Portrait of a Hipster." *Partisan Review* 15 (Jan.–Jun. 1948): 721–726. Print.

Cagle, Chris. "*Knock on Any Door*: Realist Form and Popularized Social Science." *Lonely Places, Dangerous Ground: Nicholas Ray in American Cinema*. Ed Steven Rybin and Will Scheibel. Albany: State U of New York P, 2014. 41–47. Print.

Campbell, Neil. "*The Lusty Men* and the Post-Western." *Lonely Places, Dangerous Ground: Nicholas Ray in American Cinema*. Ed. Steven Rybin and Will Scheibel. Albany: State U of New York P, 2014. 97–107. Print.

"Camera Three: Profile of Nicholas Ray." *Bigger Than Life*. Dir. Nicholas Ray. Perf. James Mason, Barbara Rush, and Walter Matthau. The Criterion Collection, 2010. Print.Canby, Vincent. "A Fine Director, Unemployed." *New York Times* 8 Jun. 1969: D1. Print.

———. "Film: The Last Months of Nicholas Ray's Life." Rev. of *Lightning over Water*, dirs. Wim Wenders and Nicholas Ray. *New York Times* 26 Sep. 1981: 13. Print.

———. "Nicholas Ray: Still a Rebel with a Cause." *New York Times* 24 Sep. 1972: D1. Print.

———. "Nicholas Ray: Subject of *Stranger Myself*." Rev. of *I'm a Stranger Here Myself*, dir. David Helpern. *New York Times* 17 Jan. 1975: 20. Print.

Chabrol, Claude. "Evolution of the Thriller." Trans. Liz Heron. *Cahiers du cinéma, the 1950s: Neo-Realism, Hollywood, New Wave*. Ed. Jim Hillier. Cambridge, MA: Harvard UP, 1985. 158–64. Print.

Charney, Leo. "Historical Excess: *Johnny Guitar*'s Containment." *Cinema Journal* 29.4 (Summer 1990). 23–34. Print.

Childs, Peter. Modernism. 2nd ed. New York: Routledge, 2000, 2008. Print.

Cocks, Jay. "Director in Aspic." *Take One* 6 (Jan. 1977): 17. Print.

Coe, Richard L. "On the Aisle: Delinquency? We're at It Again." Rev. of *Rebel without a Cause*, dir. Nicholas Ray. *Washington Post* 28 Oct. 1955: 71 Print.

Cohan, Steven. *Masked Men: Masculinity and the Movies in the Fifties*. Bloomington: Indiana UP, 1997. Print.

Cohen, Patricia. "Reclaiming Causes of a Filmmaking Rebel." *New York Times* 16 Jun. 2010. Web. 15 Jul. 2011. <http://www.nytimes.com/2010/06/17/movies/17ray.html?emc=eta1>.

Combs, Richard. "*Lightning over Water*." *Sight and Sound* 50.2 (Spring 1981): 92. Print.

Comolli, Jean-Luc, and Jean Narboni. "Cinema/Ideology/Criticism." *Film Theory & Criticism*. 7th ed. Ed. Leo Braudy and Marshall Cohen. Oxford: Oxford UP, 2009. 686–93. Print.

Conroy, Marianne. "Acting Out: Method Acting, the National Culture, and the Middlebrow Disposition in Cold War America." *Criticism* 35. 2 (Spring 1993): 239–63. Print.

Cook, Pam. "Melodrama and the Women's Picture." *Imitations of Life: A Reader on Film and Television Melodrama*. Ed. Marcia Landy. Detroit: Wayne State University Press, 1991. 248–62. Print.

Cordova, Richard de. "A Case of Mistaken Legitimacy: Class and Generational Difference in Three Family Melodramas." *Home Is Where the Heart Is: Studies in Melodrama and the Woman's Film*. Ed. Christine Gledhill. London: BFI Publishing, 1987. 255–67. Print.

Corrigan, Timothy. "Cinematic Snuff: German Friends and Narrative Murders." *Cinema Journal* 24.2 (Winter 1985): 9–18. Print.

———. "The Commerce of Auteurism: A Voice without Authority." *New German Critique* 49 (Winter 1990): 43–57. Print.

Cossar, Harper. "Ray, Widescreen, and Genre: *The True Story of Jesse James*." *Lonely Places, Dangerous Ground: Nicholas Ray in American Cinema*. Ed. Steven Rybin and Will Scheibel. Albany: State U of New York P, 2014. 189–207. Print.

"Court Throws Out Girl's Complaint against Bogart." *Los Angeles Times* 1 Oct. 1949: 3. Print.

Crowther, Bosley. "*King of Kings* Has Its Premiere at State." Rev. of *King of Kings*, dir. Nicholas Ray. *New York Times* 12 Oct. 1961: 41. Print.

———. "*Lusty Men*, Tale of Rodeo Riders with Robert Mitchum, Makes Debut at Criterion." Rev. of *The Lusty Men*, dir. Nicholas Ray. *New York Times* 25 Oct. 1952: 12. Print.

———. "Screen: Sheriff Cagney Goes It Alone." Rev. of *Run for Cover*, dir. Nicholas Ray. *New York Times* 30 Apr. 1955: 10. Print.

———. "Screen: Tax of Tedium, *Bigger Than Life* Has Debut at Victoria." Rev. of *Bigger Than Life*, dir. Nicholas Ray. *New York Times* 3 Aug. 1956: 11. Print.

———. "Screen: *The Everglades*: Schulbergs' Film Has Debut at Mayfair, The." Rev. of *Wind Across the Everglades*, dir. Nicholas Ray. *New York Times* 12 Sep. 1958: 21. Print.

———. "The Screen: Delinquency, *Rebel without Cause* Has Debut at Astor." Rev. of *Rebel without a Cause*, dir. Nicholas Ray. *New York Times* 27 Oct. 1955: 28. Print.

———. "The Screen: *East of Eden* Has Debut; Astor Shows Film of Steinbeck Novel." Rev. of *East of Eden*, dir. Elia Kazan. *New York Times* 10 Mar. 1955: 33. Print.

———. "The Screen: Three Films Make Their Bows: Humphrey Bogart Movie, *In a Lonely Place*, at Paramount—Import at Trans-Lux." Rev. of *In a Lonely Place*, dir. Nicholas Ray. *New York Times* 18 May 1950: 46. Print.

———. "The Screen in Review: Humphrey Bogart, John Derek Seen in *Knock on Any Door*, New at Tenant at Astor." Rev. of *Knock on Any Door*, dir. Nicholas Ray. *New York Times* 23 Feb. 1949: 31. Print.

———. "The Screen in Review: *Johnny Guitar* Opens at the Mayfair." Rev. of *Johnny Guitar*, dir. Nicholas Ray. *New York Times* May 28, 1954: 19. Print.

———. "The Screen in Review: *On Dangerous Ground*, Story of Detective Turned Sadist, Opens at Criterion." Rev. of *On Dangerous Ground*, dir. Nicholas Ray. *New York Times* 13 Feb. 1952: 35. Print.

———. "*They Live by Night*, Starring Cathy O'Donnell and Farley Granger, at Criterion." Rev. of *They Live by Night*, dir. Nicholas Ray. New York Times 4 Nov. 1949: 33. Print.

Criterion Collection, The. Web. 21 Feb. 2014. <http://www.criterion.com/about_us>.

Daly, Fergus. "JHL/JLG: Women and Money." *La Furia Umana* 1 (Winter 2013): 149–50. Print.

Danks, Adrian. "'God Was Wrong': Nicholas Ray's *Bigger Than Life*." *Senses of Cinema* 50 (Mar. 2009). Web. 9 Nov. 2013. <http://sensesofcinema.com/2009/cteq/bigger-than-life/>.

Davis, Evan, et al. "Homes for Strangers." *MUBI Notebook* Jul.–Aug. 2009. Web. 9 Nov. 2013. <http://mubi.com/notebook/posts/tag/Homes%20for%20Strangers>.

DeAngelis, Michael. *Gay Fandom and Crossover Stardom: James Dean, Mel Gibson, and Keanu Reeves*. Durham, NC: Duke UP, 2001. Print.

Desjardins, Mary. "Systematizing Scandal: Confidential Magazine, Stardom, and the State of California." *Headline Hollywood: A Century of Film Scandal*. Ed. Adrienne L. McLean and David A. Cook. New Brunswick, NJ: Rutgers UP, 2001. 206–31. Print.

Denning, Michael. *The Cultural Front: The Laboring of American Culture in the Twentieth Century*. London: Verso, 1997. Print.

Deutsch, James I., and Lauren R. Shaw. "Citizen Nick: Civic Engagement and Folk Culture in the Life and Work of Nicholas Ray." *Lonely Places, Dangerous Ground: Nicholas Ray in American Cinema*. Ed. Steven Rybin and Will Scheibel. Albany: State U of New York P, 2014. 109–21. Print.

Dixon, Wheeler Winston. *The Films of Jean-Luc Godard*. Albany: State U of New York P, 1997. Print.

Doane, Mary Ann, Patricia Mellencamp, and Linda Williams, eds. *Re-Vision: Essays in Feminist Film Criticism*. Frederick, MD: American Film Institute/University Publications of America, 1984. Print.

———. "The 'Woman's Film': Possession and Address." *Home Is Where the Heart Is: Studies in Melodrama and the Woman's Film*. Ed. Christine Gledhill. London: BFI Publishing, 1987. 283–98. Print.

Domarchi, Jean, et al. "Hiroshima, *notre amour*." Trans. Liz Heron. *Cahiers du cinéma, the 1950s: Neo-Realism, Hollywood, New Wave*. Ed. Jim Hillier. Cambridge, MA: Harvard UP, 1985. 59–70. Print.

Doty, Alexander. "'I've Got the Queerest Feeling' about *A Woman's Secret and Born to Be Bad*." *Lonely Places, Dangerous Ground: Nicholas Ray in American Cinema*. Ed. Steven Rybin and Will Scheibel. Albany: State U of New York P, 2014. 49–61.

Dyer, Richard. *Stars*. 2nd ed. London: BFI Publishing1979, 1998. Print.

Ebert, Roger. "Nick Ray Promises a Movie on 'Chicago Seven.'" *Los Angeles Times* 8 Mar. 1970: N14. Print.

Eells, George. *Robert Mitchum*. London: Franklin Watts, 1984. Print.

Eisenschitz, Bernard. *Nicholas Ray: An American Journey*. Trans. Tom Milne. London: Faber and Faber, 1993. Print.

Elsaesser, Thomas. *New German Cinema*. New Brunswick, NJ: Rutgers UP, 1989. Print.

———. "Nicholas Ray (Part 1)." *Brighton Film Review* 19 (Apr. 1970): 13–16. Print.

———. "Nicholas Ray (Part 2)." *Brighton Film Review* 20 (May 1970): 15–16. Print.

———. "Spectators of Life: Time, Place, and Self in the Films of Wim Wenders." *The Cinema of Wim Wenders: Image, Narrative, and the Postmodern Condition*. Ed. Roger F. Cook and Gerd Gemünden. Detroit: Wayne State UP, 1997. 240–56. Print.

———. "Tales of Sound and Fury: Observations on the Family Melodrama." *Home Is Where the Heart Is: Studies in Melodrama and the Woman's Film*. Ed. Christine Gledhill. London: BFI Publishing, 1987. 2–15. Print.

Farrell, Tom. "Nick Ray's German Friend Wim Wenders." *Wide Angle* 5.4 (1983): 60–67. Print.

———. "We Can't Go Home Again." *Sight and Sound* 50.2 (Spring 1981): 92–94. Print.

"Film 'Shot' from Helicopter." *New York Times* 23 Aug. 1947: 7. Print.

Fischer, Lucy. "Seduced and Abandoned: Recollection and Romance in *Letter from an Unknown Woman*." *Issues in Feminist Film Criticism*. Ed. Patricia Erens. Bloomington: Indiana UP, 1990. 163–82. Print.

Foucault, Michel. "Discursive Formations." *The Archeology of Knowledge and the Discourse on Language*. Trans. A. M. Sheridan Smith. New York: Pantheon, 1972. 31–39. Print.

———. "What Is an Author?" Trans. Josue V. Harari. *The Foucault Reader*. Ed. Paul Rabinow. New York: Pantheon, 1984. 101–20. Print.

Frank, Thomas. *The Conquest of Cool: Business Culture, Counterculture, and the Rise of Hip Consumerism*. Chicago: U of Chicago P, 1997. Print.

Frascella, Larry, and Al Weisel. *Live Fast, Die Young: The Wild Ride of Making* Rebel without a Cause. New York: Simon and Schuster, 2005. Print.

Fujiwara, Chris. "Bigger Than Legend." *The Boston Phoenix* 6 Jul. 2010. Web. 9 Nov. 2013. <http://thephoenix.com/boston/movies/104757-bigger-than-legend/>.

Gallagher, Cullen, et al. "The Mystic: The Films of Nicholas Ray." *Not Coming to a Theater Near You* 14 Aug. 2008. Web. 9 Nov. 2013. <http://www.notcoming.com/features/nicholasray>.

Gay, Peter. *Modernism: The Lure of Heresy: From Baudelaire to Beckett and Beyond*. New York: Norton, 2008. Print.

Geist, Kathy. "*Lightning over Water*." *Film Quarterly* 35.2 (Winter 1981–1982): 46–51.

———. *The Cinema of Wim Wenders: From Paris, France to Paris, Texas*. Ann Arbor, MI: UMI Research Press, 1988. Print.

Gemünden, Gerd. *Framed Visions: Popular Culture, Americanization, and the Contemporary German and Austrian Imagination*. Ann Arbor: U of Michigan P, 1998. Print.

Gerstner, David A. "The Practices of Authorship." *Authorship and Film*. Ed. David A. Gerstner and Janet Staiger. New York: Routledge, 2003. 3–25. Print.

Gilmore, John. *Live Fast—Die Young: Remembering the Short Life of James Dean*. New York: Thunder's Mouth P, 1998. Print.

Gledhill, Christine, ed. *Home Is Where the Heart Is: Studies in Melodrama and the Woman's Film*. London: BFI Publishing, 1987. Print.

Godard, Jean-Luc. "Beyond the Stars." Trans. Tom Milne. *Cahiers du cinéma, the 1950s: Neo-Realism, Hollywood, New Wave*. Ed. Jim Hillier. Cambridge, MA: Harvard UP, 1985. 118–19. Print.

———. *Godard on Godard*. Ed. and trans. Tom Milne. Cambridge, MA: Da Capo P, 1986. Print.

———. "Nothing but Cinema." Trans. Tom Milne. *Cahiers du cinéma, the 1950s: Neo-Realism, Hollywood, New Wave*. Ed. Jim Hillier. Cambridge, MA: Harvard UP, 1985. 116–17. Print.

Gomery, Douglas. "Nicholas Ray's *They Live by Night*." *The Velvet Light Trap* 5 (Summer 1972): 25–29. Print.

Goodman, Ezra. "Delirium over Dead Star." *Life* 41.13 (24 Sep. 1956): 75–76, 79–80, 85–86, 88. Print.

Goodwin, Michael, and Naomi Wise. "Nicholas Ray: Rebel!" *Take One* 5.6 (Jan. 1977): 7–16, 18–21. Print.

Gottheim, Larry. "Bigger Than Life: Between Ken Jacobs and Nicholas Ray." *Optic Antics: The Cinema of Ken Jacobs*. Ed. Michele Pierson, David E. James, and Paul Arthur. Oxford: Oxford UP, 2011. 89–95. Print.

Gunning, Tom. "D.W. Griffith: Historical Figure, Film Director, and Ideological Shadow." *Film and Authorship*. Ed. Virginia Wright Wexman. New Brunswick, NJ: Rutgers UP, 2003. 181–93. Print.

Guralnick, Peter. *Lost Highway: Journeys and Arrivals of American Musicians*. Edinburgh: Canongate, 2002. Print.

Hankin, Kelly. "A Rebel without a Choice?: Femme Spectatorship in Hollywood Cinema." *The Velvet Light Trap* 41 (Spring 1998): 3–18. Print.

Hansen, Miriam. "Mass Production of the Senses, The: Classical Cinema as Vernacular Modernism." *Modernism/Modernity* 6.2 (1999): 59–77 Print.

Harvey, Sylvia. "Whose Brecht? Memories for the Eighties." *Screen* 23.1 (May/Jun. 1982): 45–59. Print. Hawkins, Joan. *Cutting Edge: Art Horror and the Horrific Avant-Garde*. Minneapolis: U of Minnesota P, 2000. Print.

Higashi, Sumiko. "Cecil B. DeMille and Highbrow Culture: Authorship versus Intertextuality." *Film and Authorship*. Ed. Virginia Wright Wexman. New Brunswick, NJ: Rutgers UP, 2003. 194–222. Print.

Hillier, Jim, ed. *Cahiers du cinéma, the 1950s: Neo-Realism, Hollywood, New Wave*. Cambridge, MA: Harvard UP, 1985. Print.

———, ed. *Cahiers du cinéma, the 1960s: New Wave, New Cinema, Reevaluating Hollywood*. Cambridge, MA: Harvard UP, 1986. Print.

———. "Introduction." *Cahiers du cinéma, the 1950s: Neo-Realism, Hollywood, New Wave*. Ed. Jim Hillier. Cambridge, MA: Harvard UP, 1985. 1–17. Print.

———. "Introduction: *Cahiers du cinéma* in the 1960s." *Cahiers du cinéma, the 1960s: New Wave, New Cinema, Reevaluating Hollywood.* Ed. Jim Hillier. Cambridge, MA: Harvard UP, 1986. 1–24. Print.

———. "Part II American Cinema: Introduction." *Cahiers du cinéma, the 1950s: Neo-Realism, Hollywood, New Wave.* Ed. Jim Hillier. Cambridge, MA: Harvard UP, 1985. 73–85. Print.

Hirsch, Foster. *Otto Preminger: The Man Who Would Be King.* New York: Knopf, 2007.

Hoberman, J. "Vulgar Modernism." *Artforum* 20.6 (1982): 71–76. Print.

Hopkins, Orval. "Bogart and Grahame Combine to Make a Swift Whodunit." Rev. of *In a Lonely Place*, dir. Nicholas Ray. *Washington Post* 14 Jul. 1950: B4. Print.

Hopper, Hedda. "Keep Your Eye on James Dean." *Chicago Tribune* 27 Mar. 1955: L40. Print.

———. "Young Men of Hollywood: A Selection of Stars of Tomorrow." *Coronet* 38 (1 Jul. 1955): 51–57. Print.

Houston, Penelope. "Rebels without Causes." *Sight & Sound* 25.4 (Spring 1956): 178–81. Print.

———, and John Gillett. "Conversations with Nicholas Ray and Joseph Losey." *Sight & Sound* 30.4 (Autumn 1961): 182–87. Print.

———. "The Critical Question." *Sight & Sound* 29.4 (Autumn 1960): 160–65. Print.

Hoveyda, Fereydoun. "Nicholas Ray's Reply: *Party Girl.*" *Cahiers du cinéma, the 1960s: New Wave, New Cinema, Reevaluating Hollywood.* Ed. Jim Hillier. Cambridge, MA: Harvard UP, 1986. 122–31. Print.

"Humphrey's Snarling Again." Rev. of *In a Lonely Place*, dir. Nicholas Ray. *Wall Street Journal* 19 May 1950: 5. Print.

"In Death, James Dean a Hero to French." *Variety* 11 Jul. 1956: 2. Print.

"Jackson Pollock: Is He the Greatest Living Painter in the United States?" *Life* 27.6 (8 Aug. 1949): 42–43, 45. Print.

Jezer, Marty. *The Dark Ages: Life in the United States 1945–1960.* Boston: South End P, 1982. Print.

"Jim Jarmusch: Extended Interview." *We Can't Go Home Again / Don't Expect Too Much.* Oscilloscope Laboratories, 2011. Print.

Johnson, Paul Anthony. "'You Can't Be a Rebel If You Grin': Masculinity, Performance, and Anxiety in 1950s Rock-and-Roll and the Films of Nicholas Ray." *Lonely Places, Dangerous Ground: Nicholas Ray in American Cinema.* Ed. Steven Rybin and Will Scheibel. Albany: State U of New York P, 2014. 139–49. Print.

Jost, Jon. "Wrong Move." *Sight & Sound* 50.2 (Spring 1981): 94–97. Print.

"Just a Saloon Hassle, Mitchum Says of Fight." *Los Angeles Times* 9 Nov. 1951: 2.

Kael, Pauline. "Circles and Squares." *Film Quarterly* 16.3 (Spring 1963): 12–26. Print.

Kaplan, George. "They Live by Night." *Senses of Cinema* 59 (Jun. 2011). Web. 9 Nov. 2013. <http://sensesofcinema.com/2011/cteq/they-live-by-night/>. Print.

Kapsis, Robert E. *Hitchcock: The Making of a Reputation*. Chicago: U of Chicago P, 1992. Print.

Kashner, Sam, and Jennifer MacNair. *The Bad and the Beautiful: Hollywood in the Fifties*. Old Saybrook, CT: Konecky & Konecky, 2002. Print.

Kaufman, Anthony. "What It Takes, BAMcinemaFEST Edition." *Village Voice* (8 Jun. 2010). Web. <http://www.villagevoice.com/film/what-it-takes-bam cinemafest-edition-6429446>.

Kleinhans, Chuck. "Notes on Melodrama and the Family Under Capitalism." *Imitations of Life: A Reader on Film and Television Melodrama*. Ed. Marcia Landy. Detroit: Wayne State UP, 1991. 197–204. Print.

Klinger, Barbara. *Melodrama and Meaning: History, Culture, and the Films of Douglas Sirk*. Bloomington: Indiana University Press, 1994. Print.

———. "'Cinema/Ideology/Criticism" Revisited: The Progressive Genre." *Film Genre Reader*. Ed. Barry Keith Grant. Austin: U of Texas P, 1986. 74–90. Print.

Klinger, Gabe. "*We Can't Go Home Again*: Nicholas Ray's *Film Maudit* Restored." *CinemaScope* 48 (Fall 2011): 18–20. Print.

Kolker, Robert Phillip. "Night to Day." *Sight& Sound* 43.4 (Autumn 1974) 236–39. Print.

———, and Peter Beicken. *The Films of Wim Wenders: Cinema as Vision and Desire*. Cambridge: Cambridge UP, 1993. Print.

Korman, Seymour. "The Last Hours of James." *Chicago Daily Tribune* 5 Feb. 1956: F18. Print.

Kovács, András Bálint. *Screening Modernism: European Art Cinema, 1950–1980*. Chicago: U of Chicago P, 2007. Print.

Krohn, Bill. "The Class: Interview with Nicholas Ray." *Lonely Places, Dangerous Ground: Nicholas Ray in American Cinema*. Albany: State U of New York P, 2014. 251–66. Print.

———. "*We Can't Go Home Again*." *Kino Slang* 17 Nov. 2012. Web. 4 Jun. 2015. <http://kinoslang.blogspot.com/2012/11/we-cant-go-home-again-by-bill-krohn.html>.

Krutnik, Frank. "'A Living Part of the Class Struggle': Diego Rivera's *The Flower Carrier* and the Hollywood Left." *"Un-American" Hollywood: Politics and Film in the Blacklist Era*. Ed. Frank Krutnik, Steve Neale, Brian Neve, and Peter Stanfield. New Brunswick, NJ: Rutgers UP, 2007. 51–78. Print.

———, Steve Neale, Brian Neve, and Peter Stanfield, eds. *"Un-American" Hollywood: Politics and Film in the Blacklist Era*. New Brunswick, NJ: Rutgers UP, 2007. Print.

Kuersten, Erich. "*Bigger Than Life*: Nicholas Ray in the Heart of Gray Flannel Darkness." *Bright Lights Film Journal* 68 (May 2010). Web. 9 Nov. 2013. Print. <http://brightlightsfilm.com/68/68biggerthanlife.php#.Un3uOqWTOlI>.

Kuisel, Richard. *Seducing the French: The Dilemma of Americanization*. U of California P, 1993. Print.

Lambert, Gavin. "Good-Bye to Some of That." *Film Quarterly* 12.1 (Autumn 1958): 25–29. Print.

———. *Mainly about Lindsay Anderson*. New York: Knopf, 2000. Print.

———. *Natalie Wood: A Life*. New York: Knopf, 2004. Print.

———. "Rebels and Causes." *Twentieth Century* 159 (Mar. 1956): 275–80.

———. *The Slide Area*. New York: Serpent's Tail, 1998. Print.

Lane, Anthony. "The Current Cinema: Only the Lonely." *New Yorker* 24 Mar. 2003. Web. 21 Feb. 2014. <http://www.newyorker.com/archive/2003/03/24/030324crci_cinema>.

Leland, John. *Hip: The History*. New York: HarperCollins, 2004. Print.

Lewis, Jon. "Growing Up Male in Jim's Mom's World." Rebel without a Cause*: Approaches to a Maverick Masterwork*. Ed. J. David Slocum. Albany: State U of New York P, 2005. 89–107. Print.

Lederer, Joseph. "Film as Experience: A Director Turns Teacher." *American Film* 1.2 (Nov. 1975): 60–64. Print.

Lloyd, Ann, ed. *Movies of the Fifties*. London: Orbis Publishing, 1982. Print.

MacDonald, Scott M. *Binghamton Babylon: Voices from the Cinema Department, 1967–1977*. Albany: State U of New York P, 2015. Print.

Mailer, Norman. "The White Negro: Superficial Reflections on the Hipster." *The Time of Our Time*. New York: Random House, 1998. 211–30. Print.

Margulies, Ivone. "Delaying the Cut: The Space of Performance in *Lightning over Water*." *Screen* 34.1 (Spring 1993): 54–68. Print.

Martin, Adrian. "Disequilibrium, or: Love Interest (On *Party Girl*)." *Lonely Places, Dangerous Ground: Nicholas Ray in American Cinema*. Ed. Steven Rybin and Will Scheibel. Albany: State U of New York P, 2014. 209–217. Print.

———. "Nicholas Ray: Let It Become Clear." *Keyframe* (31 Jan. 2014). Web. Accessed 2 Feb. 2014. <http://www.fandor.com/keyframe/nicholas-ray-let-it-become-clear>.

———. "Where I Come From, Where I'm Going." *[in]Transition* 1.3 (2014). Web. Accessed 26 Aug. 2014.<http://mediacommons.futureofthebook.org/intransition/2014/09/14/inwardoutward-turn>.

Mathy, Jean Philippe. *French Resistance: The French-American Culture Wars*. Minneapolis: U of Minnesota P, 2000. Print.

McCann, Graham. *Rebel Males: Clift, Brando, and Dean*. New Brunswick, NJ: Rutgers UP, 1993. Print.

McElhaney, Joe. "Nicholas Ray: The Breadth of Modern Gesture." *Lonely Places, Dangerous Ground: Nicholas Ray in American Cinema*. Ed. Steven Rybin and Will Scheibel. Albany: State U of New York P, 2014. 19–28. Print.

———. *The Death of Classical Cinema: Hitchcock, Lang, Minnelli*. Albany: State U of New York P, 2006. Print.

McNiven, Roger D. "The Middle-Class American Home of the Fifties: The Use of Architecture in Nicholas Ray's *Bigger Than Life* and Douglas Sirk's *All That Heaven Allows*." *Cinema Journal* 22.4 (1983): 38–57. Print.

McGilligan, Patrick. *Nicholas Ray: The Glorious Failure of an American Director*. New York: Harper Collins, 2011. Print.

Medovoi, Leerom. *Rebels: Youth and the Cold War Origins of Identity*. Durham, NC: Duke UP, 2005. Print.

Metro-Goldwyn-Mayor. *The End of Violence Press Release*. 1997. Print.

Michaud, Michael Gregg. *Sal Mineo: A Biography*. New York: Crown Archetype, 2010. Print.

Mitchell, Jon. "Jim Stark's 'Barbaric Yawp': *Rebel without a Cause* and the Cold War Crisis in Masculinity." Rebel without a Cause*: Approaches to a Maverick Masterwork*. Ed. J. David Slocum. Albany: State U of New York P, 2005. 131–47. Print.

"Mitchum's Pal Ford Gets 60 Days in Jail." *Los Angeles Times* 17 Mar. 1949: 2. Print.

Mitgang, Herbert. "Strange James Dean Death Cult." *Coronet* 41 (1 Nov. 1956): 107–15. Print.

Modleski, Tania. "Time and Desire in the Woman's Film." *Home Is Where the Heart Is: Studies in Melodrama and the Woman's Film*. Ed. Christine Gledhill. London: BFI Publishing, 1987. 326–28. Print.

Morgan, Kim, and Matt Zoller Seitz. "*In a Lonely Place*." *YouTube* 16 Jul. 2009. Web. 9 Nov. 2013: <http://www.youtube.com/watch?v=jQKHrKJ7kC8>.

Morris, George. "Old Hollywood: *On Dangerous Ground*." *Film Comment* 11.2 (Mar.–Apr. 1975): 22–23. Print.

Mulvey, Laura. "Notes on Sirk and Melodrama." *Home Is Where the Heart Is: Studies in Melodrama and the Woman's Film*. Ed. Christine Gledhill. London: BFI Publishing, 1987. 75–79. Print.

Naremore, James. *Acting in the Cinema*. Berkeley: U of California P, 1988. Print.

———. "Authorship and the Cultural Politics of Film Criticism." *Film Quarterly* 44.1 (Autumn 1990): 14–23. Print.

———. *More than Night: Film Noir in Its Contexts*. Updated and expanded ed. Berkeley: U of California P, 1998, 2008. Print.

———, and Patrick Brantlinger. "Six Artistic Cultures." *Modernity and Mass Culture*. Ed. James Naremore and Patrick Brantlinger. Bloomington: Indiana UP, 1991. 1–23.

Nicholas Ray Foundation. 11 Nov. 2013. Web. <http://nicholasrayfoundation.org>. Accessed on 11 Nov. 2013.

Nielson, Evelyn Washburn. "The Truth about James Dean." *Chicago Daily Tribune* 9 Sep. 1956: L22. Print.

Nowell-Smith, Geoffrey. "Minnelli and Melodrama." *Home Is Where the Heart Is: Studies in Melodrama and the Woman's Film*. Ed. Christine Gledhill. London: BFI Publishing, 1987. 70–74. Print.

Oscilloscope Laboratories. 21 Feb. 2014. Web. <http://www.oscilloscope.net/?page_id=21>. Accessed on 21 Feb. 2014.

Palmer, James W. "*In a Lonely Place*: Paranoia in the Dream Factory." *Literature/Film Quarterly* 13.3 (1985): 200–207. Print.

Palmer, R. Barton, ed. *Larger Than Life: Movie Stars of the 1950s*. New Brunswick, NJ: Rutgers UP, 2010. Print.

Parsons, Louella. "James Dean: New Face with Future." *Cosmopolitan* 138 (1 Mar. 1955): 44.

Pells, Richard. *Modernist America: Art, Music, Movies, and the Globalization of American Culture*. New Haven, CT: Yale UP, 2011. Print.

———. *Not Like Us: How Europeans Have Loved, Hated, and Transformed American Culture Since World War II*. Basic Books, 1997. Print.

Perkins, V. F. "*55 Days at Peking*." *Movie* 11 (Jul.–Aug. 1963): 46. Print.

———. "*In a Lonely Place*." *The Movie Book of Film Noir*. Ed. Ian Cameron. London: Studio Vista, 1992. 222–31. Print.

———. "*King of Kings*." Movie 1 (Jun. 1962): 29–30. Print.

———. "Must We Say What They Mean?: Film Criticism and Interpretation." *Movie* 34 (Oct. 1990): 1–6. Print.

———. "*Nicholas Ray*." *Oxford Opinion* 40 (14 Jun. 1960): 31–34. Print.

———. "The Cinema of Nicholas Ray." *Movies and Methods*. Ed. Bill Nichols. Berkeley: U of California P, 1976. 251–62. Print.

Perry, George. *James Dean*. New York: Dorling Kindersley Ltd., 2005. Print.

Peterson, Jennifer. "The Competing Tunes of *Johnny Guitar*: Liberalism, Sexuality, Masquerade." *Cinema Journal* 35.3 (Spring 1996): 3–18. Print.

Polan, Dana. *In a Lonely Place*. London: BFI Publishing, 1993. Print.

Pomerance, Murray. "1957: Movies and the Search for Proportion." *American Cinema of the 1950s: Themes and Variations*. Ed. Murray Pomerance. New Brunswick, NJ: Rutgers UP, 2005. 177–200. Print.

———. "Introduction." *Cinema and Modernity*. Ed. Murray Pomerance. New Brunswick, NJ: Rutgers UP, 2006. 3–15. Print.

———. "James Stewart and James Dean: The Darkness Within." *Larger Than Life: Movie Stars of the 1950s*. Ed. R. Barton Palmer. New Brunswick, NJ: Rutgers UP, 2010. 61–85. Print.

———. "Stark Performance." Rebel without a Cause*: Approaches to a Maverick Masterwork*. Ed. J. David Slocum. Albany: State U of New York P, 2005. 35–52. Print.

———. "Teacup and a Kiss, A: Staging Action in *Johnny Guitar*." *Lonely Places, Dangerous Ground: Nicholas Ray in American Cinema*. Ed. Steven Rybin and Will Scheibel. Albany: State U of New York P, 2014. 23–37. Print.

———. "The Hero in the China Sea." *The Horse Who Drank the Sky: Film Experience Beyond Narrative and Theory*. New Brunswick: Rutgers UP, 2008. 36–61. Print.

———. " 'Who Lives?': Notes on a Cinematic Moment." *Flow: A Critical Forum on Television and Media Culture* 13.8 (2011). Web. 20 Sep. 2015. <http://flowtv.org/2011/02/who-lives/>.

Prince, Stephen. "The Filmmakers." *A New Pot of Gold: Hollywood Under the Electronic Rainbow, 1980–1989*. Ed. Stephen Prince. Berkeley: U of California P, 2000. 186–286. Print.

Prouse, Derek. "*Rebel without a Cause*." *Sight and Sound* 25 (Winter 1956): 161, 164. Print.

Rathgeb, Douglas L. *The Making of* Rebel without a Cause. Jefferson, NC: McFarland, 2004. Print.

Ray, Nicholas. "Always a Guest, Never a Host." *Hollywood Reporter* 29 Nov. 1962. Print.

———. *I Was Interrupted: Nicholas Ray on Making Movies*. Ed. Susan Ray. Berkeley: U of California P, 1993. Print.

———. "Rebel: The Life Story of a Film." *Daily Variety* 31 Oct. 1956. Print.

———. "Story into Script." *Sight & Sound* 26.2 (Autumn 1956): 70–74. Print.

Ray, Susan. "Out of the Box." *CinemaScope* 48 (Fall 2011): 21–25. Print.

———. "To the Viewer: On Nicholas Ray's *We Can't Go Home Again*." *Senses of Cinema* 66 (Mar. 2013). Web. 9 Nov. 2013. <http://sensesofcinema.com/2013/feature-articles/to-the-viewer-on-nicholas-rays-we-cant-go-home-again/>.

"*Rebel*'s Child-Parent Hostility Theme Drawing Lots of Mail." 14 Dec. 1955: 2, 71. Print.

Rivette, Jacques. "Notes on a Revolution." *Cahiers du cinéma, the 1950s: Neo-Realism, Hollywood, New Wave*. Ed. Jim Hillier. Cambridge, MA: Harvard UP, 1985. 94–97. Print.

———. "On Imagination." Trans. Liz Heron. *Cahiers du cinéma, the 1950s: Neo-Realism, Hollywood, New Wave*. Ed. Jim Hillier. Cambridge, MA: Harvard UP, 1985. 104–05. Print.

Robertson, Pamela. "Camping under Western Stars: Joan Crawford in *Johnny Guitar*." *Journal of Film and Video* 47.1–3 (Spring-Fall 1995): 33–49. Print.

Rockhill, Gabriel. "Modernism as a Misnomer: Godard's Archeology of the Image." *Journal of French and Francophone Philosophy* 18.2 (2010): 107–29. Print.

Rodowick, D. N. *Crisis of Political Modernism, The: Criticism and Ideology in Contemporary Film Theory*. 2nd ed. Berkeley: U of California P, 1988, 1994. Print.

———. "Madness, Authority, and Ideology in the Domestic Melodrama of the 1950s." *Home Is Where the Heart Is: Studies in Melodrama and the Woman's Film*. Ed. Christine Gledhill. London: BFI Publishing, 1987. 268–80. Print.

"Rodeo Cowboys Heroes of Film." *New York Herald Tribune* 19 Oct. 1952: D3. Print.

Rohmer, Éric. "Ajax or the Cid?" Trans. Liz Heron. *Cahiers du cinéma, the 1950s: Neo-Realism, Hollywood, New Wave*. Ed. Jim Hillier. Cambridge, MA: Harvard UP, 1985. 111–15. Print.

———. *The Taste for Beauty*. Trans. Carol Volk. Cambridge: Cambridge UP, 1989. Print.

———. "Rediscovering America." Trans. Liz Heron. *Cahiers du cinéma, the 1950s: Neo-Realism, Hollywood, New Wave*. Ed. Jim Hillier. Cambridge, MA: Harvard UP, 1985. 88–93. Print.

Rosenbaum, Jonathan. "Circle of Pain: The Cinema of Nicholas Ray." *Sight & Sound* 42.4 (Autumn 1973): 218–22. Print.

———. "Guilty by Omission." *Film Comment* 27.5 (Sep. 1991): 42–57. Print.

———. "Looking for Nicholas Ray." *American Film* 7.3 (Dec. 1981): 55–56, 71–76. Print.

Roth, Sanford Harrison. "The Late James Dean." *Colliers* (25 Nov. 1955): 62–65. Print.

Roud, Richard. "The French Line." *Sight & Sound* 29.4 (Autumn 1960): 166–71. Print.

Rybin, Steven. "Nicholas Ray's *The Lusty Men* and Cowboy Cinephilia." *Quarterly Review of Film & Video* 31 (2014): 764–78. Print.

———. "*Party Girl*." *Senses of Cinema* 59 (Jun. 2011). Web. <http://sensesofcinema.com/2011/cteq/partygirl/>.

———, and Will Scheibel, eds. *Lonely Places, Dangerous Ground: Nicholas Ray in American Cinema*. Albany: State U of New York P, 2014. Print.

———. "The Pedagogical Aesthetics of *We Can't Go Home Again*." *Lonely Places, Dangerous Ground: Nicholas Ray in American Cinema*. Ed. Steven Rybin and Will Scheibel. Albany: State U of New York P, 2014. 241–50. Print.

Sanjek, David. "*Johnny Guitar*." *Senses of Cinema* 59 (Jun. 2011). Web. 9 Nov. 2013. <http://sensesofcinema.com/2011/cteq/johnny-guitar/>.

Sarris, Andrew. "Nicholas Ray (1911–)." *Film Culture* 28 (Spring 1963): 15–16. Print.

———. "Notes on the Auteur Theory in 1962." *Film Theory and Criticism*. 7th ed. Ed. Leo Braudy and Marshall Cohen. Oxford: Oxford UP, 2009. 451–54. Print.

———. "Seditious Movie, The." *Village Voice* 12 Mar. 1970: 55. Print.

———. "The Acid Test of Auteurism." *Village Voice* (11–17 Nov. 1981): 43. Print.

———. *The American Cinema: Directors and Directions, 1929–1968*. New York: Da Capo P, 1996. Print.

Sayad, Cecilia. *Performing Authorship: Self-Inscription and Corporeality in the Cinema*. London: I. B. Tauris, 2013. Print.

Schaefer, Eric. *"Bold! Daring! Shocking! True!": A History of Exploitation Films, 1919–1959*. Durham, NC: Duke UP, 1999. Print.

Scheibel, Will. "Bigger Than Life: Melodrama, Masculinity, and the American Dream." *Lonely Places, Dangerous Ground: Nicholas Ray in American Cinema*. Ed. Steven Rybin and Will Scheibel. Albany: State U of New York P, 2014. 177–87.

Scheuer, Philip K. "Crop of Practical Young Men Displacing Old-Line of Directorial Stylists and 'Artists.'" *Los Angeles Times* 27 Mar. 1949: D1, D4. Print.

———. "Hollywood Mood Film Has Bogart." Rev. of *In a Lonely Place*, dir. Nicholas Ray. *Los Angeles Times* 25 Aug. 1950: 14. Print.

———. "James Dean Sympathetic *Rebel without a Cause*." Rev. of *Rebel without a Cause*, dir. Nicholas Ray. *Los Angeles Times* 10 Nov. 1955: B12. Print.

Schleier, Merrill. "The Griffith Observatory in Ray's *Rebel without a Cause* (1955): Mystical Temple and Scientific Monument." *Journal of Architecture* 16.3 (2011): 365–85.

Scott, John L. "Mitchum's Mobile Cabin Takes Him into Wilds He Really Loves." *Los Angeles Times* 24 Aug. 1952: E1, 3. Print.

Scullion, George. "James Dean: The Legend and the Facts." *Look* 20 (16 Oct. 1956): 120–28. Print.

Silver, Alain, and James Ursini. *Film Noir*. Ed. Paul Duncan. Los Angeles: Taschen, 2013.

Slocum, J. David, ed. Rebel without a Cause*: Approaches to a Maverick Masterwork*. Albany: State U of New York P, 2005. Print.

———. "*Rebel without a Cause*." *Senses of Cinema* 59 (Jun. 2011). Web. 9 Nov. 2013. <http://sensesofcinema.com/2011/cteq/rebel-without-a-cause/>.

Smirnova, Larysa, and Chris Fujiwara. "'As Surely as a Criminal Would Die': Nicholas Ray's *The Doctor and the Devils*." *Lonely Places, Dangerous Ground: Nicholas Ray in American Cinema*. Ed. Steven Rybin and Will Scheibel. Albany: State U of New York P, 2014. 231–40. Print.

Spoto, Donald. *Rebel: The Life and Legend of James Dean*. New York: HarperCollins, 1996. Print.

Staiger, Janet. "Authorship Approaches." *Authorship and Film*. Ed. David A. Gerstner and Janet Staiger. New York: Routledge, 2003. 27–57. Print.

Stanislavsky, Constantin. *An Actor Prepares*. Trans. Elizabeth Reynolds Hapgood. New York: Routledge, 1936, 1948. Print.

"Stars That Won't Dim." *Newsweek* 18 Jun. 1956: 122. Print.

Stearns, Peter N. *American Cool: Constructing a Twentieth-Century Emotional Style*. New York: New York UP, 1994. Print.

Sterritt, David. *The Films of Jean-Luc Godard: Seeing the Invisible*. Cambridge: Cambridge UP, 1999. Print.

Stock, Dennis. "Moody New Star." *Life* 38.10 (7 Mar. 1955): 125–28. Print.

Stone, Susan. "Scorsese Presents Restored *Rebel without a Cause* in Berlin." *Women's Wear Daily* 15 Feb. 2014. Web. 16 Feb. 2014. <http://www.wwd.com/fashion-news/fashion-scoops/scorsese-presents-restored-rebel-without-a-cause-in-berlin-7463280?module=Fashion-Fashion%20Scoops-bullet>.

Studlar, Gaylyn. "Masochistic Performance and Female Subjectivity in *Letter from an Unknown Woman*." *Cinema Journal* 33.3 (Spring 1994): 35–57. Print.

Suárez, Juan A. *Jim Jarmusch*. Urbana: U of Illinois P, 2007. Print.

Tamarin, Jean. "Nicholas Ray, Auteur." *Chronicle of Higher Education* 58.9 (21 Oct. 2011). Web. 9 Nov. 2013. <https://chronicle.com/article/Nicholas-Ray-Auteur/129410/>.

Taylor, Greg. *Artists in the Audience: Cults, Camp, and American Film Criticism*. Princeton: Princeton UP, 2001. Print.

"TCM Private Screenings." *Macao*. Dir. Josef von Sternberg. Perf. Robert Mitchum, Jane Russell, and William Bendix. 1952. DVD. Warner, 2007.

Telotte, J. P. "The Displaced Voice of *In a Lonely Place*." *South Atlantic Review* 54.1 (Jan. 1989): 1–12. Print.

Thomson, David. "Director Whose Life Could Have Been a Movie, A." *New York Times* 16 Mar. 2003. Web. 9 Nov. 2013. <http://www.nytimes.com/2003/03/16/movies/film-a-director-whose-life-could-have-been-movie.html?src=pm>.

———. "*In a Lonely Place*." *Sight & Sound* 48.4 (Autumn 1979): 215–220. Print.

———. "James Dean: The Grace of Loneliness." *Movies of the Fifties*. Ed. Ann Lloyd. London: Orbis Publishing, 1982. 80–83. Print.

———. "Nicholas Ray." *New Biographical Dictionary of Film, The*. Expanded and updated ed. Westminister, MD: Knopf, 2004. 731–33. Print.

———. "Poet of Nightfall, The." *Guardian* 27 Dec. 2003. Web. 9 Nov. 2013. <http://film.guardian.co.uk/features/featurepages/0,4120,1112652,00.html>.

———. "The Lonely Legacy of Nicholas Ray." *New Republic* 4 Aug. 2011. Web. 9 Nov. 2013. <http://www.tnr.com/article/film/93139/david-thomson-films-nicholas-rey-legacy>.

Thompson, Howard. "Another Dean Hits the Big League." *New York Times* 13 Mar. 1955: X5. Print.

Tinee, Mae. "Bogart Movie Holds Interest at a High Pitch." Rev. of *In a Lonely Place*, dir. Nicholas Ray. 5 Jun. 1950: A3. Print.

———. "James Dean's Last Movie Has an Impact." Rev. of *Rebel without a Cause*, dir. Nicholas Ray. *Chicago Daily Tribune* 22 Nov. 1955: B5. Print.

Tirro, Frank. *Jazz: A History*. 2nd ed. New York: Norton, 1977, 1993. Print.

Truffaut, François. *The Films in My Life*. New York: Da Capo P, 1994. Print.

———. "A Wonderful Certainty." Trans. Liz Heron. *Cahiers du cinéma, the 1950s: Neo-Realism, Hollywood, New Wave*. Ed. Jim Hillier. Cambridge, MA: Harvard UP, 1985. 107–10. Print.

"Vicki Evans Back, and Out of Jail." *Los Angeles Times* 28 Jan. 1949: 2. Print.

"Vicki Evans Freed on Dope Charge." *Los Angeles Times* 11 Mar. 1949: 2. Print.

Wagner, Laura. "Jane Russell: Body and Soul." *Killer Tomatoes: Fifteen Tough Film Dames*. Jefferson, NC: MacFarland, 2004. 148–67. Print.

Walker, Janet. "Hollywood, Freud, and the Representation of Women: Regulation and Contradiction, 1945–Early 60s." *Home Is Where the Heart Is: Studies in Melodrama and the Woman's Film*. Ed. Christine Gledhill. London: BFI Publishing, 1987. 197–214. Print.

Warner, Michael. "The Mass Public and the Mass Subject." *Habermas and the Public Sphere*. Ed. Craig J. Calhoun. Cambridge, MA: MIT P, 1992. 377–401. Print.

Weales, Gerald. "The Crazy, Mixed-Up Kids Take Over." *Reporter* 15 (13 Dec. 1956): 40–41. Print.

Weisman, Brad. "*Knock on Any Door*." *Senses of Cinema* 59 (Jun. 2011). Web. 9 Nov. 2013. <http://sensesofcinema.com/2011/cteq/knock-on-any-door/>.

Wenders, Wim. *On Film: Essays and Conversations*. London: Faber & Faber, 2001. Print.

Wexman, Virginia Wright. *Creating the Couple: Love, Marriage, and Hollywood Performance*. Princeton, NJ: Princeton UP, 1993. Print.

———, ed. *Film and Authorship*. New Brunswick, NJ: Rutgers University Press, 2003. Print.

———. "Introduction." *Film and Authorship*. Ed. Virginia Wright Wexman. New Brunswick, NJ: Rutgers UP, 2003. 1–18. Print.

White, Susan. "'You Want a Good Crack in the Mouth?': *Rebel without a Cause*, Violence, and the Cinema of Nicholas Ray." Rebel without a Cause*: Approaches to a Maverick Masterwork*. Ed. J. David Slocum. Albany: State U of New York P, 2005. 53–87. Print.

Willemen, Paul. "Distanciation and Douglas Sirk." *Screen* 12.2 (1971): 63–67. Print.

———. "Towards an Analysis of the Sirkian System." *Screen* 13.4 (1972–73): 128–34. Print.

Williams, Tony. "*Flying Leathernecks*: Color and Characterization." *Lonely Places, Dangerous Ground: Nicholas Ray in American Cinema*. Ed. Steven Rybin and Will Scheibel. Albany: State U of New York P, 2014. 85–95. Print.

Wilmington, Michael. "Nicholas Ray: The Years at RKO, Part One." *The Velvet Light Trap* 10 (Fall 1973): 46–53. Print.

———. "Nicholas Ray: The Years at RKO, Part Two." *The Velvet Light Trap* 11 (Winter 1974): 35–40. Print.

———. "Nicholas Ray's *Johnny Guitar*." *The Velvet Light Trap* 12 (Spring 1974): 19–25. Print.

Wilson, George M. "Nicholas Ray's *Rebel without a Cause*." Rebel without a Cause*: Approaches to a Maverick Masterwork*. Ed. J. David Slocum. Albany: State U of New York P, 2005. 109–30. Print.

Wollen, Peter. "Counter Cinema: *Vent d'est*." *Readings and Writings: Semiotic Counter-Strategies*. New York: Verso, 1997. 79–91. Print.

———. "Never at Home." *Sight & Sound* 4.5 (May 1994): 12–15. Print.

———. *Paris Hollywood: Writings on Film*. London: Verso, 2002. Print.

Wood, Robin. "Film Favorites: *Bigger Than Life*." *Film Comment* 8.3 (Sep.–Oct. 1972): 56–61. Print.

Zeitchik, Steven. "Kaufman *Interrupted*." *Variety* 8 Jan. 2006. Web. 11 Nov. 2013. <http://variety.com/2006/film/news/kaufman-interrupted-1117935715/>.

Chronological Filmography

Films Directed by Nicholas Ray

1948 *They Live by Night* (produced by RKO Radio Pictures)

1949 *Knock on Any Door* (produced by Santana Productions; distributed by Columbia Pictures)

1949 *A Woman's Secret* (produced by RKO Radio Pictures)

1950 *Born to Be Bad* (produced by RKO Radio Pictures)

1950 *In a Lonely Place* (produced by Santana Productions; distributed by Columbia Pictures)

1951 *Flying Leathernecks* (produced by RKO Radio Pictures)

1952 *On Dangerous Ground* (produced by RKO Radio Pictures)

1952 *The Lusty Men* (produced by Wald-Krasna Productions; distributed by RKO Radio Pictures)

1954 *Johnny Guitar* (produced by Republic Pictures)

1954 "High Green Wall," from *General Electric Theater* (produced by Revue Productions; distributed by the Columbia Broadcasting System)

1955 *Run for Cover* (produced by Paramount Pictures)

1955 *Rebel without a Cause* (produced by Warner Bros.)

1956 *Hot Blood* (produced by Columbia Pictures)

1956 *Bigger Than Life* (produced by Twentieth Century-Fox)

1957 *The True Story of Jesse James* (produced by Twentieth Century-Fox)

1957 *Bitter Victory* (produced by Transcontinental Films and Robert Laffont Productions; distributed by Columbia Pictures)

1958 *Wind across the Everglades* (produced by Schulberg Productions; distributed by Warner Bros.)

1958 *Party Girl* (produced by Metro-Goldwyn-Mayer)

1960 *The Savage Innocents* (produced by Gray Films, Joseph Janni-Appia Films, Magic Film, Play Art, Société Nouvelle Pathé Cinéma; distributed by Paramount Pictures)

1961 *King of Kings* (produced by Samuel Bronston; distributed by Metro-Goldwyn-Mayer)

1963 *55 Days at Peking* (produced by Samuel Bronston; distributed by Metro-Goldwyn-Mayer)

1974 "The Janitor," from *Wet Dreams* (produced by Cinereal Film, Film Group One, P. Greulich, and H. Freitag; distributed in the Netherlands by Actueel Film)

1978 *Marco* (filmed at the Lee Strasberg Institute)

1980 *Lightning over Water*, codirected with Wim Wenders (produced by Road Movies Film Produktion, Viking Film, and Wim Wenders Productions; distributed by Gray City)

2011 *We Can't Go Home Again* (filmed at Harpur College of the State University of New York in Binghamton; completed, restored, and reconstructed by Susan Ray; distributed by Oscilloscope Pictures)

Films about or Influenced by Ray

1960 *Breathless* (Dir. Jean-Luc Godard)

1975 *I'm a Stranger Here Myself* (Dir. David Helpern)

1977 *The American Friend* (Dir. Wim Wenders)

1984 *Stranger Than Paradise* (Dir. Jim Jarmusch)

2011 *Don't Expect Too Much* (Dir. Susan Ray)

Index

www.ingramcontent.com/pod-product-compliance
Lightning Source LLC
LaVergne TN
LVHW010631190926
848399LV00033B/298